THE M. & E. HANDBOOK

KV-578-782

MERCANTILE LAW

P. W. D. REDMOND, LL.M.

*Barrister-at-Law, Formerly Senior Lecturer in Mercantile Law
at the City of London College*

SECOND EDITION

MACDONALD & EVANS LTD.

8 John Street, London WC1N 2HY

1968

First published December 1964
Reprinted August 1965
Second Edition August 1968
Reprinted March 1969
Reprinted May 1970
Reprinted August 1971
Reprinted November 1971

©

MACDONALD AND EVANS LTD
1964

S.B.N. 7121 1337 1

This book is copyright and may not be
reproduced in whole or *in part* (except for
purposes of review) without the express
permission of the publisher in writing.

HANDBOOK *Conditions of Sale*

This book is sold subject to the condition
that it shall not, by way of *trade or otherwise*, be lent, re-sold, hired out or otherwise *circulated* without the publisher's
prior consent in any form of binding or
cover other than that in which it is
published *and without a similar condition
including this condition being imposed on
the subsequent purchaser.*

*Printed in Great Britain by Richard Clay (The Chaucer Press), Ltd.,
Bungay, Suffolk*

GENERAL INTRODUCTION

The **HANDBOOK** Series of Study Notes

HANDBOOKS are a new form of printed study notes designed to help students to prepare and revise for professional and other examinations. The books are carefully programmed so as to be self-contained courses of tuition in the subjects they cover. For this purpose they comprise detailed study notes, self-testing questions and hints on examination technique.

HANDBOOKS can be used on their own or in conjunction with recommended text-books. They are written by college lecturers, examiners and others with wide experience of students' difficulties and requirements. At all stages the main objective of the authors has been to prepare students for the practical business of passing examinations.

P. W. D. REDMOND
General Editor

NOTICE TO LECTURERS

Many lecturers are now using **HANDBOOKS** as working texts to save time otherwise wasted by students in protracted note-taking. The purpose of the series is to meet practical teaching requirements as far as possible, and lecturers are cordially invited to forward comments or criticisms to the Publishers for consideration.

AUTHOR'S PREFACE TO
SECOND EDITION

THE success of the first edition of this book clearly evidenced the wide-spread need for study notes on Mercantile Law among all kinds of students in Britain and overseas. A new edition has been necessitated to incorporate both significant recent cases and changes in statute law effected by the *Hire Purchase Act*, 1965, and the *Misrepresentation Act*, 1967.

The book is intended as a series of concise and comprehensive lecture or study notes for students preparing for professional and other examinations in Mercantile Law. It follows the pattern of the author's **HANDBOOK** on *General Principles of English Law*, so as to facilitate the studies of those who have already used the more elementary book.

Before commencing to work through this book the student is advised to study the syllabus for his particular examination, since the detailed requirements of different institutions vary considerably. Most examinations in commercial law cover Contract, Agency, Partnership, Sale of Goods, and Negotiable Instruments with the addition of one or some of the other topics covered in this book. The student should therefore compare his syllabus with the contents pages of this book to see what, if anything, he can safely leave out.

As to the method of study, the student is advised to go through this **HANDBOOK** chapter by chapter. Read first through the section headings and bold-printed paragraph heads to see what the chapter is about. Then do a slower detailed reading (ignoring references to cases and statutes) and concentrating on understanding the text. Only at the third reading should the student commence memorisation (leaving cases and statutes to the end).

Case and statute references are given throughout the text, and the most important are starred. Those which are starred *must* be memorised, and all references should be memorised if the student can manage it.

Progress Tests are placed at the end of each Part for self-examination and revision. Try to answer each question and

then check your answer with the text (by means of the section
and paragraph references given). The easiest way to memorise
the subject is to make constant use of the Progress Tests in this
way.

In addition a large number of specimen questions from actual
examination papers are printed throughout the book (with
references to show where the answers are to be found in the
text). These questions are printed by permission of the bodies
concerned, and I gratefully acknowledge my debt to the
following:

Institute of Chartered Accountants (C.A.)
Association of Certified & Corporate Accountants (A.C.C.A.)
Institute of Cost & Works Accountants (I.C.W.A.)
Institute of Bankers
Chartered Institute of Secretaries (C.I.S.)
Corporation of Secretaries (C.S.)

November, 1968   P. W. D. REDMOND

CONTENTS

xi

PART ONE

THE LAW OF CONTRACTS

NATURE AND CLASSIFICATION OF CONTRACTS

SECTION 1. NATURE OF CONTRACTS

1. Definition of contract. A contract is a legally binding agreement. That is, an agreement which will be enforced by the courts. Sir William Anson, in his *Principles of the Law of Contract*, defined a contract as "a legally binding agreement made between two or more persons, by which rights are acquired by one or more to acts or forbearances on the part of the other or others."

2. Consensus ad idem. An agreement occurs when two minds meet upon a common purpose. This *meeting of minds* is called *consensus ad idem, i.e.* consent to the matter.

Absence of consensus may make a contract null and void, *e.g.* where the parties are fundamentally mistaken as to each other's intentions: *Raffles* v. *Wichelhaus* (1864), *see s.* **15.**

3. Agreements which are not contracts. Mere domestic or social agreements are not usually intended to be binding, and therefore are not contracts.

EXAMPLES:
(a) A husband promised to pay a housekeeping allowance to his wife. HELD: A mere domestic arrangement, with no intention to create legally binding relations, therefore no contract: *Balfour* v. *Balfour* (1919).
(b) Three friends joined to enter a newspaper competition and agreed to share any winnings. HELD: They intended to create legal relations and their agreement was therefore a binding contract: ✱ *Simpkins* v. *Pays* (1955).

PROBLEM: X invites his friends to a party at his house. When they arrive, after expensive train journeys, they find that he has forgotten the invitation and is away from home. Can they sue him for breach of contract?

4. Intention to create legal relations. A binding contract is usually in the nature of a commercial bargain, involving some exchange of goods or services for a price (called the *consideration*).

But even such commercial bargains will not be legally binding if the parties intend otherwise, *i.e.* do not intend to create legal relations.

EXAMPLES:

(a) A written commercial agreement described itself merely as an "honourable pledge" and stated expressly that it was not "to be subject to the jurisdiction of any court." HELD: The parties did not intend to create legal relations, and the agreement was not a contract: ✳ *Rose & Frank Co.* v. *Crompton Bros.* (1923).

(b) A condition imposed by a football pool laid down that the relationship should not be legally binding. HELD: No intention to create legal relations: *Appleson* v. *Littlewoods Ltd.* (1939). (This is a common condition of entrance in football pools, etc.)

SECTION 2. CLASSIFICATION OF CONTRACTS

1. Contracts of record. These are obligations whose terms are recorded by a *court of record, e.g.* the Supreme Court or a County Court.

They are not true contracts, since the obligations of the parties arise independently of any agreement and solely by reason of entry upon the court records. Two types are:

(a) *Judgments:* by which a court imposes on some person a legal obligation, *e.g.* to pay damages. This judgment, when enrolled on the court records, constitutes a contract of record between the parties to the action in which the judgment was pronounced.

(b) *Recognisances:* written acknowledgement of a debt due to the Crown, made before a judge or authorised officer, and enrolled on the court records, *e.g.* a promise to "keep the peace" or to attend court when called (an accused person in a criminal case is sometimes released on bail pending trial, on his own recognisance, *i.e.* a promise to attend when called, or to forfeit a stated sum of money).

2. Contracts by deed (specialty contracts). A contract by deed is a promise written on paper or parchment, signed, sealed, and delivered (either actually or constructively) by the promisor to the promisee or his agent.

- (a) *Execution of deed:* when a deed has been "signed, sealed, and delivered" it is said to be *executed*, and it becomes legally binding immediately (unless it is directed to be held by the recipient in *escrow*).
- (b) *Escrows:* an escrow is a deed executed subject to a condition that it is not to become effective until the condition is satisfied, *e.g.* the occurrence of a certain event, or the expiry of a period of time. Escrows are usually delivered to a neutral intermediary, with instructions not to complete delivery to the promisee until further instructions from the promisor.
- (c) *Sealing & delivery:* sealing a deed is usually done by affixing a disc or wafer of red paper to the bottom of the deed (next to the signature of the person signing). Delivery is largely a matter of intention; thus, it may be by actually handing over the deed to the promisee, or by giving him the keys to a box in which the deed is kept (*constructive* delivery).
- (d) *Indentures and deeds poll:* a deed to which there is only one party is called a Deed Poll, *e.g.* a deed of gift. A deed to which there are two or more parties is called an Indenture, *e.g.* any contract by deed.

3. Characteristics of contracts by deed.

- (a) *Consideration:* a deed does not require to be supported by valuable consideration, like simple contracts: see below.
- (b) *Merger:* a special contract absorbs, or merges into itself, any earlier simple contract made between the same parties and on the same terms.
- (c) *Limitation of actions:* an action for breach of a specialty contract can be commenced at any time within 12 years of the breach occurring; but an action for breach of a simple contract must generally be commenced within 6 years: *Limitation Act,* 1939, and *see s.* **24.**

NOTE: Formerly a person who had signed a deed could not thereafter deny the accuracy of statements made therein, *i.e.* he was *estopped* from denying the accuracy of the deed. This was called *estoppel by deed.* The rule is now obsolete and evidence is admissible to show that the deed is inaccurate, like any other contract.

4. Simple contracts. Simple or "parol" contracts are by far the most common and important variety. They are informal contracts and may be made in any way—orally, in writing, or by implication from conduct. A person who takes a seat in a bus is entering into an implied contract to pay his fare.

A simple contract must possess the following essentials:

(a) An offer and unqualified acceptance thereof: *see ss.* **5** *and* **6**.

(b) Intention to create legal relations.

(c) Valuable consideration: *see s.* **12**.

(d) Genuineness of consent (consensus ad idem), *e.g.* the agreement must not have been induced by fraud or coercion: *see Chapter IV*.

(e) Capacity of parties: *see ss.* **13** *and* **14**.

(f) Legality of objects: *see Chapter IV, s.* **18**.

(g) Possibility of performance: *see Chapter IV, s.* **15**.

(h) Certainty of terms: *see s.* **8**.

SECTION 3. VOID, VOIDABLE, AND UNENFORCEABLE CONTRACTS

1. Void contracts. A void contract is one which is *destitute of legal effect, i.e.* of which the court will take no notice, for example, contracts void on the grounds of fundamental mistake: *see s.* **15**.

Property transferred under a void contract can usually be recovered as the transferee can have no legal right to it: *Chappell* v. *Poles* (1837) (but if the contract is void on the grounds that its object is illegal or contrary to public policy property transferred is generally irrecoverable; *see s.* **18**).

2. Voidable contracts. A voidable contract is one which can be made void by one party, at his option. Thus a contract induced by fraud can be avoided by the party misled whenever he chooses: *see s.* **16**.

3. Unenforceable contracts. An unenforceable contract is one which, though perfectly valid in all other respects, lacks some technical requirement needed to make it enforceable, *e.g.* some necessary written evidence. Such a contract will not be enforced by the courts unless and until the defect is rectified.

Thus contracts for the sale of land or any interest therein must be evidenced in writing, signed by the defendant, before they can be the subject of a successful action at law: ✱ *Law of Property Act*, 1925, *s.* 40.

But such unenforceable contracts are not void, and therefore if they have been performed and property has been transferred the court will not intervene to set the agreement aside. Thus if A orally agrees to buy B's house and pays a deposit to B, then later changes his mind and refuses to sign a written contract to purchase the house, B will be unable to sue A for damages or performance of the contract but will be able to keep A's deposit, and the court will not assist A to recover it: *Monickendam* v. *Leanse* (1923).

SECTION 4. QUASI-CONTRACTS

Sometimes the law imposes obligations of a contractual nature even where no true agreement exists between the parties. The object of such imposition is to prevent a person obtaining "unjust enrichment" merely because there is no contract between himself and the person seeking the court's aid. The chief examples of such artificial or *quasi-contracts* are given below.

1. Money paid to the use of another. If A, at the express or implied request of B, pays to X a sum of money legally owed by B to X, the law implies a quasi-contract between A and B under which B must compensate A for the sum paid, *e.g.* where A pays rent owed by B to prevent the landlord seizing A's goods, which are stored at B's premises: *Edmunds* v. *Wallingford* (1885).

2. Accounts stated. Where there has been a series of transactions between A and B and they agree a balance, showing a sum payable by A to B, the agreed balance constitutes an "account stated." If B now has occasion to sue A for the amount so stated, he does not need to prove the details of the transactions between them but can rely entirely on the *account stated* as an admission of indebtedness.

3. Total failure of consideration. Where a valid contract has been made between A and B (supported by consideration) but

subsequently B fails to provide any of the promised consideration, there is said to be a *total failure of consideration* and A
can sue for the recovery of any money he has paid.

(Contrast the situation where the consideration has only
partially failed, *e.g.* where A pays money for goods to B, who
later delivers *some* but not all of the goods ordered. Here A
can only sue for damages for breach of contract, and the
damages will be measured as the amount needed to compensate
him for his loss, *i.e.* he is unlikely to recover *all* the money he
has paid.)

4. Money had and received. If A wrongfully obtains money
to which B is legally entitled, B can sue A for recovery of the
money in a quasi-contractual action for *money had and received*, *e.g.* where an employee receives money on behalf of his
master and refused to pass it on to the proper recipient.

Thus where B used the authority of his army uniform to
assist him in smuggling activities, it was *held* that the army, as
his employer, was entitled to the profits he had made out of
the smuggling: *Reading* v. *Attorney-General* (1951).

5. Money paid under mistake of fact. Where money is paid
under a mistake of fact it is generally recoverable by the payer,
e.g. where an employer overpays wages under a mistake as to
the employee's entitlement: *Lerner* v. *L.C.C.* (1949).

NOTE: Money paid under *mistake of law* is generally irrecoverable, since ignorance of the law is no excuse (*ignorantia juris
neminem excusat*). But to this rule there are the following
exceptions:

(*a*) Where the payee knew of or induced the payer's mistake.
(*b*) Where the money was paid to an officer of the court, *e.g.* a
    trustee in bankruptcy: The Rule in *ex parte James* (1874).
(*c*) Where money was paid under unjustified threat of legal
    proceedings against the payer.
(*d*) Where the payee was under a fiduciary duty to the payer,
    e.g. where paid by a client to his solicitor.
(*e*) Where the mistake of law is treated as one of fact, *e.g.* (i)
    mistakes of foreign law, (ii) mistakes as to private pro-
    prietary rights.

6. Quantum meruit. Where there is a breach of an essential
condition in a contract, the injured party may either (*a*) seek

to enforce the contract and sue for damages by way of compensation, or (b) treat the contract as discharged, in which case he cannot sue for damages for its breach.

However where he treats the contract as discharged, and has incurred expenses under it, he is entitled to bring a quasi-contractual action for compensation for work done. This is called a *quantum meruit* action (literally "how much is it worth?"); *see s.* **26.**

In addition to providing a remedy in certain cases of breach of contract like those above, *Quantum meruit* may also be used by the court to impose *quasi-contractual* liability where there is *no* contract between the parties but justice requires that some remuneration should be paid for work done.

EXAMPLE: L, a builder, did certain work for D on the understanding that D would give him a contract later for some major building work. D did not give L the expected contract and L sued for (i) damages for breach of contract or (ii) *quantum meruit* relief. HELD: There was no contract between L and D and therefore L could not get damages, but he was entitled to reasonable remuneration on a quasi-contract: *William Lacey Ltd.* v. *Davis* (1957).

FORMATION OF CONTRACTS

In order to constitute a contract there must be an *offer*, express or implied, by one person (the "offeror"), and unqualified *acceptance*, express or implied, by the person to whom the offer is made (the "offeree").

SECTION 5. RULES GOVERNING OFFERS

1. How made. An offer may be *oral, written, or implied from conduct*. Thus an implied offer is made by a bus company when it sends its buses along the street and stops them at fixed places to let people get on (the people who then get on a bus are thus accepting the offer by implication).

2. To whom. An offer may be *specific*, *i.e.* to a particular person or group of persons, or *general*, *i.e.* to the world at large.

(a) *A specific offer* can usually be accepted only by the person or persons to whom it was made: *Boulton* v. *Jones* (1857).
(b) *A general offer* can be accepted by anyone (and usually without prior notification of intention to accept).

Thus a newspaper advertisement offering £100 to anyone who contracted influenza despite using a patent medicine in a specified way was *held* to be (i) a general offer, (ii) which could be accepted by conduct, (iii) without previously notifying the offeror of the acceptance: ✻ *Carlill* v. *Carbolic Smoke Ball Co.* (1893).

3. Communication to offeree. The offer must be communicated to the offeree before it can be accepted.

EXAMPLE: A seaman helped to navigate a ship home, and before sailing wrote to the owners telling them of his intention and asking a particular wage for his services. The owners did not receive the letter of offer until the ship was nearly home. HELD: The owners had no reasonable opportunity to accept or reject the offer, therefore the seaman could not compel them to pay him wages for navigating the ship: ✻ *Taylor* v. *Laird* (1856).

4. Certainty of offer. The offer must be definite, not vague or illusory. Thus a promise to pay an increased price for a horse "if it proves lucky to me" is too vague: *Guthing* v. *Lynn* (1831).

5. Intention to create legal relations. The offeror must intend the creation of legal relations, *i.e.* must intend that if his offer is accepted a legally binding agreement shall result: see *Balfour* v. *Balfour, s.* **1.3.** *ship of different names implied*:

6. An offer must be distinguished from:

(a) *An invitation to treat* (invitation to make offers), *e.g.* an auctioneer's request for bids (which will themselves be offers): *Payne* v. *Cave* (1789); or the display of goods in a shop window with prices marked upon them: ∗ *Fisher* v. *Bell* (1961); or the display of priced goods in a self-service store: *Pharmaceutical Soc.* v. *Boots, etc.* (1953).
(b) *A mere statement of intention, e.g.* an announcement of a forthcoming auction sale. Thus a person who attends the advertised place of auction could not sue for breach of contract if the sale were cancelled: *Harris* v. *Nickerson* (1873).
(c) *A mere communication of information* in the course of negotiations, *e.g.* a statement of the price at which one is prepared to *consider* negotiating the sale of a piece of land: *Harvey* v. *Facey* (1893).

PROBLEM: A puts a notice in his window saying "Special offer! Washing Machine £20." B enters, puts £20 on the counter and attempts to take the washing machine, but A restrains him and demands £25. Can B sue him for breach of contract? *No, invitation to treat.*

7. An offer lapses:

(a) *If either offeror or offeree dies before acceptance: Kennedy* v. *Thomassen* (1929).
(b) *If it is not accepted within* (i) the specified time (if any), or (ii) a reasonable time, if none is specified.
    What is a *reasonable time* depends on the circumstances. Five months has been held to be an unreasonable delay in accepting an offer to take shares in a company: ∗ *Ramsgate Hotel* v. *Montefiore* (1866).

(c) *If the offeree does not make a valid acceptance, e.g.* makes
a *counter-offer* or *conditional acceptance*; or, if a particular
manner of acceptance has been requested, he accepts in
some other manner, *e.g.* by sending a letter by mail when
a reply by hand was requested: *Eliason* v. *Henshaw*
(1819), U.S.A. case.

8. An offer may be revoked any time before acceptance:

(a) *Revocation must be communicated.* Until the offeree
actually receives the revocation, he is entitled to accept
and so create a binding contract:

EXAMPLE: A sent an offer by cable to B on the 1st October
requesting acceptance by the same method. B received the
offer on 11th October and immediately cabled acceptance. On
8th October A had posted a letter revoking the offer, which did
not reach B till after he had cabled his acceptance. HELD: B
had accepted before receiving the revocation, therefore a contract was made and the revocation was ineffective: * *Byrne* v.
Van Tienhoven (1880).

(b) *Indirect communication.* If the offeree learns of the revocation, he cannot later accept, even though he learns
indirectly, *e.g.* where a prospective purchaser of land
learns through a reliable third party that the offeror has
sold the land to someone else, he cannot then accept the
offer and sue the offeror for damages: * *Dickenson* v.
Dodds (1876).

NOTE: An offer for shares or debentures in a public company
made as a result of an advertisement or prospectus, cannot be
revoked until the 3rd day after the opening of the subscription
lists: *Companies Act*, 1948, *s.* 50 (5).

9. Options. An offer to keep an offer open for a specified
time (an *option*) is not binding unless (i) made under seal, or
(ii) supported by valuable consideration, like any other simple
contract: *Routledge* v. *Grant* (1828).

PROBLEMS:

(a) A wrote offering to sell a car to B and to keep the offer open
"till Wednesday noon." On Tuesday B learned through
overhearing a conversation that A had sold the car to C on
Monday. Can B now accept A's offer and sue A for damages

for breach of contract? (*See* 8 above.) Would it make any difference to your answer if B had paid A 5*s*. to keep the offer open till Wednesday? (*See* 9 above.)

(*b*) A published an advert saying that he would pay £100 to the first person to swim a particular lake on 1st April. B swims the lake and claims the reward. A now says the advert was a joke. Can B compel payment of the reward? (*See* 2 and 5 above.)

SECTION 6. RULES GOVERNING ACCEPTANCE

1. How made. Acceptance may be oral, written or implied from conduct: ✱ *Carlill* v. *Carbolic Smoke Ball Co.* (1893).

But if a particular method of acceptance is required the offeree must accept in the prescribed manner: *Eliason* v. *Henshaw* (1819).

2. Unqualified acceptance. Acceptance must be unqualified and must correspond with all the terms of the offer.

A *counter-offer* or *conditional acceptance* operates as a *rejection* of the offer, and causes it to lapse. Thus where a house is offered for sale at £1000 and the offeree counter-offers £950, the offer lapses: *Hyde* v. *Wrench* (1840).

Similarly a conditional acceptance "subject to a proper contract being drawn up" causes lapse of offer: *Eccles* v. *Bryant* (1948) (but an agreement "subject to contract" would be binding if the phrase simply meant the agreement was to be subject to the terms of a contract already existing).

3. Positive conduct. There must be active acceptance: mere passive intention to accept is ineffective.

Thus an offer by letter containing the words, "If I hear no more, I shall consider the horse is mine," is incapable on its own of constituting its own acceptance. There must be some positive communication of acceptance by the offeree; it would not be enough to show that the offeree intended to accept but died before writing a letter of acceptance: ✱ *Felthouse* v. *Bindley* (1862).

4. Communication of acceptance. Normally an acceptance is ineffective unless and until it is communicated to the offeror.

EXCEPTIONS:

(*a*) Where the offeror expressly or impliedly *waives* communication, *e.g.* where a general offer requires merely conduct as its acceptance: * *Carlill* v. *Carbolic Smoke Ball Co.* (1893).

Similarly an offer of a reward is accepted by doing what is required, without any previous communication: *Williams* v. *Carwardine* (1833).

(*b*) Where the contract is made by post, or the post is envisaged as the means of communication, *e.g.* in most commercial contracts today. Here acceptance is complete *as soon as it is posted*, provided it is properly stamped and addressed: * *Household Fire Insurance Co.* v. *Grant* (1879).

In postal cases therefore it does not matter if the letter of acceptance is lost in the post and never reaches the offeror: the contract is complete as soon as the letter of acceptance is posted. As a matter of commercial expediency the Post Office is treated as agent for the offeror, and communication to the agent is treated as communication to the principal.

The same rule applies to telegrams (but where the method of communication is instantaneous, *e.g.* Telex or telephone, acceptance is *not* complete until it actually reaches its destination: *Entores* v. *Miles Far East Corpn.* (1955)).

PROBLEM: A writes offering to sell his house to B, and on Wednesday B posts a letter of acceptance. On Tuesday A posted a letter revoking his offer but this did not reach B until he returned home from work on Wednesday. Can B enforce a contract against A? (5.7; 6.4.)

5. Motive for acceptance. No one can accept an offer in ignorance of its existence, but provided he knows of the offer his *motive* for accepting is usually irrelevant.

EXAMPLE: C offered a reward for information leading to the arrest of a criminal. W provided the information (knowing of the offer) but saying that she did so simply "to ease her conscience." Therefore C refused to pay the reward. HELD: Since W knew of the offer and accepted it, her motive for doing so was irrelevant and she was entitled to the money: *Williams* v. *Carwardine* (1833).

6. Tenders. A tender is a form of offer for the supply of goods or services, usually made in response to a request for tenders.

Tenders take the following forms:

(a) *Single offer, e.g.* a tender to build a factory. Acceptance of such a tender constitutes a contract.

(b) *Standing offer, e.g.* a tender to supply goods as and when required. Here the tenderer must supply as and when agreed, whenever an order is made. But he cannot insist on *any* orders being made at all.

EXAMPLE: P tendered to supply goods up to a certain amount to the L.C.C. over a certain period. The L.C.C.'s orders did not come up to the amount expected and P sued for breach of contract. HELD: Each order made a separate contract and P was bound to fulfil the orders made, but there was no obligation to make any orders at all: *Percival Ltd.* v. *L.C.C.* (1918).

(c) *Sole supplier.* The person seeking the tender may agree to take all his requirements for certain goods from the tenderer. This agreement does not oblige him to make any orders at all, but if he does require goods within the category agreed he *must* take them from the tenderer: *Kier* v. *Whitehead Iron Co.* (1938).

SECTION 7. STANDARD FORM CONTRACTS

There is an increasing tendency for an offeror to write out the contract entirely himself, and then demand that the offeree shall accept the detailed terms of the offer without modification.

The offeror may state all his terms in one document or, as in the case of railway tickets, may simply incorporate by reference certain standard conditions contained in another document. These "offers with terms annexed" are subject to special rules. They include most forms of transport ticket, by air, sea, or rail, many printed leases, and most contracts for the supply of gas, electricity, etc.

1. If the contract is signed by the offeree he is bound by all the conditions contained in the document signed *even if he has not read them*: ✱ *L'Estrange* v. *Graucob* (1934).

EXCEPTIONS:

(a) Where he can prove he signed the document under a *fundamental mistake as to its nature* (not merely as to its *contents*). This is the Common Law defence of *non est factum*. It covers, for example, cases where a person is induced to sign a cheque

on the mistaken assumption that it is merely a guarantee: *
Foster v. *McKinnon* (1869), and *see s.* **15**, 7.

(b) Where he can prove that he was induced to sign as a result
of a *misrepresentation* by the offeror, or the offeror's agent,
whether innocent or fraudulent: *Curtis* v. *Chemical Cleaning
& Dyeing Co. Ltd.* (1951).

(c) Where, in a *hire purchase contract*, the hirer signed the contract at a place other than the trader's place of business,
the hirer can cancel his signature within 4 days of signing:
see s. **48,** 3.

2. If the contract is unsigned, *e.g.* railway tickets, etc., the
offeree is bound by all the terms in the document or annexed
to it if:

(a) *A reasonable man would assume the document to be contractual, e.g.* not merely a receipt for money: * *Chapelton*
v. *Barry U.D.C.* (1940).

(b) *Reasonable care was taken by the offeror* to bring the terms
of the offer to his attention, *e.g.* by a notice "for conditions see Company's rules and regulations" clearly displayed on the face of the ticket.

If the notice given is reasonable the contract is binding
whether the offeree reads the conditions or not: *Parker*
v. *S.E. Railway* (1877), or even whether the offeree is
illiterate and unable to read them: *Thompson* v. *L.M.S.
Railway* (1930).

(c) *Notice of annexed conditions must be contemporaneous
with the* making of the contract: *Olley* v. *Marlborough
Court Ltd.* (1949).

NOTE: An *oral* contract could also contain exemption clauses,
but they would clearly be harder to prove.

EXAMPLES:

(a) C took a deck-chair from a pile under a notice, "Hire of
chairs—2*d.*" Later an attendant came round to collect the
money and C paid him, receiving in return a ticket which
said on it, "The Council will not be liable for any accident
or damage arising from hire of chair." C put the ticket in his
pocket without reading it, thinking it was merely a receipt.
The chair collapsed and he was injured and sued the Council. HELD: The Council could not rely on the exclusionary
notice on the ticket, since none of rules (*a*), (*b*), or (*c*) above
were satisfied: *Chapelton* v. *Barry U.D.C.* (1940).

(b) O registered at a hotel by signing the visitor's book, and then went to his room where was displayed a notice excluding the hotel's liability for articles lost. HELD: He made his contract when he signed the book, and the hotel could not rely on the exclusionary notice since it was not brought to his attention contemporaneously with the making of the contract: *Olley* v. *Marlborough Court Ltd.* (1949).

3. Exemption clauses. Annexed conditions are usually aimed at exempting the offeror from some legal liability to which he would otherwise be liable, *e.g.* liability for negligence in carrying out the contract. The courts view such attempts to evade liability with suspicion and interpret exemption clauses *contra proferentem, i.e.* against the offeror. But where the clause is clear and unambiguous and reasonable notice has been given to the offeree, the courts are usually bound by the clause and will enforce it.

The attitude of the courts is seen in the "Doctrine of the Fundamental Term," under which an exemption clause will not usually be enforced so as to protect a party who has committed a *fundamental breach* of the contract, *i.e.* a breach which destroys the business efficacy of the contract. Yet it has been recently held that even here, if the exemption clause is sufficiently clear and unambiguous it may cover a fundamental breach: see the *Suisse Atlantique* Case below.

EXAMPLES:

(*a*) W obtained a car on hire-purchase, the contract stipulating that no condition or warranty was given that the car was roadworthy. The car appeared to be roadworthy when W saw it, but it was delivered at night and W found that it had been towed to his house, would not go, and lacked various important parts. HELD: The exemption clause did not protect the defendants since the court, as a matter of construction, refused to read it so as to cover the case where the car would not work at all: *Karsales (Harrow) Ltd.* v. *Wallis* (1956).

(*b*) A ship charter contract contained a clause limiting damages to 1000 dollars a day for *demurrage* (delay in loading and unloading). The charterers made *fewer voyages* than the contract required, and the owner sued them for damages higher than the stipulated sum claiming that the charterers had committed a fundamental breach disentitling them from claiming the benefit of the exemption clause. HELD (H.L.): On the construction of the contract, the breach was clearly covered by the exemption clause: *Suisse Atlantique etc. S.A.* v. *Rotterdamsche Kolen Centrale* (1966).

SECTION 8. CERTAINTY OF TERMS

1. Terms must be certain. It is for the parties to make their intentions clear in their contract. The court will not enforce a contract the terms of which are uncertain.

Thus an *agreement to agree* in the future ("a contract to make a contract") will not constitute a binding contract, *e.g.* a promise to pay an actress "a West End salary *to be mutually agreed* between us" is not a contract, since the salary is not yet agreed: * *Loftus* v. *Roberts* (1902).

Similarly, where the terms of a final agreement are too vague, the contract will fail for uncertainty, *e.g.* sale of a van "on hire-purchase terms" is too vague, since there are several types of hire-purchase agreement: *Scammell* v. *Ouston* (1941).

2. Id certum est quod certum reddi potest (*that is certain which can be reduced to certainty*).

An agreement which at first sight appears to be too vague may be enforced if:

(a) *The parties themselves have provided machinery* in the contract for resolving the uncertainty, *e.g.* where no price was fixed for the sale of petrol, but the agreement stated that all disputes should be referred to arbitration, it was HELD that the arbitrator could fix the prices and so resolve the uncertainty: * *Foley* v. *Classique Coaches Ltd.* (1934). Also where a 5-year contract for the supply of chickens failed to state the number of chickens, but contained an arbitration clause, it was HELD that the numbers could be fixed by arbitration: *F. & G. Sykes (Wessex) Ltd.* v. *Fine Fare Ltd.* (1966).

(b) *The deficiency can be remedied by the court implying a term*, either (i) from the course of dealing between the parties in the past (if any), or (ii) from trade usages in the particular trade (if any), or (iii) where certain terms are implied by statute in similar contracts, *e.g.* the Sale of Goods Act, 1893.

The court may always imply a term into a contract to save it from collapse, but will do so only where it is clearly necessary and equitable: *The Moorcock* (1889).

3. Meaningless clauses. An agreement which is definite on the whole will be enforced, notwithstanding the presence of some meaningless or unnecessary words or phrases. The court in such a case will ignore the meaningless words and enforce the contract without them: *Nicolene Ltd.* v. *Simmonds* (1953).

SECTION 9. TERMS OF A CONTRACT

1. Express or implied terms. The parties may expressly state every term of their contract with varying degrees of precision; or they may simply agree the basic purpose of the contract and leave the detailed terms to be deduced from the surrounding circumstances.

Contractual terms are of two kinds: (i) conditions (main terms), or (ii) warranties (subordinate terms). Whether a term is a condition or a warranty is a question of intention to be deduced by the court in the light of the surrounding circumstances (mistaken use of the words "condition" or "warranty" by the parties will not be regarded as conclusive).

2. Conditions. A condition is an *essential term*, which goes to the root of the contract, *i.e.* it may constitute the main purpose of the agreement, or one of several main purposes.

Breach of condition entitles the injured party to treat the contract as at an end: *Behn* v. *Burness* (1863), and *see s.* **26.**

3. Kinds of condition.

(a) *Condition precedent:* a condition that the contract shall not bind one or both of the parties until such condition is fulfilled, *e.g.* "this contract is not to be binding until the war ends."

(b) *Condition subsequent:* a condition under which the contract shall cease to be binding at the option of one party on the happening of a certain event, *e.g.* "this contract shall cease to be binding if war breaks out." This is called a *determinable contract* and remains binding until the condition subsequent is fulfilled: contrast a voidable contract, which can be made completely void at the option of one party—*s.* **3.**

(c) *Condition concurrent:* a condition under which performance by one party is made dependent on performance by the other at the same time, *e.g.* payment of price upon delivery of goods ordered.

4. Warranties. A warranty is a *subordinate term*, subsidiary to the main purpose of the contract; *S.G.A.*, 1893, *s.* **62.**

Breach of warranty entitles the injured party to sue for damages, but he cannot regard the contract as at an end and must perform his part of it.

EXAMPLE: B promised to attend rehearsals for six days before a concert, but arrived in London only in time for two days' rehearsals, whereat G claimed the contract was discharged by breach of condition. HELD: Attendance at rehearsals was a warranty only, and therefore the contract was not discharged, though G was entitled to damages: * *Bettini* v. *Gye* (1876).

5. Ex post facto warranties. Where a breach of condition occurs the injured party can (*a*) treat the contract as discharged, or (*b*) if he prefers he may treat the breach as breach of a warranty, go on with the contract and sue for damages.

In some cases he *must* adopt the second alternative, *e.g.* where in a contract for sale of goods the purchaser has accepted a substantial part of the goods, before discovering a breach of condition, he must treat the breach as a breach of warranty: * *S.G.A.*, 1893, *s.* 11 (1).

This treating a breach of condition after it has occurred as though it were a breach of warranty is called treating it as breach of an *ex post facto* warranty, *i.e.* a warranty *after the event*.

6. Implied terms. The general rule is that the parties are presumed to have expressed their intentions fully.

The courts will only imply additional terms where it is strictly necessary to give effect to the clear intentions of the parties, or where custom or statute requires the implication: *The Moorcock* (1889), and *see s.* **8**.

7. Terms and representations. Frequently during preliminary negotiations one of the parties (*e.g.* the seller of goods) may make a series of statements, or representations, to help persuade the other party to enter the contract. Whether such representations become terms in the contract (and so binding the maker) depends on the construction which the court puts upon them.

The test is: Did the plaintiff accept the representations as mere inducements, or did he insist that he would not enter into the contract unless the representations could be regarded as binding conditions or warranties?

The following rules apply:

(*a*) A representation will not be regarded as a term of the contract unless the parties so agree, expressly or by implication.

(b) If a representation is treated as a *mere inducement*, the plaintiff cannot sue for breach of contract if it proves untrue. (Though he may be able to *avoid* the contract and obtain damages on the grounds of *Misrepresentation*: *Misrepresentation Act*, 1967, *see s.* **16.**)

(c) If a representation is agreed by the parties to be a term of the contract, the plaintiff's remedies will depend on whether it is regarded by the court as a *condition* or as a *warranty*: *see* **4** and **5** above, and *s.* **26.**

8. Construction of terms. In construing the terms of a contract the courts apply the following rules:

(a) Language used must be construed as far as possible in such a way as to give effect to the *intentions of the parties*.

(b) Words used must be presumed to have their *normal literal meaning*, unless the contrary is proved.

(c) Where there are *two possible meanings*, one legal and the other unlawful, the lawful meaning is to be preferred so as to render the contract enforceable (illegal contracts are void: *see s.* **18**).

(d) The contract is to be construed most strongly against the party who drew it up (the *contra proferentem* rule: *see s.* **7,** 3).

(e) Contracts are to be construed according to their *proper law*, *i.e.* usually the law of the country in which they were made: *see s.* **10.**

(f) If the contract fails to express the undoubted intentions of the parties, the court will *rectify* it so as to make it express such intentions: *see* 9 below.

9. Collateral contracts. Where A and B enter into a contract the rights and duties arising will normally affect only A and B: *see* Privity of Contract, *s.* **27.** But sometimes if A was induced to enter into this contract by the representations of X, the court may *imply a collateral contract* between X and A, the consideration for which is A's agreement to enter into the contract with B.

EXAMPLE: X induced A to buy a car from B on hire-purchase. The hire-purchase contract was between A and B and X was not a party to it. The car was defective and injured A. X's statements as to the condition of the car were found to be false. HELD: A had no remedy against B, by reason of an exemption clause. But there was an implied collateral contract between X and A, under which A promised to buy the car from B; X was

B

liable in damages for his false statements: *Andrews* v. *Hopkinson* (1956).

NOTE: Under the *Hire Purchase Act*, 1965, B would now be liable in contract for misrepresentations by his agent, X: *see s.* **48** below.

SECTION 10. CONFLICT OF LAWS

1. Conflict of laws. There is an increasing tendency for mercantile contracts to be made between people in different countries and the question may then arise: which of several possible systems of law should the English court apply to resolve a dispute upon the contract?

The general rule is that the "proper law" of a commercial contract is that which the parties have expressly or impliedly chosen (this will usually be the *Lex Loci Contractus*—"the law of the place of contracting").

2. Rules applicable to commercial contracts.

(a) *Contractual capacity of a party* is generally governed by the law of his domicil (the *Lex Domicilii*).

    A person's domicil is the country in which he *resides with intention to remain there permanently*.

(b) *Whether the contract itself is valid* or not depends on the *proper law* of the contract, *i.e.* whether it is void, voidable, or enforceable.

(c) Questions relating to the *form of the contract* are decided by reference to the *Lex Loci Contractus*.

(d) *Procedural matters* and questions relating to the evidence required to prove the contract are governed by *English law*.

(e) *Questions relating to construction and discharge* of the contract are governed by its *proper law*.

(f) *The legality of the contract* is assessed by the following rules:

    (i) If the contract is illegal by the *Lex Loci Contractus* it will not be enforced in Britain.

    (ii) If the contract is legal where made, but would be illegal in the country in which it is to be performed, it will not be enforced in Britain.

    (iii) A contract valid by its proper law but illegal by English law will not be enforced in Britain.

FORM, CONSIDERATION, AND CAPACITY

GENERALLY a contract can be made in any form, but in exceptional cases the law lays down a particular requirement, *e.g.* that the contract shall be by deed.

All simple contracts must be supported by consideration, that is by some element of exchange which is measurable in money or money's worth, *e.g.* goods in return for cash, or services in return for wages or goods.

Generally any person can make any sort of contract, *i.e.* has full capacity to contract. But certain special classes of person suffer from contractual incapacities of various kinds, *e.g.* infants or minors.

SECTION 11. FORMAL REQUIREMENTS

1. Generally no formality. Most contracts can be made in any form, *i.e.* orally, by writing, by telephone, telegram, or by deed.

But in the following special cases the law requires that a particular form shall be adopted, usually to provide better evidence of the terms and so prevent disputes.

2. Contracts void unless made by deed.

(*a*) Promises of gifts: * *Rann* v. *Hughes* (1778).
(*b*) Transfers of British ships or shares therein.
(*c*) Conditional bills of sale: *see s.* **72**.
(*d*) Certain documents creating or transferring estates or interests in land, *e.g.* conveyances of land, legal mortgages, and leases for more than three years: *Law of Property Act*, 1925.

Note that *corporations' contracts* formerly had to be made by deed if the contract was other than of day-to-day or trivial importance. This rule has been abolished and corporations can now make their contracts in whatever form would be appropriate to private individuals: * *Corporate Bodies Contracts Act*, 1960.

3. Contracts void unless fully written. These include:

(*a*) Bills of exchange: *Bills of Exchange Act*, 1882, *s.* 3(1).
(*b*) Assignments of copyrights: *Copyright Act*, 1956, *s.* 36.
(*c*) Contracts of marine insurance: *Marine Insurance Act*, 1906.
(*d*) Transfers of shares in registered companies: *Companies Act*, 1948.
(*e*) Acknowledgements of statute-barred debts: *Limitation Act*, 1939.
(*f*) Articles of association of registered companies.

NOTE: *Hire purchase contracts*, credit sales and conditional sales are *unenforceable* unless written in proper form and signed by the hirer (or purchaser): *Hire Purchase Act*, 1964, and *see s.* **48, 3.**

4. Contracts unenforceable unless "evidenced" in writing.
Note that these contracts are merely *unenforceable* unless in the required form, while those in paragraphs 2 and 3 above are *void*: *see s.* 3 (meaning of void, etc.).

Contracts in this class are:

(a) *Contracts of guarantee* (*see below*): * *Statute of Frauds*, 1677, *s.* 4.
(b) *Contracts for the sale or other disposition of land* or any interest therein. This includes contracts to grant mortgages, leases, etc.: *L.P.A.*, *s.* 40. (Notice that the *contract* to dispose of land must be evidenced in writing, while the conveyance which effects the actual transfer must be by deed: *see 2 above*.)

NOTE: *Sect.* 4, *Statute of Frauds*, originally applied to several types of contract besides guarantees, *e.g.* contracts for sale of goods worth more than £10, contracts not to be performed within one year of their making, executors' promises to pay a deceased's debts out of their own pocket, etc. But the * *L.R.* (*Enforcement of Contracts*) *Act*, 1954, reduced this list to guarantees only; the other contracts formerly covered by the Statute of Frauds can now be made in any form.

5. Contracts of guarantee. A guarantee is a contract *"to answer for the debt, default or miscarriage of another"*: *s.* 4, *Statute of Frauds*; that is, a contract to discharge another's obligations *if that other fails to do so* himself, *i.e.* a contract of secondary liability (for guarantees generally, *see* Chapter XVI).

Contrast *contracts of indemnity*: promises to discharge another's obligation or to ensure that it is discharged, *i.e.* a contract in which the indemnifier accepts primary liability (indemnities do not need to be evidenced in writing).

NOTE: Guarantees do not need to be evidenced in writing if they are merely part of larger transactions, *e.g.* where, on his appointment, an agent guarantees to make good losses incurred by his employer if any of the clients introduced by the agent fail to pay their debts. Here the guarantee is merely part of the contract of agency and therefore the whole contract can be oral if so desired: *Eastwood* v. *Kenyon* (1840).

6. Meaning of "evidenced in writing." The minimum of necessary written evidence suffices, provided it contains all the material terms of the contract, *i.e.* any *signed note or memorandum of material terms* on any scrap of paper.

The note or memorandum must contain the following:

(a) *The signature of the "party to be charged"* or of his agent, *i.e.* the signature of the defendant in any action brought upon the contract. It need not be signed by the plaintiff in the action.

(b) *All material terms* of the contract, *i.e.* (i) *names* of the parties or sufficient identification (ii) *description of the subject-matter, e.g.* the address of a house being sold (iii) *the price* or other consideration.

NOTE: Although, like other simple contracts guarantees must be supported by consideration, the consideration does not need to be expressly *stated* in the memorandum of guarantee: *Mercantile Law Amendment Act*, 1856.

7. When and how made. The note or memorandum can be made *at any time* after the contract is agreed, providing it is made (and signed by the defendant) before the contract is disputed in court.

It may consist of several documents, provided there is sufficient evidence to connect them beyond reasonable doubt, *e.g.* a letter headed "Dear Sir" might be linked to the envelope which contained it, so identifying the recipient: *Long* v. *Millar* (1879).

PROBLEM: A contracted to buy a house from B, vacant possession to be given on completion. A paid a 10% deposit and B gave him a signed receipt which identified the parties, stated the purpose of the deposit, but contained no mention of vacant possession. Would this receipt be a sufficient memorandum? Would it be sufficient if it mentioned the requirement as to vacant possession?

8. Effect of non-compliance. If a contract required to be evidenced in writing is not so evidenced it is *unenforceable.* Therefore, although it may be perfectly lawful, if one party breaks the contract the other cannot sue him for damages for breach of contract in the normal way (but he would be entitled to keep any deposit he had obtained: *see s.* **3.3**).

BUT NOTE:

(a) *The parties retain all other rights*, except action in the courts. Thus, in an oral contract for the sale of land which fails through the fault of the purchaser, the vendor would be entitled to retain a deposit the purchaser had put down (normally 10%) and the court would not assist the purchaser to recover it: *Monickendam* v. *Leanse* (1923) and *see s.* **3. 3**.

(b) *If one party has fully performed his part of the contract* the court may give him an order for *specific performance*, commanding the defendant to perform his side of the bargain despite the absence of written evidence (this is the *Equitable Doctrine of Part Performance*, and it applies only to contracts for the transfer of some interest in land).

9. The Doctrine of Part Performance. An oral contract for the transfer of any estate or interest in land is unenforceable: *L.P.A.*, *s.* 40. (Breach of such contract does not give rise to any action for damages.)

But if A has performed his part of the contract and B then refuses to perform his part, the court will intervene to save A from hardship by ordering B to perform his side of the bargain.

Such an order for specific performance is discretionary, and will only be granted where:

(a) *The contract is one of which specific performance can be ordered, i.e.* where damages would be inadequate to compensate the plaintiff, and performance can be compelled without requiring constant supervision by the court: *see* Specific Performance, *s.* **26**, **9**.

(b) *The act of part performance relied on is referable to the contract alleged:* ✱ *Wakeham* v. *McKenzie* (1968).

(c) The act of part performance relied on is such that it would *amount to fraud on the part of the defendant* to take advantage of the absence of writing.

(d) *There is sufficient oral evidence* of the material terms of the contract.

EXAMPLES:

(i) X orally promised a woman to leave her his house in his will, if she gave up her own house and came to keep house and care for him until his death. She did so, but paid for her own board. When he died his will made no mention of the bargain. She sued the executors. HELD: Her actions were sufficiently clear part performance of the oral contract: ✱ *Wakeham* v. *McKenzie* (1968).

(ii) P wrote asking C to come and live with him, and promised to leave his house to C. C sold his own home and went to live with P. Later P ejected C, who sued for specific performance. HELD: C's sale of his own home taken in conjunction with P's request and promise constituted a binding contract, under which C was entitled to live in P's house and to inherit it on P's death: *Parker* v. *Clarke* (1960).

SECTION 12. VALUABLE CONSIDERATION

1. Importance of consideration. The courts will not enforce a simple contract unless it is supported by valuable consideration, which is therefore an essential element in most contracts.

(Consideration is not necessary in specialty contracts or contracts of record: *see s.* **2.**)

2. Meaning of "valuable consideration." It has been defined as *the price for which a promise is bought* (Sir Frederick Pollock).

Consideration itself means "some right, interest, profit, or benefit accruing to one party or some forbearance, detriment, loss or responsibility given, suffered or undertaken by the other": *per Lush, J.*, ✱ *Currie* v. *Misa* (1875).

Consideration therefore means the *element of exchange* in a bargain, and in order to satisfy the requirements of English

law it must be *valuable* consideration, *i.e.* something which is
capable of being valued in terms of money or money's worth,
however slight. It may take the form of money, goods, services, a promise to marry, a promise to forbear from suing the
promisee, etc.

3. Kinds of consideration.

(a) *Executory consideration, i.e.* where the consideration
   consists of a *promise* to do something in the future (such
   as an engagement to marry someone).

(b) *Executed consideration, i.e.* where the act constituting the
   consideration is wholly *performed*.

Thus if X pays a shopkeeper now for goods which are
promised to be delivered later, X has *executed* his consideration,
but the shopkeeper is giving *executory* consideration, *i.e.* a
promise to be executed in the future.

4. Rules governing consideration. These require to be fully
learned and understood, and are set out in detail below.

RULES RELATING TO CONSIDERATION

A. Necessity for consideration. Every simple contract must
be supported by valuable consideration, otherwise it is normally void.

EXCEPTIONS:

(a) *Gratuitous bailments.* A bailment is the delivery of a chattel
   to a hirer or borrower for some limited purpose or period.
   Most bailments are for *reward, i.e.* are supported by some
   payment, but even where the bailment is *gratuitous* it is
   still recognised as an enforceable contract: *Bainbridge* v.
   Firmstone (1838). (In such cases the courts tend to regard the
   owner's parting with possession of his chattel as sufficient
   notional consideration, so that this is not a real exception to
   the doctrine of consideration.)

(b) *Gratuitous services, when performance commenced.* If A
   gratuitously promises to dig B's garden, and fails to do so,
   B cannot sue A for breach of contract since there is no
   consideration for A's promise. But it has been suggested
   that if A once commenced the digging, he would be under
   an obligation to exercise reasonable care in the work and
   could be sued for damages if he were negligent.

B. Legality of consideration. The consideration must be lawful, *e.g.* not some illegal act, such as paying someone to commit a crime.

If the consideration is unlawful, the contract is void: *see s.* **18.**

C. Consideration must move from the promisee. That is, a person seeking to enforce a simple contract in court must prove that he himself has given consideration in return for the promise he is seeking to enforce.

EXAMPLE: D had supplied goods to a wholesaler, X, on condition that any retailer to whom X resupplied the goods should promise X not to sell them to the public without fulfilling stated conditions. X supplied goods to S upon this condition, but nevertheless S sold them in breach of stated conditions. HELD: There was a contract between D and X, and a contract between X and S, but none between D and S. Therefore D could not obtain damages from S. The main reason for this decision was the fact that D could not show that he himself had given any consideration for S's promise to X: ✱ *Dunlop Tyre Co.* v. *Selfridges Ltd.* (1915) (reaffirmed in *Midland Silicones Ltd.* v. *Scruttons Ltd.* (1962), *H.L.*).

NOTE: Compare this rule with the *Doctrine of Privity of Contract, see s.* **27.** In effect, in any contractual action, the court asks two implied questions which must be satisfied before the plaintiff can succeed in his action: (i) Is the plaintiff a party to the contract he seeks to enforce? (privity of contract) and (ii) if so, has he given consideration for the promise he seeks to enforce? In *Dunlop* v. *Selfridges* the plaintiff failed to supply satisfactory answers to both questions.

D. It must be something more than the promisee is already bound to do for the promisor.

That is, the person seeking to enforce the promise must show that he himself has undertaken some obligation to the promisor *beyond* what he was already bound to do either (*a*) as part of his legal duty as a citizen, or (*b*) as part of a private contractual duty owed to the promisor.

EXAMPLE: If a seaman deserts his ship—so breaking his contract—and is induced to return to his duty by the promise of extra wages, he cannot later sue for the extra wages since he has only done what he was already contracted for: *Stilk* v. *Myrick* (1809).

BUT NOTE: performance by A of an existing duty owed to B
will suffice to support a promise by C to A.

Thus where A was engaged to marry B, and C promised A a
sum of money to carry out this promise to B, it was HELD that
A could sue C for the money as soon as he had performed his
promise and married B: * *Shadwell* v. *Shadwell* (1860).

E. Consideration must be real. That is, it must not be *vague,
indefinite, or illusory, e.g.* a son's vague promise to "stop being
a nuisance" to his father: *White* v. *Bluett* (1853).

Although the consideration must be real, it *need not be
adequate, i.e.* it is up to the parties to fix their own prices, and
providing there is some definite valuable consideration the
court will not set a contract aside merely because the price is
inadequate: *Haigh* v. *Brooks* (1839).

But a *ridiculously* inadequate consideration may be prima
facie evidence of misrepresentation or coercion: *see s.* **17.**

EXAMPLE: A bought a guarantee contract from B which later
turned out to be unenforceable. HELD: A had got what he
wanted and could not later rescind the contract merely because it turned out to be worth less than he thought: * *Haigh* v.
Brooks (1839).

F. Consideration must not be past. That is, a promise made
in return for some *past* service is unenforceable, *e.g.* where,
having bought a horse, the purchaser promised to give the
seller an extra sum because of his satisfaction with the purchase it was HELD that the promise was unenforceable since it
related to a past sale, and the purchaser was therefore receiving
no new benefit as consideration for his new promise: *Roscorla*
v. *Thomas* (1842).

EXCEPTIONS: *Past consideration is sufficient* in the following
cases:
(a) *To revive a statute-barred claim*, a mere written acknowledge-
    ment is enough without any fresh consideration: *Limitation
    Act*, 1939 (for limitation of actions, *see s.* **24**).
(b) *A bill of exchange can be supported by* any antecedent debt
    or liability: *B.E.A.*, 1882, *s.* 27.
(c) Where the past consideration was rendered in response to *an
    earlier request* by the person who subsequently promises to
    pay for the service rendered: * the rule in *Lampleigh* v.
    Braithwaite (1616). Here the promisor's request is held to
    imply a promise to pay a reasonable sum later and the
    subsequent promise to pay merely fixes the sum: *Stewart* v.
    Casey (1892).

EXAMPLE: A asked B to use his influence to obtain a royal pardon for A, who had committed a crime. B did as he was asked, and later (in consideration of this past service) A promised to pay B £100. HELD: B could enforce payment: *Lampleigh* v. *Braithwaite*.

G. Payment of a smaller sum will not discharge a liability to pay a larger: *the Rule in* ✱ *Foakes* v. *Beer* (1854).

Thus if A owes B £100 and B agrees to accept £50 in complete discharge of the debt, there is nothing to stop B later changing his mind and suing for the remaining £50.

EXCEPTIONS:

(a) *Where the smaller sum is paid in a form or manner different* from that originally intended, *e.g.* where the smaller sum is paid earlier than the debt was due, or where a money debt is settled in goods or by cheque to a smaller value, or is paid by handing over "a horse, hawk, or robe": ✱ *Pinnel's Case* (1602).

But it is important to note that the creditor's acceptance of the smaller sum *must be voluntary*. Thus where a debtor put pressure on his creditor to accept a smaller sum, it was held that the acceptance was not binding: *D. & C. Builders Ltd.* v. *Rees* (1966).

(b) Where (i) the creditor *promises* to accept a smaller sum (ii) intending his promise *to be relied upon*, and (iii) the debtor *alters his financial position* in reliance on the promise, *the creditor may be estopped* from going back on his promise, even though it was unsupported by consideration.

EXAMPLE: A leased property to B at a rent of £2,500 p.a. but promised to accept half this sum during the war years, and B relied on this promise, making no attempt to earn the money necessary to pay the full rent. If later A went back on his promise and sued for the full rental, the court would exercise its equitable discretion and estop A from retracting his promise: ✱ *The Hightrees Case (Central London Property Trust* v. *Hightrees, etc.,* 1947).

This is an application of the principle of *equitable estoppel,* whereby a man may be prevented from denying any promise unconscionably, even though it was unsupported by consideration. But the Hightrees rule can only be raised as a defence, and not as a cause of action by the debtor, *e.g.* where a creditor has retracted his promise to accept a smaller sum and has forced the debtor to pay him the full amount, the debtor could not use the Hightrees rule as the basis of an action to recover the extra money paid: *Combe* v. *Combe* (1950).

SECTION 13. CONTRACTUAL CAPACITY

The general rule is that all persons have full capacity to make binding contracts, but the following exceptional cases exist: *see also* Infants, *s.* **14** below.

1. Aliens. They have full capacity, save that they cannot own or hold shares in British ships: *Merchant Shipping Act*, 1894, *s.* 1.

Aliens residing in countries at war with Britain are classed as *enemy aliens* (whatever their nationality). They cannot sue in British courts during war-time, but can be sued; and if sued they can defend the action, appeal, and lodge counter-claims in the normal way, either personally or through agents: *Porter* v. *Freudenberg* (1916).

2. Foreign sovereigns and diplomats. They have diplomatic immunity and cannot be sued in British courts, unless they voluntarily submit to the jurisdiction: *Diplomatic Privileges Act*, 1964.

3. Married women. They now have full contractual capacity, can sue or be sued in their own names, can be bankrupted for their debts, etc.: *L.R.* (*Married Women & Tortfeasors*) *Act*, 1935.

Formerly a husband was responsible for his wife's contracts, but since 1935 this liability no longer arises unless the wife is acting as her husband's agent. Such agency is implied in contracts relating to the purchase of household necessaries: *see* Chapter VII, *s.* **29**.

4. Mental patients and drunkards. Their contracts are voidable, if (i) they were so drunk or mentally unbalanced as not to understand what the contract was about, and (ii) the other party was aware of this: *Imperial Loan Co.* v. *Stone* (1892). Such voidable contracts can be ratified during lucid or sober intervals.

∗ *The Sale of Goods Act*, 1893, *s.* 2, lays down that lunatics, drunkards, and infants are bound to pay a reasonable price for necessaries (*see* Infants, *below*).

5. Corporations. A corporation is an artificial personality recognised by the law. Consequently they can only contract through human agents.

Under the *Ultra Vires Doctrine* a statutory or registered corporation can only contract validly within the powers conferred upon it. Any contract which is *ultra vires* ("beyond the powers") is *void*. (Corporations created by royal charter are not subject to the doctrine, though if they exceed their authority their charter may be revoked.)

NOTE:

(i) *Statutory companies, i.e.* those created by special Act of Parliament: the statute will define the company's powers, and any contract beyond those powers is void absolutely.

(ii) *Registered companies, i.e.* those incorporated by registration under the *Companies Acts*: their powers are not usually expressly stated, but such companies must register a *memorandum of association* in which the *objects* of the company must be stated. The powers of the company will then be *such powers as are necessary to the achievement of its objects*. Any contract which exceeds such powers is void and cannot be ratified even by the unanimous vote of all the members: * *Ashbury Carriage Co.* v. *Riche* (1875).

Registered companies must also have *articles of association* which govern the internal regulations of the company, *e.g.* the rights of members and the powers of directors. If the directors exceed the powers delegated to them by the articles, the contract is *voidable* by the company and is said to be "*ultra vires* the directors" (but if the contract in question is within the powers of the company itself, it can ratify such contract if it wishes).

SECTION 14. CAPACITY OF MINORS

1. Infants' contracts. An infant or minor attains his majority at the first instant of his 18th birthday: *Family Law Reform Act*, 1969. (Formerly the age of majority was 21.)

Minors' contracts are roughly divisible into *three classes*: *binding, voidable, and void.*

2. Contracts binding on minors.

(a) *Contracts for "necessaries,"* i.e. *goods and services* necessary to maintain the infant, having regard to his social position. (A married minor would also be liable for necessaries supplied to his wife and children, and for such things as funeral and legal expenses.)

Goods: A minor must pay (i) a reasonable price for goods (ii) suitable for his condition in life and (iii) to his actual requirements, at the time of (iv) sale and (v) delivery: ∗ *S.G.A.*, 1893, *s*. 2, (before he can be made to pay for goods, the supplier must prove all five points).

Goods may be classed as necessaries even if they are *luxurious*, provided they have some actual utility and fit the actual requirements of the minor, *e.g.* an engagement ring: *Elkington* v. *Amery* (1936).

EXAMPLE: A minor ordered eleven fancy waistcoats, which could have been considered necessaries having regard to his financial position. HELD: He could not be made to pay for them, as he was already sufficiently supplied with articles of this kind: *Nash* v. *Inman* (1908).

NOTE: Goods necessary when ordered might have ceased to be necessary by the time they were delivered, *e.g.* where a minor orders a suit from a tailor but buys other suits before that ordered is actually delivered. Here the minor could not be made to pay the tailor.

(b) *Beneficial contracts relating to education or training, e.g.* contracts intended to assist the minor in training for adult life or for a career (non-educational contracts would not be binding, even if beneficial).

These contracts are binding even if they contain one or two *burdensome terms*, provided they are on the whole beneficial to the minor.

EXAMPLES: (i) A contract signed by an infant boxer, which was intended to protect him from exploitation during his minority, contained a clause by which he was to forfeit his pay for a fight if disqualified for fouling. HELD: This clause was burdensome but was binding since the contract as a whole was beneficial: ∗ *Doyle* v. *White City Stadium* (1935).

(ii) C contracted with a publisher to publish his autobiography, since his wife and child needed money. Later C tried to avoid the contract. HELD: It was binding, as beneficial in earning C a livelihood: *Chaplin* v. *Leslie Frewen* (*Publishers*) *Ltd*. (1966).

3. Contracts void against minors. The following are absolutely void against a minor:

(a) *Contracts to repay money* lent or to be lent.
(b) Contracts for *goods* supplied or to be supplied, *other than necessaries*.

(c) *All accounts stated, e.g.* IOUs: ✳ *Infants Relief Act*, 1874, *s.* 1.

NOTE ALSO:

(a) A minor incurs no liability by signing a *bill of exchange* (such as a cheque) whether as drawer, indorser, or acceptor: *B.E.A.*, 1882, *s.* 22.

(b) If a minor fraudulently misrepresents his age in order to obtain a loan of money, he cannot be made to repay the loan; nor can he be sued for damages for fraudulent misrepresentation, since this would amount to indirect enforcement of the void contract of loan: ✳ *Leslie* v. *Sheill* (1914).

(c) If a minor obtains unnecessary goods under a void contract, he must return them if possible. If it is impossible (perhaps because the goods have been consumed), he cannot be made to pay any compensation for them: *Stocks* v. *Wilson* (1913). But if he has sold such goods to another person, he is liable for damages for the *tort of conversion* since he had no right to the goods and has dealt with them in a manner inconsistent with the rights of the true owner: ✳ *Ballett* v. *Mingay* (1943).

(d) A minor can only recover money he has transferred under a void contract if he has received no benefit under the contract: *Steinberg* v. *Scala Ltd.* (1923).

(e) If an adult guarantees a loan made to a minor, the guarantee is void as well as the contract of loan: ✳ *Coutts & Co.* v. *Browne-Lecky* (1947).

(f) If a minor borrows money to buy necessaries he must repay the loan, as the lender is placed in the position of the seller of the necessaries, *i.e.* is subrogated into the position of the seller.

4. Contracts voidable by a minor.

(a) *Contracts requiring express repudiation* before or within a reasonable time after reaching 18, *e.g.* contracts involving a continuing interest in property of a permanent nature, such as leases of land or contracts to take shares in a company.

Such contracts will become binding unless repudiated by the infant within a reasonable time after his 18th birthday. Thus if a minor leases a flat, he must pay rent while he is in occupation but can repudiate the lease and escape liability for future rent any time until a few weeks after his 18th birthday; if he fails so to repudiate he will become liable for all the rent up to his majority and for the whole of the lease thereafter: ✳ *Davies* v. *Beynon-Harris* (1931).

(b) *Contracts not requiring express repudiation*, *e.g.* trading contracts and promises to marry. These *remain voidable*, even after the 18th birthday and even if confirmed by a fresh promise after 18, unless such promise was supported by fresh and *additional consideration* (otherwise any purported ratification by the minor after 18 is ineffective: *Infants Relief Act*, 1874, *s.* 2).

Thus a trading contract is not binding on a minor even if beneficial to him. And if a minor in business receives payment for goods sold by him, but refuses to deliver them, he cannot usually be sued for their value: *Cowern* v. *Nield* (1912).

VOID, VOIDABLE, AND ILLEGAL CONTRACTS

THESE include contracts invalidated because they rest upon some fundamental mistake of fact (void), contracts induced by misrepresentation or coercion (voidable), and contracts which are contrary to some statute or to Common Law (void and illegal).

SECTION 15. MISTAKE

1. Effect of mistake. The general Common Law rule is that mistake made by one or both parties in making a contract has no effect on the validity of the contract, *e.g.* where a person pays an excessive price for goods under a mistake as to their true value: *Leaf* v. *International Galleries* (1950).

However where the parties contracted under a fundamental mistake of fact, the contract may be *void if*:

(a) *the mistake is one of fact,* and not of law or opinion, and

(b) *the mistake is so fundamental* as to negative the agreement.

Mistake which thus renders a contract void is called "operative mistake."

2. Mistakes of law and of fact. Mistakes of law generally have no effect, since "ignorance of the law is no excuse" (*ignorantia juris haud excusat*).

In two exceptional cases, however, mistakes of law are treated as though they were mistakes of fact:

(a) *Mistake of foreign law*, since the laws of a foreign country require to be proved in British courts as ordinary facts.

(b) *Mistake as to private rights*, *e.g.* a right of property, as where a purchaser buys property which already belongs to him: *Cooper* v. *Phibbs* (1867) (*see note,* "Money paid under mistake of law," *s.* **4**).

3. Operative mistakes of fact. It is difficult to deduce consistent principles from the numerous cases on this subject, but it is fairly well established that in the following cases a fundamental mistake of fact will avoid a contract:

(a) *Common mistake as to the existence of the subject-matter of the contract.*

(b) *Mutual mistake as to the terms of an offer, or the identity of the subject-matter.*

(c) *Unilateral mistake as to the identity of the person contracted with.*

(d) *Unilateral mistake as to the nature of a contract signed.*

NOTE: *Common mistake* is where both parties make the same mistake. *Mutual mistake* is where each makes a different mistake, *i.e.* they misunderstand one another.

Unilateral mistake is where only one party is mistaken. Unilateral mistake is generally of no effect, unless (i) it concerns some fundamental fact, and (ii) the other party is aware of the mistake. Thus unilateral mistake has no effect where it relates merely to an error of judgment by one of the parties.

4. Common mistake as to existence of subject-matter, *i.e.* where, unknown to both parties, the subject-matter has been destroyed before the contract was made.

EXAMPLES:

(a) The sale of a life insurance policy on the life of a person who, unknown to purchaser or seller, is already dead: *Scott* v. *Coulson* (1903).

(b) The sale of goods which, unknown to the contractors, have already been destroyed: *Couturier* v. *Hastie* (1857), and *Sale of Goods Act*, 1893, *s.* 6 (*see s.* 42).

NOTE: Mistakes as to the *quality* of the subject-matter generally have no effect. The general maxim of English law is *caveat emptor* ("let the buyer beware") and if a man mistakenly pays an unduly high price for something he has only himself to blame for the bad bargain.

EXAMPLES:

(a) L paid a senior employee £50,000 compensation for loss of office when dismissing him before his contract had expired. Later L discovered that the employee had committed breaches of duty which would have entitled L to dismiss him without compensation. HELD: L could not recover the money on discovering the truth, since the House of Lords considered that the mistake related only to the quality of what was purchased, namely release from the contract of employment: ✱ *Bell* v. *Lever Bros.* (1931).

(b) L bought from G a painting which both mistakenly believed to be by Constable and of great value. Later L discovered it was by an unknown artist and comparatively worthless. HELD: L could not avoid the contract, as his mistake related only to the quality of the subject-matter: ✱ *Leaf* v. *International Galleries* (1950).

5. Mutual mistake.

(a) *As to the terms of the offer.* Where the parties *misunderstand each other* as to the terms of the offer, the contract will be void if the mistake is sufficiently fundamental.

Here there is no real concurrence of offer and acceptance, since the offeree is accepting on a mistaken understanding of what the offeror intended.

EXAMPLE: A and B contracted to ship a cargo on the *Peerless* from Bombay. Unknown to either party there were two ships of the same name, and both were at Bombay and were due to sail on different dates. A had in mind one of the two ships, and B had in mind the other. HELD: The contract was void: ✱ *Raffles* v. *Wichelhaus* (1864).

(b) *As to the identity of the subject-matter, i.e.* the parties misunderstand each other as to what is to constitute the subject-matter of the contract.

EXAMPLE: At an auction X, misled by the catalogue, bid an absurdly high price for some tow (thinking it was hemp) and the auctioneer accepted the bid thinking that X was merely mistaken as to the value of tow. HELD: Contract void: ✱ *Scriven* v. *Hindley* (1913).

6. Unilateral mistake as to the identity of the person contracted with. Such mistake will only operate to avoid the contract where:

(a) The identity of the person contracted with is of *fundamental importance*; and

(b) *This is made clear* by the party mistaken before or at the time of contracting (so that the other party knows of the mistake).

Contrast the following two cases:

(i) A rogue, X, entered a jeweller's and offered to buy goods. His offer was accepted, and he then offered to pay by cheque. The jeweller accepted the cheque, but said delivery would be delayed until the cheque was cleared. The rogue then said he was a well-known person and asked to take some of the jewels immediately. Deceived as to his identity, the jeweller let him take some of the jewels. X took the goods and sold them to a pawnbroker, and the cheque proved worthless. HELD: The contract was made before the identity became important, therefore it was *not void* on the grounds of mistake: ✱ *Phillips* v. *Brooks* (1919) (the contract was probably voidable on the grounds of misrepresentation): *see also s.* **43**.

(ii) A rogue, X, offered to buy a car from I and to pay by cheque. I refused the offer and the cheque, since she did not know X. X then convinced her that he was a well-known person, and being convinced, she accepted his cheque and let him take the car. He sold the car to L and the cheque proved worthless. HELD: The contract between X and I was void for mistake, since the mistake occurred during the negotiations, and I would not have accepted X's offer if she had not been convinced of his identity: ✱ *Ingram* v. *Little* (1961). Consequently, X never had any right to the car and could not lawfully sell it to L, so that in the action in court I was allowed to recover the car from L.

7. Unilateral mistake as to nature of a contract signed. Generally a person who signs a contract is bound by it, even if he has not read it: *L'Estrange* v. *Graucob, see s.* **7**, **1**.

But a person who signs a document under a fundamental mistake *as to its nature* may have it avoided, *e.g.* where A is induced to sign a negotiable instrument believing it is merely a guarantee: ✱ *Foster* v. *McKinnon* (1869).

Contrast a mistake merely as to *the contents* of the document, *e.g.* where A signed a document, knowing it disposed of an interest in land but thinking it merely a mortgage, when in fact it also bound him to pay money. HELD: the mistake was inoperative, since it related merely to the contents of the document, and A knew the nature of what he was signing: *Howatson* v. *Webb* (1907), see also *Gallie* v. *Lee* (1969).

NOTE: Carelessness does not exclude the defence, providing the mistake is fundamental: *Carlisle, etc., Banking Co.* v. *Bragg*

(1911) (but if the document signed is a negotiable instrument carelessness might negative the defence).

8. Mistake in equity. The Common Law rules relating to mistake stated above render the contract either completely void or completely valid, even though neither conclusion may be completely just.

But since the *Judicature Acts* (1873–75) allow equity to be administered in all courts to modify the Common Law in the interests of justice, the courts have used equitable principles to achieve a compromise result where it would be unjust to one or both of the parties to apply the Common Law doctrine rigidly in cases of mistake.

Equity will thus intervene:

(a) *To rectify* (amend) a written instrument containing patent errors of expression.

(b) *To set aside an agreement on terms* fair to all parties, where Common Law will not declare it void: ✸ *Solle* v. *Butcher* (1950). See also *Grist* v. *Bailey* (1966) where a sale of a house was held voidable on grounds of common mistake as to value, which was not sufficient to render the contract void at law.

(c) *To refuse to order specific performance* of a contract against a defendant who is labouring under a mistake such that it would be grossly unjust to compel him to perform his contract, *e.g.* where A, by a slip of the pen, writes offering to sell land to B for "£1,250" when he meant to write "£2,250." Here if B tries to enforce a contract at the lower price equity will refuse to help him and will protect A against the consequence of his mistake: *Webster* v. *Cecil* (1861).

9. Rectification. Where a written contract does not accurately express the intentions of the parties, the court will amend (rectify) the contract to make it express the true intentions. The party seeking rectification *must prove*:

(a) The mistake to be rectified lies *only* in the words used.

(b) There is a complete and final contract between the parties.

(c) There is clear oral or written evidence of the true intention of the parties.

(d) The mistake is *common* to both parties: *Craddock Bros.* v. *Hunt* (1923).

SECTION 16. MISREPRESENTATION AND FRAUD

1. Caveat emptor. In English law a person is generally under no duty to disclose all facts in his possession to the other contracting party. Each must protect his own interests un- aided. The rule is "buyer beware" (*caveat emptor*). Keeping silent therefore is generally not actionable, even though it causes damage to the other party.

> EXAMPLE: H sold pigs "with all faults" to W, knowing that they had swine fever, and that W was unaware of this. HELD: W could not have the contract set aside: *Ward* v. *Hobbs* (1878).

2. Misrepresentation. But where one party makes a *positive false statement* which deceives the other, this may amount to *misrepresentation* rendering the contract voidable at the option of the party misled.

The deceived party may also be entitled to damages: (i) for *deceit*, if he can prove fraud, or (ii) for *negligence*, if he can prove that the representation—though believed by the maker —was made negligently: *Misrepresentation Act, 1967*.

3. What is misrepresentation? A misrepresentation is (i) a false statement (ii) of material fact, (iii) made by a party to the contract or his agent, (iv) which induces the other party to enter into the contract.

Misleading conduct may also amount to misrepresentation, if it presents a misleading picture about material facts and satisfies (iii) and (iv) above.

NOTE:

(a) *The statement must be of fact*, not of law or opinion (but an opinion expressed by a person who might be expected to know the facts, *e.g.* by a technical expert on his own sub- ject, may amount to a statement of fact: *Brown* v. *Raphael* (1958)).

(b) *It must be of material importance* in the transaction, *e.g.* in the sale of a car a statement that the car is in good working order. But representations relating to trivial matters, such as the condition of the windscreen wipers, would not amount to actionable misrepresentation.

(c) *It must be made by a party to the contract* or his agent, *i.e.*

not by a mere bystander. Thus where A invests money in a
company in reliance on a false statement by the company's
auditor in the company's balance sheet, A cannot sue the
company for misrepresentation because the contract is
between him and the company and the auditor is not an
agent for the company for the purpose of making statements to lure investors: *Candler* v. *Crane Christmas* (1951)
(but an action might be possible against the auditor for the
tort of negligence: ✱ *Hedley Byrne & Co.* v. *Hellers, etc.*
(1963), *H.L.*).

(d) *It must be relied upon, i.e.* it must succeed in inducing the
offeree to enter into the contract. Thus, A sold a broken gun
to B and patched the barrel with clay to conceal the crack.
B did not examine the gun and therefore was not deceived
by the patch. HELD: The misrepresentation was not
actionable, since it had no effect on B: *Horsfall* v. *Thomas*
(1862).

(e) *It must be by positive words or conduct,* not by mere silence
unless the silence amounts to active concealment of facts,
or silence about some facts puts those revealed into a false
and deceptive light. Thus where a company's prospectus
showed that it had paid dividends for several years, without
disclosing that these had been paid out of reserves as the
company was trading at a loss, it was HELD that the om-
mission was deceptive and amounted to misrepresentation:
R. v. *Kylsant* (1923).

(f) *Statements true when made but becoming false before the contract is made must be corrected.* Thus R arranged to sell a
business to Y and estimated profits at £2,000 p.a. By the
time the sale was completed the profits had fallen considerably. HELD: A's failure to disclose the change amounted to
misrepresentation: *With* v. *O'Flanagan* (1936).

Thus an exceptional duty of disclosure is imposed in (e) above
where silence is actually deceptive, and in (f) where facts true
when stated subsequently become untrue before negotiations
are completed. A further duty of disclosure is imposed in
uberrimae fidei contracts: *see* 10 *below.*

4. Innocent misrepresentation. If a person makes a misrepresentation *believing* what he says is true he commits innocent
misrepresentation.

The party misled may:

(a) *affirm the contract* and treat it as binding, *or may rescind*
the contract by notifying the other party and—where

necessary—obtaining the court's assistance to secure restitution.

(b) *sue for damages* under the *Misrepresentation Act*, 1967, s. 2.

5. Damages for innocent misrepresentation. Formerly a plaintiff could not secure damages for innocent misrepresentation, but the *Misrepresentation Act*, 1967, gives a right to damages in certain cases:

(a) *Where the misrepresentation was made negligently.* Note that negligence is presumed; the defendant can only escape liability for damages if he can show that he had *reasonable grounds* for believing what he said was true *at the time the* contract was made: *s.* 2 (1).

(b) *Where the plaintiff has sought rescission*, the court has power to award damages *in lieu* of rescission: s. 2 (2).

NOTE: Any *exemption clause* seeking to exclude liability for misrepresentation is *void unless* it is deemed *fair and reasonable* in the circumstances: s. 3.

Damages are also obtainable against the makers for innocent misrepresentations made in a company prospectus: *Companies Act*, 1948, *s.* 43.

6. Fraudulent misrepresentation. "An untrue statement made knowingly, or without belief in its truth, or recklessly, careless whether it be true or false": *per Lord Herschel*, ✻ *Derry* v. *Peek* (1889).

Thus if the maker believes that his representation is true, he cannot be guilty of fraud, even if he was negligent or unreasonable in saying what he did: *Akerhielm* v. *De Mare* (1959). (But in such cases he may be liable for damages for the tort of negligence: ✻ *Hedley Byrne & Co.* v. *Hellers, etc.* (1963).)

7. Remedies for fraudulent misrepresentation.

(*a*) The plaintiff may sue for damages for the tort of deceit (fraud).

(*b*) The plaintiff may repudiate the contract or have it rescinded by the court (with or without claiming damages for deceit).

(*c*) The plaintiff may affirm the contract and still claim damages for deceit.

8. Limits to the right of rescission. Although the misled party can generally get the contract rescinded (set aside by the court) this right is lost in the following cases:

(a) *Affirmation:* where the injured party has expressly or impliedly affirmed the contract after learning of the misrepresentation.

(b) *Restitution impossible:* where the parties cannot be restored to their original position, *i.e. restitutio in integrum* (total restitution) is impossible.

(c) *Prejudice of third parties:* where an innocent third party has obtained an interest in the subject-matter of the contract in good faith and for value: see *Phillips* v. *Brooks, s.* **15** (in that case the innocent purchaser of the jewels from the rogue was held entitled to them since he had bought them from a person with a voidable title to them before that title was avoided and without notice of the fraud: *see s.* **43**, 6).

(d) *Undue delay:* where in a case of innocent misrepresentation the plaintiff delays unreasonably in seeking rescission, the court may refuse to grant him the discretionary remedy of rescission: ✱ *Leaf* v. *International Galleries* (1950).

NOTE: Formerly rescission was unobtainable where a contract had been performed under the Rule in *Sedāon* v. *N.E. Salt Co.* (1905). This rule has been abolished by the 1967 *Act*, *s.* 1.

9. Representations as terms of a contract. If a misrepresentation is made during negotiations and is later incorporated as a term of the contract, the remedies of the injured party will be basically those for breach of contract. The remedies available will then depend on whether the term concerned is a condition or a warranty: *see s.* **9.**

10. Contracts uberrimae fidei ("of the utmost good faith"). Although there is no general duty of disclosure, in some exceptional contracts the law imposes a special duty to act with the utmost good faith, *i.e.* to disclose all material information.

Failure so to disclose renders the contract *voidable* at the option of the other party (and note the duty of disclosure imposed in ordinary contracts in certain circumstances: *see* 3 (e) and (f) *above*).

EXAMPLES:

(a) *Contracts of insurance.* The insured must disclose all facts which might influence the judgment of a prudent insurer, whether to decline the risk or to increase the premium.

(b) *Contracts of family arrangement,* for the settlement of family property, etc. Each member of the family must disclose any portions he or she has already received without the knowledge of other members of the family.

(c) *Company prospectuses.* Directors, promoters, etc. must make full disclosure of material facts in any prospectus inviting the public to subscribe for shares in the company: *Companies Act*, 1948, *s.* 43. Failure to do so renders the contract voidable and makes the directors, etc., liable for damages.

(d) *Contracts for sale of land.* The vendor must disclose any defects in his title to the land, of which he knows. The duty does not extend to other matters, *e.g.* there is no obligation to disclose physical defects in the property sold.

(e) *Suretyship and partnership contracts.* These contracts are not *uberrimae fidei* at their formation, but since made they impose a duty of utmost good faith on the parties to disclose to each other all material facts coming to light after the making of the contract (*see* Partnership, *s.* 34, and Guarantees, *s.* 74).

SECTION 17. DURESS AND UNDUE INFLUENCE

1. Duress. This means actual or threatened violence to the person (not the property) of the party coerced or to his wife, children, or parents, and its effect is to render the contract voidable at the option of the party coerced.

Threats of imprisonment are included under this head, *e.g.* where A was induced to part with valuable documents by threats of continued confinement: *Cummings* v. *Ince* (1847).

2. Undue influence. This means any pressure or coercion, not amounting to duress, which prevents the party coerced from exercising free judgment, and it makes the contract voidable by him at the discretion of the court (thus a plaintiff who proves duress is entitled to rescission, while one who can only prove undue influence is dependent on the discretion of the court).

Undue influence covers all types of pressure not amounting to duress, *e.g.* moral pressure, threats of violence to property, playing on victim's superstitions, etc.

To be actionable the undue influence need not have been exercised by a party to the contract (cx. misrepresentation).

EXAMPLE: A mother coerced her daughter into making a money-lending contract with X, a money-lender, who knew of the mother's actions. HELD: The contract was voidable by the daughter: *Lancashire Loans Ltd.* v. *Black* (1934).

3. Undue influence may be presumed. The court presumes that undue influence has been available to one party (and exerted) in contracts between persons in a fiduciary relationship, *i.e.* where one party is in a position to influence the other unfairly. Wherever undue influence is thus presumed, the burden of proof will lie on the defendant to disprove its exercise if he wishes to preserve the contract.

Undue influence is *presumed* in contracts between parent and child, trustee and beneficiary, solicitor and client, doctor and patient, priest and communicant, teacher and pupil, etc.

The defendant can *disprove* undue influence by showing that:

(a) full disclosure of all material facts was made;
(b) the consideration was adequate, and
(c) the weaker party was in receipt of independent legal advice.

4. Other cases of undue influence. Even where it is not presumed, undue influence may still be alleged. In such cases the burden of proof lies on the plaintiff to show that such influence existed and was exerted.

EXAMPLE: A nephew managing the affairs of an elderly aunt persuaded her to give him some shares, for the purpose of getting control of the company. HELD: The contract was voidable, despite the fact that she had received independent legal advice, since the lawyer who advised her to make the contract was not informed that the shares were virtually all the property the woman possessed: *Inche Noriah* v. *Shaik Ali Bin Omar* (1929).

5. Right to relief lost. Since remedies for undue influence are discretionary, they will only be awarded where the plaintiff's own conduct is equitable. A claim for relief may be disallowed where:

(a) the plaintiff's conduct has been tricky or unfair, or
(b) the plaintiff has delayed unreasonably in seeking rescission of the contract: *Allcard* v. *Skinner* (1887).

SECTION 18. ILLEGALITY

1. Meaning of "illegality." An illegal contract is one which is void because (*a*) it is for an illegal purpose, or (*b*) it is contrary to some rule of public policy.

The courts will generally give the parties to such contracts no protection at all, even to prevent hardship (except as stated in 5 below). Contrast contracts which are void for some other reason than illegality, *e.g.* mistake, or by *s.* 1 Infants' Relief Act, *see s.* **14**; in these cases the court will assist the parties to the extent of ordering the return of property transferred under the contract: *Chappell* v. *Poles* (1837).

2. The Doctrine of Severance. Where a contract is for several independent purposes, some of which are lawful and others unlawful, the court may sever the illegal terms from the contract and enforce the remaining lawful terms: *Pickering* v. *Ilfracombe Rail Co.* (1868), and *see s.* **21. 5.**

But this is only possible where the lawful and unlawful terms are clearly independent. The court will not re-write the main terms of the contract so as to make it lawful: *Napier* v. *National Business Agency* (1951).

3. Presumption in favour of validity. The courts are reluctant to declare any contract void on the grounds of illegality and will do so only where:

(*a*) *a statute* clearly prohibits the contract, or
(*b*) a well-established rule of *Common Law* makes such contract unlawful on grounds of public policy.

Otherwise the general attitude of the courts has been stated thus: "You have this paramount policy to consider—that you are not lightly to interfere with the freedom of contract": *per Lord Jessel, in Printing & Numerical Co.* v. *Sampson* (1875).

This legal presumption in favour of validity is sometimes expressed in Latin as *ut res magis valeat quam pereat* ("it is better to preserve than to destroy").

4. Consequences of illegality.

(*a*) *The contract is entirely void*, unless the Doctrine of Severance can be applied to save part of it.
(*b*) *Money paid or property transferred under an illegal contract cannot be recovered* (subject to the exceptions in 5 below).

The maxim is *in pari delicto, potior est conditio defendentis* ("in cases of equal guilt, more powerful is the condition of the defendant"). Thus where the parties are equally guilty, if the plaintiff is suing for the return of money paid under the illegal contract, the court will usually allow the defendant to keep it. (For the rules applicable where the parties are not equally guilty, see 5 below.)

(c) *Negotiable securities,* such as cheques and other bills of exchange, transferred between the parties to the contract are void as between them. But an innocent third party who acquires such securities in good faith and for value can usually enforce them: see Bills of Exchange, s. 62. Thus where A pays a gambling debt to B by cheque, B cannot enforce payment against A; but if B sells the cheque to C, who buys in good faith and without notice of any irregularity, C will be able to enforce the cheque.

(d) *Ex turpi causa non oritur actio* ("from an evil cause, no action arises"). Where a plaintiff seeking the court's assistance has to base his claim on his own illegal or immoral act, his claim will fail.

EXAMPLE: A rented a flat to R at £1,200 p.a. To avoid tax they agreed to describe the money as £450 for rent and £750 for "services." Later R attempted to bilk A by refusing to pay the £750 on the grounds that he had received no services, and A sued for the money. HELD: The contract was illegal as an attempt to defraud the revenue, and A could not recover the money since he could only get it by admitting that it was really rent and this involved admitting his own guilt. But to prevent R benefiting from this situation the court terminated his tenancy on the grounds that it was illegal, and offered him a new one at the full rent: ✳ *Alexander* v. *Rayson* (1936).

5. Recovery of property transferred. Money paid or property transferred under an illegal contract is normally irrecoverable.

EXCEPTIONS:

(a) Where the transferor *repents* of making the contract before any part of the illegal purpose is carried out, or

(b) Where:

    (i) He is not *in pari delicto* (equally guilty) with the defendant, *e.g.* where he was induced to make the contract by the fraud of the defendant; or

(ii) The transferee was under a *fiduciary duty* to protect the plaintiff's interests, and has abused this duty by making the illegal contract, *e.g.* where he is the plaintiff's solicitor or trustee; or

(iii) The contract is made illegal by *a statute intended to protect* a class of which the plaintiff is a member, *e.g.* a borrower suing to recover excessive interest from a moneylender under a contract illegal under the Moneylenders' Acts (which are intended to protect borrowers).

SECTION 19. CONTRACTS FORBIDDEN BY STATUTE

1. Contracts for trading or selling on a Sunday: The Sunday Observance Act, 1677. But many of these are in fact made lawful under the Shops Act, 1950, under which shops may be licenced to remain open on Sundays.

2. Registration of Business Names Act, 1916. Any person trading under a name other than his real name must register such trade name. If he, or his firm, fails to do so any contracts made under the trade name are void: *see* Partnership, *s.* 34.

3. Moneylenders Act, 1900. This lays down restrictions upon professional moneylenders. A contract made in contravention of the Act is void.

NOTE:

(*a*) A moneylending contract is not enforceable unless *in writing signed by the borrower*, and the borrower must receive a copy of the contract within 7 days of making it: *Moneylenders Act*, 1927, *s.* 6.

(*b*) Moneylenders are persons whose *main business is the lending of money: M.A.*, 1900. Moneylenders must be licensed, and any contracts with unlicensed moneylenders are void. (Contrast banks, insurance companies, finance companies, etc., to whom the lending of money is merely subsidiary to their main business: *U.D.T. Ltd.* v. *Kirkwood* (1966).)

(*c*) The moneylender's right to sue for the debt is *statute-barred* 12 months after the right of action accrued: *M.A.*, 1927, *s.* 13. Contrast actions for breach of ordinary contracts, where the limitation period is usually 6 years: see s. **24**.

(*d*) *The maximum rate of interest* chargeable by a moneylender is 48% p.a.; *M.A.*, 1927, *s.* 10. A non-professional lender of money however might lawfully charge more.

(e) Wherever a moneylending contract is *harsh or unconscionable* the court may set it aside and either invalidate it completely or, more usually, substitute more equitable terms, *e.g.* where interest is excessive: *M.A.*, 1900.

4. Gaming and wagering contracts. A wager is a promise to give or pay something on the ascertainment of an uncertain future event, *e.g.* a horse race. A bet is a wager on the result of a game.

Such contracts are void under the Gaming and Wagering Acts, 1835–1960. The position is complex, but the following basic rules apply:

(a) *Money earned as commission* on bets and wagers is irrecoverable: *Gaming Act*, 1892. An agent cannot therefore recover his commission from his principal. But the principal can recover any winnings received on his behalf by the agent: *De Mattos* v. *Benjamin* (1894).

(b) *Negotiable instruments* given for a bet are given for an illegal consideration and are void as between the parties: *Gaming Act*, 1835, but an innocent third party who becomes a holder in due course of such an instrument may be able to enforce it fully: *see* Bills of exchange, *s.* **65**, 10.

(c) *Money lent to a loser* to pay his bets is recoverable: *Re O'Shea* (1911); but not if the lender himself pays the winner, since he is then participating in the forbidden transaction: *Macdonald* v. *Green* (1957).

(d) *The winner of a wager cannot sue the loser* for his winnings, even though the loser later makes a fresh promise to pay supported by fresh consideration: *Hill* v. *William Hill Ltd.* (1949).

This rule still applies, even though the Betting Act, 1960, legalises gambling in certain circumstances, *i.e.* the contracts resulting from such legalised gambling are still void.

(e) *Money paid to a stakeholder* to retain pending the result of a wager can be recovered from the stakeholder by the payer at any time before he has handed it over to the other party to the wager: *Burge* v. *Ashley & Smith Ltd.* (1900).

(f) *The essence of a wager is* that neither party has any legitimate interest in the uncertain event wagered upon, except the money staked. Where a party has something to gain or lose apart from the money staked, the agreement is not a wager, *e.g.* insurance contracts. Thus if A insures his life, his ship, or his house against death, loss, or damage, he stands to lose the value of his ship or house (or his life) quite apart from the wager. Although this insurance contract is similar in its other characteristics to a wager, it is valid and enforceable: *see* Insurance, *s.* **54**.

SECTION 20. CONTRACTS ILLEGAL AT COMMON LAW

1. Contracts tainted with sexual immorality. A contract superficially lawful will be void if, to the knowledge of the parties, its ultimate purpose was immoral, *e.g.* an ordinary lease of a house would be void if the house was to be used as a brothel.

EXAMPLE: A hired a carriage to a woman knowing that she was a prostitute and would use the carriage for the purpose of soliciting. HELD: The contract was void and he could not recover unpaid hiring charges: ✱ *Pearce* v. *Brooks* (1866). This is an example of the working of the maxim *In pari delicto, potior est conditio defendentis*: *see s.* **18**, 4, *above*.

2. Contracts tending to interfere with the sanctity of marriage, *e.g.* a promise by a married man to marry another woman as soon as his wife is dead: *Wilson* v. *Carnley* (1908).

Where a married man promises to marry another woman, the other woman could not sue him for breach of promise if she knew he was married when he made the promise. But she probably could sue him if he deceived her into thinking he was single.

3. Contracts for the sale of public offices or titles of honour, *e.g.* a promise to use influence to obtain a title or commission for the promisee in return for money: *Parkinson* v. *College of Ambulance Ltd.* (1925).

4. Contracts to commit crimes or torts, whether in Britain or in any foreign friendly nation, *e.g.* a contract to smuggle goods into the United States of America: *Foster* v. *Driscoll* (1929).

5. Contracts to obtain an unfair benefit from the government, *e.g.* a promise to use influence to obtain exemption from a legal duty, such as military service: *Montefiore* v. *Motor Components Ltd.* (1918).

6. Contracts involving trade with an enemy nation are illegal at Common Law and also under the *Trading with the Enemy Act,* 1939.

7. Contracts to defraud the Revenue, *see Alexander* v. *Rayson, s.* **18**, 4.

8. Contracts tending to impede the administration of justice, *e.g.* a promise by an accused person to indemnify someone who has stood bail for him: *Herman* v. *Jeuchner* (1885).

9. Contracts prejudicial to the freedom of marriage, *e.g.* imposing a general restraint upon a person to prevent marriage, though a particular restraint might be valid if not unreasonable, *e.g.* a contract forbidding a girl from marrying a particular man.

Marriage brokage contracts are also in this category and are void, *i.e.* contracts to arrange marriages for a reward: *Herman* v. *Charlesworth* (1905).

10. Contracts involving champerty or maintenance. *Maintenance* means giving financial or other assistance to a party to a law suit, where the maintainor has no sufficient legal or moral interest in the case. *Champerty* means maintenance with a view of sharing the profits of the action.

NOTE: A shared commercial interest is sufficient to negative maintenance: *Martell* v. *Consett Iron Co. Ltd.* (1955).

(A person guilty of champerty or maintenance can also be sued in tort by the person injured by the action brought with the assistance of the maintainer.)

11. Contracts in restraint of trade. These are contracts which seek to restrict a person from freely exercising his trade or profession. For students of Mercantile Law this is the most important category of illegal contracts and is dealt with separately in *s.* **21** below.

SECTION 21. CONTRACTS IN RESTRAINT OF TRADE

1. Restraints prima facie void. All restraints on trade are prima facie void, though they may be enforceable if they seek

C

merely to protect some legitimate commercial interest. By contrast, a restraint which seeks merely to prevent competition is always void: * *Morris* v. *Saxelby* (1916).

A restraint may be (a) *general*, *i.e.* forbidding trading throughout a large area, such as throughout the United Kingdom, or Europe, or (b) *particular*, *i.e.* forbidding trade in some localised area, such as a particular town and its environs. General restraints are more disfavoured than particular restraints.

2. When restraints are valid. A restraint will be held *void unless* the party seeking to enforce it can prove:

(a) That it is *reasonable in the public interest*.

(b) That it is *reasonable as between the parties*, *i.e.* seeks to provide reasonable protection for some legitimate interest of the plaintiff, such as trade secrets or business goodwill.

(c) That the plaintiff has given *valuable consideration* for the promise he seeks to enforce. In this type of contract consideration is necessary even if the contract is under seal.

Whether a restraint is reasonable or not is a question of law to be decided by the judge; whether the individual restraint under dispute is in fact reasonable is a question of fact in each case.

A restraint which is reasonable between the parties is presumed to be reasonable in the public interest, unless there is some rule of law to the contrary: *Attorney General of Australia* v. *Adelaide S.S. Co.* (1913).

3. Kinds of restraint. Restraints can be grouped roughly into three categories:

(a) *Between employer and employee*, to prevent the employee competing with his employer after leaving his job: *see 4 below*.

(b) *Between the vendor and the purchaser of a business*, to prevent the seller harming the goodwill of the business sold: *see 6 below*.

(c) *Between traders, to regulate conditions of trade*. These are now largely governed by statute, *e.g.* the *Restrictive Trade Practices Act*, 1956, and the *Resale Prices Act*, 1964: *see 7 below*.

4. Restraints upon employees. An employer may compel an employee to sign a covenant promising not to injure the employer's interests either (a) *during the continuance of the employment* (*e.g.* by passing confidential information to outsiders), or (b) *after leaving the employment* (*e.g.* by luring away his former employer's customers).

Such agreements are *viewed with disfavour* by the courts because of the element of coercion: *see* Undue Influence, *s.* **17**. They will only be enforced if they satisfy the tests set out in 5 below.

NOTE: Apart from any express covenant, an employer is entitled to prevent an employee from disclosing trade secrets during the employment or after leaving: *Amber Size & Chemical Co.* v. *Menzel* (1913); or from making a list of the employer's clients with a view to competition after leaving: *Robb* v. *Green* (1895). But even if an express covenant exists and is enforceable, the employer loses the right to enforce it if he himself breaks the contract of employment, *e.g.* by wrongfully dismissing the employee: *General Billposting C.* v. *Atkinson* (1909).

5. Restraints upon employees: when enforceable. Restraints upon employees will only be enforced if they satisfy the following tests:

(a) *The restraint is void unless supported by valuable consideration.* The payment of wages is the usual consideration given by the employer. If therefore the covenant is only imposed when the employee is leaving, there may be no consideration for it (unless some special payment is made to bind the contract).

(b) *The restraint is void unless the employee has some real capacity to damage the employer* and the covenant seeks to guard against such damage.

Thus a master is entitled to protection of trade secrets, or to a covenant that an employee in an influential position will not use his influence to seduce the master's clients.

Therefore the employee must generally be in some confidential capacity, *e.g.* a solicitor's managing clerk: ✱ *Fitch* v. *Dewes* (1921); but not a mere door-to-door salesman: *Mason* v. *Provident Clothing Co.* (1913); nor a newspaper correspondent: *Leng* v. *Andrews* (1909) (though a newspaper editor might be in a sufficiently confidential capacity).

(c) *The restraint is void if it seeks merely to restrict or prevent competition.*

(d) *The restraint must be reasonable*, having regard to:

    (i) the *type* of employment: *Mason* v. *Provident Clothing Co.*

    (ii) the *period* of restraint: *Kores Ltd.* v. *Kolok Ltd.* (1959).

    (iii) the *area* of restraint, *e.g.* a solicitor's managing clerk covenanted not to open a competing practice within 7 miles of his former employers. HELD: Reasonable and enforceable: *Fitch* v. *Dewes* (1921).

EXAMPLES:

    (*a*) A tailor's assistant covenanted not to open a competing business within 10 miles of his former employer's. HELD: Void, because in this particular case the assistant had no confidential relationship with customers and the covenant was therefore aimed merely at preventing ordinary competition: *Attwood* v. *Lamott* (1920).

    (*b*) S was an estate agent with offices at Dartmouth and Kingsbridge. J was employed at the Kingsbridge office and covenanted not to open a competing business within 5 miles of *Dartmouth or Kingsbridge* within 3 years of leaving the employ. HELD: The restraint was too wide, since J had never worked at *Dartmouth*, but was valid in so far as it related to Kingsbridge. (This was an application of the Doctrine of Severance: *see s.* **18.** 2 above.) *Seymour* v. *Seymour-Jones* (1966).

6. Restraints on sale of a business. Restraints imposed by the purchaser of a business on the seller, preventing the latter from opening another business in such a way as to damage the goodwill of the business sold, are enforced if reasonable in the circumstances.

Restraints of this kind are more readily enforced than those between employer and employee, because they lack the element of coercion which may be present between the parties in contracts of employment.

A restraint of this kind will be reasonable if (*a*) it satisfies the tests set out in 2 above, and (*b*) it is intended merely to protect the purchaser's investment in the goodwill of the business bought, *i.e.* not intended to protect other businesses the purchaser already owned, or merely to prevent ordinary competition.

EXAMPLES:

    (*a*) N, an inventor of guns, sold his world-wide business to M and promised not to manufacture guns anywhere in the

world for 25 years. HELD: Reasonable and binding: *
Nordenfelt v. *Maxim-Nordenfelt* Co. (1894), *H.L.*
(*b*) S sold his localised business to C (who already had branches
all over Britain) and promised not to open a competing
business anywhere within 10 miles of any of C's branches.
HELD: Void. The restraint was more than was necessary to
protect the goodwill of the small local business purchased
from S: * *British Concrete Co.* v. *Schelff* (1921).

7. Restraints regulating trading conditions. Sometimes
traders enter into agreements to regulate conditions of trading
between themselves, and in trading with the public. Such
agreements are generally considered contrary to the public
interest, and are attacked by the * *Restrictive Trade Practices
Act*, 1956, and the * *Resale Prices Act*, 1964: *see* **8** and **9** below.

A further type of restraint is a *solus* agreement, under
which a retailer contracts to obtain all his supplies of stated
commodities from one supplier, *e.g.* where a garage proprietor
obtains finance from a petrol company in return for *solus*
terms. These agreements are valid if reasonable in the circumstances.

EXAMPLE: M obtained finance from P, a petrol company, to
open a garage and promised to sell no other petrol than P's
for 12 years, and to impose a similar solus condition on any
person to whom he sold the garage. HELD: The agreement was
unreasonable in detail and was therefore void: *Petrofina (G.B.)
Ltd.* v. *Martin* (1966).

8. Contracts contrary to the R.T.P. Act, 1956. The Act covers
agreements by which producers, suppliers or exporters of goods
restrict the manufacture, supply or distribution of goods by
collective agreements between themselves (such agreements
usually relate to the fixing of prices).

NOTE:

(*a*) All agreements covered by the Act must be *registered* with
the Registrar of Restrictive Trading Agreements, otherwise
they are void.
(*b*) Once registered such agreements are submitted for consideration by the *Restrictive Practices Court* (consisting of
one High Court judge and two lay members) which may
pronounce the agreement void as contrary to the public
interest, or valid.
(*c*) All agreements between *two or more persons* carrying on

business in the United Kingdom are registrable if they relate
to:

(i) prices to be charged for goods, or processes of manufacture (ii) conditions of supply (iii) quantities and descrip-
tions of goods (iv) processes of manufacture to be applied to
goods (v) persons with whom the parties may deal. (The Act
does not cover agreements relating to conditions of employment or remuneration.)

(d) If an agreement is *pronounced valid* by the Court it becomes
binding even on persons who were not parties to it, providing that when they took the goods affected by the
agreement they had notice of the agreement: *s.* 25.

(e) *Private agreements* relating to exclusive selling or distribution rights were expressly excluded from the Act, with
the result that many manufacturers desiring to enforce
resale price maintenance made such private agreements with
retailers. To stop this loophole, the *Resale Prices Act,* 1964,
was passed: *see below.*

9. Resale Prices Act, 1964. The purpose of this Act is to
prohibit resale price maintenance, except where it can be
shown to be in the public interest.

The main provisions of the Act are as follows:

(a) Any term in a contract for sale of goods which imposes on
the purchaser an obligation to charge any *minimum price* on
any subsequent resale is void: *s.* 1.

(b) *Discrimination* by a supplier against a dealer who resells
below the prices fixed by the supplier is unlawful, and actionable by any person injured thereby or by the Crown: *s.* 4.

(c) Goods may be *exempted* from the provisions of the Act by
decision of the Restrictive Practices Court, if in the opinion
of the court such exemption is in the public interest: *ss.* 5–7.

DISCHARGE OF CONTRACTS

SECTION 22. DISCHARGE BY PERFORMANCE

1. Complete performance. In order to effect discharge, performance must be complete and exactly in accord with the terms of the contract.

Partial performance, even if substantial, will not discharge the contract (except in the special cases stated below).

> EXAMPLE: A sailor, having signed on to receive a lump sum payment for a complete voyage, died before he completed the journey. HELD: His widow could not claim any part of his wages since he was entitled to payment only if he completed his contracted obligations: *Cutter* v. *Powell* (1807) (NOTE: On the facts this case would now be decided differently, but the general rule it lays down is still valid).

2. Exceptional cases.

(a) *Performance prevented by the promisee.* Here the promisor can obtain compensation for work actually done in pursuance of the contract by suing on a *quantum meruit* claim: see *s.* **26, 8.**

(b) *Partial performance accepted.* If the promisee *voluntarily* accepts less than complete performance where he had genuine freedom of choice, the promisor is entitled to claim payment on *quantum meruit, e.g.* A contracted to erect a building for B, and when the work was half done A abandoned the job. B had to complete the building himself, but A sued him for work done. HELD: B need pay nothing under the contract, as he had not freely chosen to complete the building himself, but had been compelled to do so by A's breach: ✱ *Sumpter* v. *Hedges* (1898); and *see s.* **22. 8.**

(c) *Substantial performance, i.e.* where performance is as complete as a reasonable man could expect, even though not strictly in accord with every detail of the contract. This is a question of fact, *e.g.* A decorated B's flat for £750, but because of faulty workmanship B had to pay an extra £290 to complete the job. B refused to pay any money at all to

A. HELD: A was entitled to recover the £750, less the £290 paid to make good his defective workmanship: *Hoenig* v. *Isaacs* (1952).

(d) *Divisible contracts*. If performance is to be by instalments payment can be recovered for instalments actually completed (unless the intention of the parties appears to be to the contrary).

3. Tender of performance and payment.

(a) *Tender of performance*. It is sometimes sufficient if the promisor attempts to perform his side of the contract. Then, if performance is rejected, the promisor is discharged from further liability and may sue for breach of contract if he so wishes.

(b) *Tender of payment* relieves the promisor from future liability to make further tenders, but does not discharge him from liability to pay.

Under the *Coinage Act*, 1870, *s.* 4, gold coins are legal tender up to any amount, silver coins up to 40s., and bronze coins up to 1s. Bank of England notes are legal tender for any amount.

4. Time for performance or payment. Failure to perform or pay on time may be a *breach of warranty* but is rarely a breach of condition, *i.e.* is rarely "of the essence" of the contract.

(a) *Time of payment* is not of the essence unless otherwise agreed expressly or impliedly. (This rule is statutorily applied to contracts for the sale of goods: *S.G.A.*, 1893, *s.* 10.)

(b) *Time of performance* is not usually of the essence but may be made so by agreement, and this is usually done in mercantile contracts.

EXAMPLE: O waived the original delivery date but stipulated a later date as final. HELD: This made the later date of the essence, *i.e.* a condition, of the contract and failure to deliver on the new date entitled O to rescind the contract: *Richards* v. *Oppenheim* (1950).

5. Rules re payment of money.

(a) *Payment of a smaller sum* will not usually discharge liability to pay a larger: **✱** *Foakes* v. *Beer* (1884), except where the rules in *Pinnel's Case* or the *Hightrees Case* apply; *see s.* 12.

(b) *Payment to an agent* is usually a good discharge, if the agent is held out by the creditor as having authority to receive money.

(c) *Payment by a third party* is not a good discharge, unless he pays as agent for the debtor: *Smith* v. *Cox* (1940).

(d) *Payment to one joint creditor* discharges liability to the others: *Kendall* v. *Hamilton* (1879).

(e) *Payment by negotiable instrument* is conditional payment only, *until* the negotiable instrument is cashed (or as otherwise agreed).

The creditor can always refuse to take a negotiable instrument such as a cheque and can insist on cash.

(f) *Payment by post* is ineffective if the letter is lost in the post, unless the creditor requested this method of payment: *Pennington* v. *Crossley & Son* (1897).

But if the creditor did request payment by post, payment is effective once posted, even if the letter is lost in the post: *Newman* v. *Ricketts* (1886).

(g) *Payment by cheque* is prima facie evidence of receipt (once the cheque has been cashed) but a formal receipt can also be demanded: *Cheques Act,* 1957, *s.* 3.

6. Appropriation of payments. Where there are several debts outstanding between the parties, it is sometimes important to ascertain what payment has discharged what debt.

The following legal rules apply:

(a) *The debtor* can appropriate any payment to any debt, no matter which is the longest outstanding.

(b) If the debtor makes no appropriation, *the creditor* can appropriate in any way he chooses, *e.g.* applying the money to pay off a statute barred debt: *Seymour* v. *Pickette* (1905).

(c) *The Rule in* ✳ *Clayton's Case* (1816). If there is a current account between the parties, subject to constant incomings and outgoings, then if neither party makes any express appropriation the law presumes that the first payment in discharges the earliest outstanding debt.

SECTION 23. DISCHARGE BY AGREEMENT

1. Executory contracts, *i.e.* those wholly unperformed by either side, can be discharged by simple waiver. Consideration for the waiver lies in the exchange of promises not to sue to enforce the contract.

2. Executed contracts, *i.e.* those wholly or partly performed by one party. Discharge of such contracts must be supported by consideration, or must be under seal.

(a) *Deed of release,* for which no consideration is necessary.
(b) *Accord and satisfaction, i.e.* a simple contract agreement (the accord) + valuable consideration (the satisfaction) other than performance of the actual obligations under the original contract. The consideration may take the form of some alternative method of performance, or mere executory promises. But some consideration is necessary to prevent the rule in *Foakes* v. *Beer* coming into operation: *see s.* **12**.

3. Substituted agreement. A contract can also be discharged by the parties making a fresh contract in substitution for the old. But this method is available on where the contract is not yet wholly performed on either side, *i.e.* is still partly executory on both sides.

A new contract substituted for an earlier in this way is called a *novation*.

4. Variation of contracts. Discharge by agreement may be total or partial.

Variation (which may amount to partial discharge) can generally take *any form,* except that contracts unenforceable unless evidenced in writing can only be varied in writing: * *Morris* v. *Baron* (1918).

(Total rescission can always be made in any form, *e.g.* a specialty contract can be rescinded orally: *Berry* v. *Berry* (1929).)

5. Unauthorised alteration. If one party makes a material alteration to a contract without the consent of the other, the contract is automatically discharged.

A material alteration is one which alters the effect of the contract, *e.g.* altering the crossing or the amount payable on a cheque.

SECTION 24. DISCHARGE BY OPERATION OF LAW

1. By merger. A contract is discharged if it is merged in a higher obligation, *e.g.* a deed swallows or merges into itself a simple contract on the same terms and between the same parties.

2. Contracts for personal services. These are automatically discharged by death in most cases. Contracts of a non-personal nature may survive for the benefit of the deceased's estate.

3. Discharge in bankruptcy. Where a bankrupt obtains his discharge the order automatically cancels liability on all provable debts existing at that date: *see s.* **78, 7.**

4. Lapse of time: * Limitation Act, 1939. The Act lays down that actions for breach of contract must be commenced within a certain time after the breach occurs, otherwise the right of action lapses, *i.e.* is statute-barred. (The right of action is not destroyed by lapse of time, it simply cannot be enforced: *see* 6 *below.*)

The more important periods of time laid down by the Act are as follows:

(a) *Six years* for actions for breach of *simple contracts.*
(b) *Twelve years* for actions for breach of *special contracts.*
(c) *Thirty years* in actions for recovery of land where the Crown is the plaintiff; *twelve years* in other cases.

5. When time runs. The limitation period under the Act is generally calculated from the moment the breach occurs, except where:

(*a*) The plaintiff was under a *legal disability* at the date of the breach, *e.g.* infancy or lunacy. Here time runs from the date when the disability ceases, or the plaintiff dies while still disabled: *s.* 22.
(*b*) The action is based on *fraud, mistake, etc.* Here time begins to run from the date when the fraud or mistake is discovered by the plaintiff, and not from the date when the cause of action arose: *L.A., s.* 26.

6. Acknowledgments and part payments. When a right of action has lapsed it may be revived by:

(a) *A written acknowledgment* constituting an express or implied admission of liability. Thus a letter admitting liability but refusing to pay and relying on the Limitation Act has been held to be a sufficient acknowledgment for this purpose: *Re Coliseum (Barrow) Ltd.* (1930). (If the written acknowledgment is lost, its contents can be proved by oral evidence: *Reas* v. *Price* (1909).)

(b) *A part-payment* of a statute barred debt.

Where there is an acknowledgment or part payment, it *starts time running again, i.e.* the plaintiff has a further six years (or twelve if a special contract is involved) in which to commence action: *L.A., ss.* 23–25.

Note: a part payment into a bank current account which is overdrawn operates to revive the right of action for the whole account, including debts incurred more than 6 years previously: *Re Footman Bower & Co. Ltd.* (1961).

PROBLEMS:

(a) A is employed as a clerk in a grocer's shop run by B and his wife. B dies but his widow wishes to continue the business. Will A's contract of employment continue?

(b) C's bank account was overdrawn in 1950 when he went to Australia. In 1964 he returned to England and paid in some money, stipulating that this was not to be appropriated by the bank to payment of any indebtedness incurred before 1964. Can this be regarded as a part payment under the Limitation Act? (*See* 6 *above*, and *s.* 22, 6.)

SECTION 25. FRUSTRATION OF CONTRACTS

1. Supervening impossibility of performance. Where at the outset it is clearly impossible to perform a contract, such contract lacks an essential element and is void, *e.g.* contracts to walk across the Atlantic.

But sometimes a contract possible when made, subsequently becomes impossible to perform, *e.g.* a lawful contract involving trade between Britain and Russia became impossible to perform when the Crimean War broke out between the two countries: * *Avery* v. *Bowden* (1856).

The general rule is that supervening impossibility of performance *does not discharge the contract, except where the Doctrine of Frustration applies.*

2. Doctrine of Frustration. This has been developed to mitigate hardship which might be caused by the supervening impossibility rule stated above.

Under the doctrine of frustration the courts will imply a term into a contract providing for the discharge of the contract if certain types of impossibility arise after the contract is made: *Cricklewood Property Co.* v. *Leighton's Investment Trust* (1945).

3. Frustration occurs where:

(a) *Basis destroyed.* If the contracts depends on the continued existence of some thing, and that thing is destroyed, *e.g.* hire of a theatre frustrated by the theatre being burned down: ✱ *Taylor* v. *Caldwell* (1863).

(b) *Non-occurrence of an essential event.* If the contract depends on the occurrence of an event which does not in fact happen, *e.g.* hire of rooms to watch the coronation procession of Edward VII, frustrated by cancellation of the procession: ✱ *Krell* v. *Henry* (1903); contrast *Herne Bay S.S. Co.* v. *Hutton* (1905), see problems below.

(c) *Death or illness.* A contract for personal services may be frustrated by death or unduly prolonged illness of the employee. What amounts to unduly prolonged illness is a question of fact in each case, *e.g.* if a concert pianist hired for three performances is ill when due to play at the first, this might amount to frustration: *Robinson* v. *Davison* (1871).

(d) *Government interference.* Where the government prohibits performance for such a period that it would be unreasonable to expect performance after, the prohibition ceases: *Metropolitan Water Board* v. *Dick Kerr & Co. Ltd.* (1918).

(e) *Change in law.* Where a contract legal when made subsequently becomes unlawful through a change in the legal situation: ✱ *Avery* v. *Bowden* (1856).

(f) *Method of performance impossible.* If a particular manner of performance is essential, and when the time comes for performance this particular method has become impossible.

4. Limits of the Doctrine. Frustration does not occur in the following cases:

(a) *Express terms may cover the contingency* complained of. The court will refuse to treat the contract as frustrated where to do so would be contrary to the express terms of the contract: ✱ *British Movietonews Ltd.* v. *London, etc., Cinemas Ltd.* (1951), *H.L.*

(b) *Self-induced frustration* cannot be pleaded as grounds for discharge, as it may amount to breach of contract: *see s.* **26.**

(c) Leases are not subject to frustration: *Paradyne* v. *Jayne* (1647).

5. Effect of frustration. The contract is discharged for the future (from the date of the frustrating event), but is not void *ab initio*. Therefore it may be important to ascertain who should bear the loss and who should pay for any services rendered up to the time of frustration.

(a) *Before* 1943. At Common Law the loss lay where it fell, *i.e.* money which had become payable before frustration remained payable, and money paid before frustration was irrecoverable, but money not due until after frustration ceased to be payable: *Chandler* v. *Webster* (1904).

This harsh rule was later modified to allow apportionment of loss where there had been total failure of consideration: *Fibrosa Case* (1943).

(b) ✱ *L.R. (Frustrated Contracts) Act,* 1943, reformed the above position by providing:

   (i) Money paid before frustration is prima facie recoverable (unless its retention can be justified by expenses incurred by the recipient before frustration).

   (ii) Money due before frustration ceases to be payable (unless needed to cover expenses as in (i) above).

   (iii) Benefits received before frustration must be paid for, and a party who has incurred expense before frustration is entitled to compensation therefore.

NOTE: The Act can be excluded by express agreement, and in any case it does not apply to (i) charter parties, (ii) carriage of goods by sea, (iii) sales of specific goods, (iv) insurance contracts.

SECTION 26. BREACH OF CONTRACT AND REMEDIES

1. Breach of contract occurs where one party

(a) *repudiates* his obligations;

(b) *disables* himself from performing his part of the contract; or

(c) *fails to perform* his part of the contract as and when agreed.

2. Anticipatory breach. In (a) and (b) above the breach may occur before the date fixed for performance, *e.g.* where A hired B to act as a courier commencing employment 1st June but wrote to B in May repudiating the agreement, it was HELD that B was immediately entitled to sue, and need not wait till the 1st June for his right of action to accrue: * *Hochster* v. *De La Tour* (1853).

3. Effect of breach. The effect depends largely on whether the breach is of a condition or of a warranty: *see s.* **9.**

(a) *Breach of warranty:* the injured party can only sue for damages and must go on with the contract, *i.e.* the breach does not operate to discharge the contract.

(b) *Breach of condition:* the injured party can choose whether

    (i) to treat the breach as a breach of ex post facto warranty (and sue for damages while going on with the contract), or

    (ii) to treat the breach of condition as automatically discharging the contract.

NOTE: *If he chooses alternative* (ii) he cannot also sue for damages for breach, since he has indicated a willingness to regard the contract as dead and has therefore waived his right of action for damages (but if he has incurred expense under the contract he can bring a quasi-contractual quantum meruit action for compensation).

If he chooses alternative (i) he keeps the contract alive, and should immediately commence action to enforce it, *i.e.* should sue for damages or specific performance. If he delays suing he takes the risk that some unforeseen event may occur to discharge the contract by frustration, thus depriving him of his right of action.

EXAMPLE: A hired B's ship to carry a cargo from Russia. Later B repudiated the contract, thus entitling A either to treat the contract as discharged or to sue for damages. A delayed a decision hoping B would change his mind before the performance date. War broke out between Russia and Britain before the performance date, frustrating the contract. HELD: A had lost his right to sue for damages by his delay: * *Avery* v. *Bowden* (1856).

4. Remedies for breach. The Common Law remedy is damages by way of compensation. In addition there are the discretionary equitable remedies of specific performance and injunctions, which are usually available where damages are inadequate to compensate the plaintiff for the breach.

5. Damages for breach of contract. The plaintiff can recover financial compensation for his actual loss, provided it is not too remote.

Under the ∗ *Rule in Hadley* v. *Baxendale* (1854) damage is not too remote if:

(a) *It is the natural consequence of the breach, e.g.* B unduly delayed delivery of a mill-shaft to A's mill, whereby the mill was out of action for a considerable time. A had not informed B that lack of the shaft would necessitate closure of the mill. HELD: A could recover damages for the delay in delivery, but not for loss of profits occasioned by closure of the mill, since there was no way B could have foreseen that his delay would cause the closure: *Hadley* v. *Baxendale.*

(b) Although not arising naturally from the breach, the damage caused was something which was *within the contemplation of the parties when making the contract.* (Thus in *Hadley* v. *Baxendale* the mill-owner could have recovered damages for loss of profits if he had informed the carrier of the likely result of delayed delivery.)

EXAMPLE: A contracted to supply a boiler to B's laundry and was five months late in delivery. HELD: B could recover damages for loss of ordinary profits occasioned by the delay since A knew the laundry would be closed pending delivery of the boiler (but B could not recover damages for loss of exceptional profits expected to arise under a valuable contract of which A was not informed): *Victoria Laundry* v. *Newman Industries* (1949).

6. The measure of damages. Damages for breach of contract are intended to compensate the plaintiff, not to punish the defendant (though in the special case of actions for breach of promise to marry, an additional sum called a solatium or solace may be awarded to the jilted woman as solace for her injured feelings).

NOTE:

(a) *The plaintiff must mitigate* or minimise his loss as far as he reasonably can; he cannot recover additional damages for loss occasioned by his failure to do so.

Thus if an employee is *wrongfully dismissed* he can recover damages for loss of wages, but must reduce his loss as much as he can by seeking new employment. He will not recover extra heavy damages if he is out of work for a long time by reason of his own failure to seek work: *Brace* v. *Calder* (1895).

(b) *Interest on any sum* claimed is not allowed unless:

    (i) the parties have previously so agreed, or

    (ii) the claim is on a bill of exchange or promissory note, or

    (iii) the court exercises its statutory discretion to award interest under the *L.R. (Miscellaneous Provisions) Act*, 1934.

7. Penalties and liquidated damages. Where the amount of compensation claimed is left to be assessed by the court, damages claimed are called unliquidated damages.

But sometimes the parties agree in advance the amounts payable in the event of breach. Such an amount is called liquidated damages, and in any action for breach of such contract the court will award the pre-assessed sum unless it has been fixed in such a way as to break the rules against penalties.

Liquidated damages are a genuine pre-estimate of the measure of loss which a breach of the contract is likely to cause. *A penalty* on the other hand is a sum fixed at random to frighten a party into performing his contract: ✱ *Dunlop Pneumatic Tyre Co.* v. *New Garage Co.* (1915).

A sum is a penalty if:

(a) It is extravagant having regard to the maximum possible loss which could result from the breach.

(b) If failure to pay a sum of money results in liability to pay a larger sum.

(c) If a single sum is payable on the occurrence of any of several events of differing degrees of importance: *Kemble* v. *Farren* (1829).

If a sum is held to be a penalty the court will not award it, but will make its own assessment of damages. The fact that the parties describe a sum as a penalty or a clause as a "penalty clause" is not decisive. The court will apply the above tests in each case, and if satisfied that the sum is a genuine pre-estimate of loss the court will award it to the plaintiff as liquidated damages.

8. Quantum meruit. Where there has been a *breach of condition* and the injured party has elected to treat the contract as at an end, he cannot later sue for damages for breach of the contract since he has already accepted breach as terminating the contract's existence. However, in such cases, if he has incurred loss, he can bring a quasi-contractual quantum meruit action for compensation for work done, expense incurred, etc.: *see s.* **4**.

A quantum meruit (literally "how much is it worth?") claim can thus arise where:

(a) *The defendant has abandoned or repudiated* the contract, *e.g.* where after commissioning a writer to do a series of articles, a magazine closes down before the series is completely written: *Planché* v. *Colburn* (1831). The writer could not sue for breach of contract here because he had not completed his own side of the bargain.

(b) Under *a void contract* one party has done work and the defendant has received the benefit of it: *Craven-Ellis* v. *Canons Ltd.* (1916). Here again the plaintiff could not have sued on the contract since it was void.

(c) The parties have *agreed to terminate* the contract but the plaintiff has performed a substantial part of his own side of the bargain. Here he can sue on a *quantum meruit* claim, but not on the contract since he has accepted termination: *Dakin* v. *Lee* (1916).

(d) One party has *obtained a benefit* which he could not reasonably expect to get without paying for it, *e.g.* where a builder leaves building materials on X's land and X uses the materials, the builder can sue for the value of the materials: **✱** *Sumpter* v. *Hedges* (1898) and *see s.* **22**, 2 *above*.

    Similarly if a grocer by mistake leaves goods at the wrong house and the occupant uses the goods, the grocer could sue for their value.

9. Specific performance. This is a *discretionary remedy* for breach of contract and consists in a *court order* compelling the defendant to perform his side of the bargain. It may be awarded in *addition to or instead of damages*.

Specific performance will only be awarded where:

(a) *Damages would be inadequate* to compensate the plaintiff, *e.g.* in contracts to sell or lease land, or for the sale of valuable and unique chattels such as rare paintings.

    It will not be awarded in ordinary contracts for sale of goods where the plaintiff could easily obtain replacement articles with the money received as damages, *e.g.* in sales of ordinary cars, books, furniture, etc.

(b) The enforcement of the order *would not require constant supervision* by the court, *e.g.* not in building contracts or contracts of employment.

(c) The contract is *equally enforceable by both parties.* Thus an infant plaintiff cannot obtain specific performance of a contract which would not be enforceable against him, since it would be impossible for the adult defendant party to claim specific performance against the infant (in such cases the infant can of course obtain damages).

(d) *The plaintiff himself has acted fairly and equitably.* He cannot obtain specific performance if his own conduct has been tricky or unfair: *Webster* v. *Cecil* (1861), *see s.* **15**, 8.

10. Injunctions. An injunction is a discretionary court order and is either:

(a) *Prohibitory:* forbidding a person to do something, or

(b) *Mandatory:* commanding a person to do something.

Mandatory injunctions are rarely granted since they might call for supervision by the court, which may not have the resources to enforce the injunction adequately.

Injunctions may take the following forms:

(a) *Quia timet injunctions:* issued to prevent an apprehended injury before it has occurred, but where there is reasonable ground for fearing a breach of contract may occur.

(b) *Interim or interlocutory injunctions:* usually granted pending the decision of a case, *e.g.* prohibiting the defendant from taking disputed property overseas until the dispute as to its ownership has been settled in court.

(c) *Perpetual:* issued when a dispute has been finally settled, *e.g.* where an interim injunction is made perpetual when the dispute has been finally settled in court.

11. Injunctions to restrain breaches of contract. An injunction is a suitable additional or alternative remedy to damages where the plaintiff wants to prevent the defendant breaking the contract, or continuing to break it.

Injunctions may be available where specific performance is not. Thus a contract of personal services cannot be enforced by an order for specific performance, since this would necessitate constant supervision by the court. But the court might in such a case grant a prohibitory injunction, forbidding the defendant from breaking the contract (and threatening him with imprisonment if he disobeys).

An injunction will only be granted to restrain a breach of contract if the clause the plaintiff seeks to enforce is *negative in substance*, though it may be positive in form. Thus a contract under which a film star is to work exclusively for a plaintiff company appears positive in form, but has a negative meaning, *i.e.* that the film star shall not work for anyone else. An injunction could be granted therefore to prevent the film star working for anyone else: *Warner Bros.* v. *Nelson* (1936).

PRIVITY, ASSIGNMENT, AND NEGOTIABILITY

SECTION 27. PRIVITY OF CONTRACT

1. Doctrine of Privity. A contract is a private relationship between the parties who make it, and no other person can acquire rights or incur liabilities under it.

> *Compare* this rule with the separate rule that "*consideration must move from the promisee.*" The two rules together mean that a person seeking to sue upon a contract must satisfy the court: (a) *that he is a party to* the contract he seeks to enforce, and (b) *that he has given consideration* for the promise he seeks to enforce (or that the contract is under seal): *see s.* **12.**
>
> *Contrast a legal duty with a contractual duty.* A legal duty is one which, if not performed, can be sued upon by any person injured by the breach of duty; actions for tort are actions for breach of this sort of duty. A contractual duty is one which is owed only to the other party to the contract, and only that party can sue to enforce it (also contractual duties arise by agreement, while legal duties are imposed by the law independently of any agreement between the parties).

2. Scope of Doctrine. The Doctrine of Privity has two aspects:

(a) *No one can acquire rights* under a contract to which he is not a party.
(b) *No one can incur liabilities* under a contract to which he is not a party.

3. Acquisition of rights. If A and B make a contract whereby B is to pay A to do something for X, X cannot sue A if he fails to do what he promised. It makes no difference if X has given consideration for the promise—he cannot sue unless he is a party to the contract: *Price* v. *Easton* (1820), nor that B and X are closely related: *Tweddle* v. *Atkinson* (1861).

73

EXCEPTIONS:

(a) *Constructive trust.* Where B is regarded as a trustee for X, X may sue A (and join B as co-defendant) if the contract between B and A is broken. (A constructive trust is one imposed by the courts to prevent injustice, and arises independently of any agreement between the parties.)

(b) ✱ *Restrictive Practices Act*, 1956, *s*. 25. A retailer who obtains goods from a wholesaler with notice of restrictive conditions imposed on resale of the goods by the original supplier may be bound by such conditions, even though they arose from the contract between the wholesaler and the supplier (to which the retailer was not a party): *Goodyear Tyre & Rubber Co. Ltd.* v. *Lancashire Batteries Ltd.* (1958): *see s.* **21,** 8.

(c) *Negotiable instruments.* If X is the holder for value of a bill of exchange he may sue the drawer (A) upon the bill: *see s.* **65.**

(d) *Agency.* Where B is secretly acting as agent for X, X can intervene to enforce the contract between A and B, in which case B drops out and the contract subsists directly between A and X. This is called the Doctrine of the Undisclosed Principal: *see s.* **32.**

(e) *Road Traffic Act*, 1960, *s*. 207. Persons specified in a third party car insurance policy can sue the insurance company to enforce the policy for their own benefit.

(f) *Law of Property Act*, 1925, *s*. 56, states that a person may take "an immediate or other interest" under a contract, providing it is in *writing*. The C.A. has interpreted this as offering an exception to the privity rule, *e.g.* P sold his business to J, the written contract providing that after P's death J would pay an annuity to P's widow (who was not a party to the contract). HELD: After P's death the widow could enforce the annuity under *s*. 56, *L.P.A.: Beswick* v. *Beswick* (1966).

4. Acquisition of liabilities. A contract between A and B cannot impose liabilities on X, save in the following exceptional cases:

(a) *R.T.P. Act*, 1956, *s*. 25: *see above.*

(b) Commercial usage or trade customs may so provide.

(c) Sale of ships. If X buys a ship from B which has previously been chartered by A, he may be bound by the terms of the charterparty if he has notice of its terms: *Strathcona S.S. Case* (1926).

(d) *Restrictive covenants affecting land.* These may run with the land, *i.e.* if X buys land he may be bound by a covenant between A and B, the seller of the land, provided (i) X accepts the covenant when buying the land, or (ii) the covenant is registered at the Land Charges Registry under the *Land Charges Act*, 1925.

SECTION 28. *TRANSFER AND ASSIGNMENT OF CONTRACTS*

1. Transfer of contracts. Rights and liabilities under a contract can be transferred in some cases. In this situation, in accordance with the Doctrine of Privity, if in a contract between A and B, B transfers the contract to X, B drops out of the contract which now subsists between A and X. B thereafter generally has no further rights or obligations under the contract.

2. Transfer of liabilities. This is only possible where:

(*a*) the contract so provides, or

(*b*) the parties later so agree.

Transfer is effected by cancellation of the existing contract between A and B and substitution of a new agreement between B and X, *i.e.* a novation.

NOTE: In a contract between A and B, if performance is not a personal matter, B can always delegate performance to some other person, *e.g.* his employee. This does not involve transfer of the contract, and privity still exists between A and B who remain fully liable on the contract.

3. Assignment of rights: choses in action. A right or benefit arising under a contract is called a *chose (or "thing") in action*, *i.e.* a personal right of property which can usually be enforced only by suing (by action) and not by taking physical possession: *Torkington* v. *Magee* (1902). Contrast a *chose in possession*, which is a piece of property capable of actual physical possession, *e.g.* goods, ships, etc.

Whether the benefit of a contract can be assigned depends on the intention of the parties. Thus a contract of employment cannot usually be assigned, unless otherwise agreed.

Choses in action can be assigned in two ways: (*a*) in accordance with *s.* 136, *Law of Property Act*, 1925, and (*b*) in accordance with rules of *equity* (*i.e.* any assignment not complying with *s.* 136, *L.P.A.*).

4. Statutory assignments: ✶ L.P.A. 1925, s. 136. Such an assignment operates to transfer (i) the full legal obligation (ii) the right to enforce the obligation, and (iii) power to give a valid discharge.

REQUIREMENTS:

(a) The assignment must be *absolute*, *i.e.* of the whole debt or other obligation.
(b) The assignment must *not be by way of charge only*.
(c) It must be *in writing, signed by the assignor*.
(d) *It need not be supported by valuable consideration*.
(e) *Express notice in writing* must be given to the obligee by the assignee, to avoid the obligee performing the contract for the benefit of the assignor.

Thus if A owes B £100, B can sell his right to collect payment to X (in the form set out above), and this will entitle X to enforce the debt against A. But X should notify A of the assignment to avoid A paying B.

5. Effect of statutory assignments.

(a) The assignee (X) can *sue in his own name* to enforce the chose in action, *e.g.* by suing A for debt.
(b) The assignee (X) takes *subject to equities* having priority over his assignment, *e.g.* if A has paid part of his debt to B before receiving notice of the assignment X cannot compel A to pay the full amount (but must try and recover the money from B).

6. Equitable assignments. This means any assignment which though valid fails to comply with the requirements of *s.* 136 *L.P.A.*, *e.g.* an oral assignment.

In an equitable assignment the assignee (X) cannot sue in his own name, but must join the assignor (B) as co-plaintiff in any action against the debtor or other obligee (A), or as co-defendant if he refuses. Thus the action will be either X and B *v.* A, or X *v.* B and A.

ESSENTIALS:

(a) *Intention* to assign (no particular form is necessary).
(b) *Notice* is necessary to the obligee to prevent him paying the assignor: the Rule in *Dearle* v. *Hall* (1823).
(c) *Value* is necessary only in *assignments of future rights*, *e.g.* the assignor's expectations under a will.

7. Negotiable instruments. Some choses in action possess the quality of negotiability, *e.g.* cheques and other bills of exchange. These negotiable instruments are *freely transferable by mere delivery* (with or without indorsement by the transferor), and the transferee usually obtains an *indefeasible title free of equities*, etc.

Negotiability must therefore be distinguished from assignability. If a chose is merely assignable, the assignee obtains no better rights to the chose than were possessed by the assignor; but if the chose is negotiable, the transferee may obtain a better right than that possessed by the transferor: *see* Negotiable Instruments, *s.* **62.**

THE LAW OF CONTRACTS

LAW OF CONTRACTS

1. How does a binding contract differ from other agreements? **(1. 1–4.)** What kinds of contract are there, and what are their characteristics? **(2.)**

2. What is a quasi-contract? When if ever can money be recovered on the grounds of mistake in payment? **(4. 5.)**

3. Distinguish an offer from: (a) an invitation to treat, and (b) a statement of intention. **(5.)**

Apply the rules of offer and acceptance to the following situations:

   (i) Bidding at an auction.
   (ii) Putting a coin in a slot machine.
   (iii) Display of goods in a shop or self-service store.

4. Comment on the statement that there cannot be a contract to make a contract. **(8. 1.)**

A agreed orally to sell his house to B for £5000 "subject to contract." The next day C offered A £5500 for the house, and A accepted this offer and sold the house to C. Can B sue A for breach of contract? **(6. 2.)**

Would it make any difference to your answer if the agreement between A and B was in writing? **(11. 4.)**

5. In what circumstance may an offer: (a) lapse, and (b) be revoked? **(5. 6.)**

6. A wrote to B offering to sell his house for £5000, the offer to remain open "until Wednesday noon." On Tuesday A sells his house to C. What remedies, if any, has B against A? **(5. 9.)** Would it make any difference to your answer if B had paid A 1s. to keep the offer open till Wednesday?

7. When if ever may communication of acceptance be dispensed with? **(6. 4.)**

8. What is a tender, and what forms may a tender take? **(6. 6.)**

9. In what circumstances may an offeree be bound by the terms of a written offer which he has not read? Where such terms are designed to limit the liability of the offeror, what is meant by saying that they are interpreted *contra proferentem*? **(7. 2, 3.)**

10. In what circumstances may the court imply a term in a contract? **(8. 2.)**

11. Distinguish between conditions and warranties in a contract, and explain what is meant by *ex post facto* warranties. **(9. 2–5.)**

Why is it important to distinguish between a term of a contract and a mere representation made during negotiations? **(9. 7.)**

12. What is meant by the proper law of a contract, and why is it important? **(10.)**

13. What contracts are void unless made (a) by deed, or (b) in writing. What contracts are merely unenforceable unless supported by written evidence? What is the distinction between void and unenforceable contracts? **(11. 1–4; 3. 1, 3.)**

14. Define consideration. When if ever is a simple contract enforceable when unsupported by valuable consideration? **(12. 1, 2, 4.)**

15. What is a guarantee, and how does it differ from an indemnity? **(11. 5.)** Is it true to say that a guarantee does not need to be supported by consideration?

16. What is meant by evidence in writing, in contracts covered by *s.* 40, Law of Property Act? How does the doctrine of part performance modify the application of this section? **(11. 6, 7, 9.)**

17. Explain the difference between executory, executed, and past consideration. Why is the distinction between executed and past consideration important? **(12. 3, 4.)**

A fell into a river and shouted for help. B hearing the cry rescued him, and in gratitude A promised B £1000. A now refuses to pay the money. Can B recover it by an action for breach of contract?

18. Explain briefly the rule in *Foakes* v. *Beer* (1854) and any exceptions of which you know. **(12. 4.)**

19. What contracts are (a) binding on an infant, (b) voidable at the infant's option? What must be proved by a shop-keeper suing an infant for the price of goods supplied? **(14. 2. 4.)**

20. When, if ever, may a contract be avoided at Common Law on the grounds of mistake (a) of law, or (b) of fact? What relief is available in Equity in cases of mistake? **(15. 1–3, 8; 4. 5.)**

21. When if ever may a person who has signed a written acceptance of an offer evade the consequences of his signature? **(7. 1; 15. 7.)**

22. "Mistakes in the formation of contracts may be common, mutual or unilateral." Discuss this statement, and explain the cases where such mistakes may avoid a contract. **(15.)**

23. What is "misrepresentation"? When, if ever, is there a positive duty of disclosure imposed on a party to a contract? **(16. 3, 10.)**

24. Distinguish between innocent and fraudulent misrepresentation and explain the remedies available for each. **(16. 4–8.)**

25. Explain the importance of the distinction between a *mere* misrepresentation, and a misrepresentation which has become a term of a contract. **(16. 9; 9. 2–7.)**

26. "Adequacy of consideration is of itself no grounds for avoiding a contract, but it may be evidence of undue influence." Explain this statement. (12. 4; 17.)

27. What is meant by an "illegal" contract, and what are the consequences of illegality? (18. 1–5.)

28. Explain briefly the main provisions of the Moneylenders Acts in regard to loans by professional moneylenders. (19. 3.)

29. Summarise briefly the rules relating gaming and wagering contracts and their effects. (19. 4.)

30. "Restraints of trade are prima facie void." How far is this true? (21. 1–3.)

31. Explain briefly the cases in which the courts will enforce covenants by an employee not to compete with his former employer. (21. 4, 5.)

32. Summarise briefly the main provisions of the *Restrictive Trade Practices Act*, 1956, and the *Resale Prices Act*, 1964. (21. 7–9.)

33. State briefly the five ways in which a contract may be discharged. (22; 23; 24; 25; 26.)

34. "To effect discharge, performance must be complete." What exceptions are there to this rule? (22. 1, 2.)

35. Explain briefly the rules relating to the appropriation of payments by a debtor, or creditor. How does the rule in *Clayton's Case* affect the position? (22. 6.)

36. Explain what is meant by: (a) Deed of Release; (b) Accord and satisfaction; (c) Novation; (d) The rule in *Morris* v. *Baron*. (23. 2–4.)

37. When are rights of action arising under a contract liable to lapse? How may such lapsed rights be revived? (24. 4–6.)

38. "Supervening impossibility of performance has no effect on contracts." Discuss this statement. (25. 1–5.)

39. A, in Whiteland, and B, in Redland, made a contract for the supply of machines by A, for which B paid in advance. The contract contained a clause stating: "this contract shall be avoided and the loss shall lie where it falls if war breaks out between Whiteland and Redland." War does break out, when A has supplied only half the machines. The contract was made in England, and B wants to know whether he can recover any of his money under the L.R. (Frustrated Contracts) Act, 1943. Advise him. (10; 25, 4, 5.)

40. What is meant by anticipatory breach of contract? A was due to perform a contract on the 1st May, but in April repudiated his obligations. On 29th April the contract became illegal through a change in the law. B, the other party to the contract, commenced an action for breach of contract on 30th April. Discuss. (26. 2; 25. 3.)

41. Explain briefly the rule in *Hadley* v. *Baxendale* (1854). What is meant by saying that the plaintiff must mitigate his loss? (26. 5, 6.)

42. Distinguish between penalties and liquidated damages in the law of contracts, and explain when interest may be allowed on sums claimed by way of unliquidated damages. (26. 6, 7.)

43. "You cannot both treat a breach of condition as discharging a contract and also sue for damages for the breach." Discuss this statement. Explain how the plaintiff might have a right of action on a *quantum meruit* claim in these circumstances. (26. 3, 8.)

44. Explain when the court may award the discretionary remedies of specific performance or injunctions in actions upon contracts. (26. 9, 10.)

45. The rule that an outsider cannot claim benefits or incur liabilities under a contract is not invariably applicable. Discuss. (27. 1–5.)

46. Why is it easier to transfer the benefit than the burden of a contract? (28. 1–3.) Distinguish between legal and equitable assignments of choses in action, and explain how the effects differ. (28. 4–6.)

SPECIMEN QUESTIONS

1. Explain the statement that for a contract to be binding the terms must be definite or capable of being made definite without further agreement of the parties.

V sold to P, a motor coach proprietor, a plot of land which P required for an extension to his garage. It was agreed that P should purchase all his petrol from V at a price to be agreed by the parties from time to time, and that any dispute should be referred to arbitration. No price was agreed, and P refused to purchase petrol from V.

Explain the legal position. *C.I.S. Final; June* 1961. (8. 1–3.)

2. What is the legal position where, although there is no contract between A and B, B has derived benefit from expenditure made on his behalf by A?

C imported carpets from Persia, and stored them in D's bonded warehouse. The carpets were stolen from the warehouse, without any negligence on the part of D. After the theft had been discovered, D was required to pay Customs Duty on the carpets. Is D entitled to recover from C the amount of the duty so paid? *C.I.S. Final, Dec.* 1961. (4, 1–6.)

3. (*a*) Explain the meaning of "valuable consideration," and its importance in the law of contract.

(*b*) Meeson has for a long time owed a debt of £1000 to Welsby, who now agrees to accept £900 in settlement. If Meeson pays £900 and gets a receipt "in full settlement," could Welsby later successfully claim the balance of £100? *I.C.W.A. Final, June 1961.* (**12.** 1–4.)

4. A customer arranged with his bank for an overdraft against the security of a guarantee to be executed by a well-known local tradesman. The bank allowed the customer to have the form of guarantee so that he could take it to the tradesman for signature. A few days later the customer returned the form of guarantee to the bank signed by the tradesman.

The customer has now defaulted, and the bank has called upon the guarantor to pay. He states that he signed the form when he was very busy without knowing that it was a guarantee, and that he had been told by the customer that the form related to some insurance matter.

Advise the bank whether the tradesman is liable on the guarantee. *Inst. of Bankers—Diploma Part II*, 1964. (**15.** 7.)

5. Explain the general principles governing the enforceability of a covenant in restraint of trade as between an employer and an employee after the latter has left the employer's service. *I.C.W.A. Final, Dec.* 1962. (**21,** 1–5.)

6. (*a*) Certain contracts are not enforceable in a court of law unless evidenced in writing. Name the contracts to which this principle applies and indicate the nature and the contents of the written evidence that has to be available if the contract is to be enforced.

(*b*) E, by an oral agreement, sold two houses to F for £10,000. F drew a cheque for £1000 by way of deposit, the cheque being made payable to E's solicitors. E personally made out a receipt for this amount, indicating the names of the parties, the description of the properties, the purchase price and the amount of the deposit. F subsequently refused to complete the contract. Discuss whether E (the vendor) has a right of action for breach of contract against F (the purchaser). *C.I.S., June* 1966. (**11,** 4–8.)

7. Summarise and explain the remedies, other than damages, available to a litigant in an action for breach of contract. *A.C.C.A., December* 1967. (**26.** 8–11.)

8. Jack, aged 20, promised to marry Jill, aged 19, who accepted his promise. Their parents consented to the marriage. For six months after he attained his majority Jack and Jill continued their engagement but then Jack refused to marry Jill. May Jill sue him successfully for breach of promise? *Inst. of Bankers—Intermediate, April*, 1967. (**14.** 4.)

9. What effect has impossibility of performance on a contract: (*a*) where it exists *before* the making of the contract; (*b*) where it occurs *after* the making of the contract? *A.C.C.A., December* 1967. (**2.** 4; **15.** 4; **25.** 1, 2, 5.)

PART TWO

AGENCY AND PARTNERSHIP

AGENCY

SECTION 29. FORMATION OF AGENCY

1. Definition of agency. An agent is a person who is employed to bring his principal into contractual relations with third parties.

Since the agent does not contract on his own behalf, he does not need to possess full contractual capacity, *e.g.* he may be a minor. But the principal must have full capacity to make the contract in question.

2. Kinds of agency.

(a) *Universal:* an agent appointed to handle all the affairs of his principal. This kind of agency is very rare: it has to be created by deed, and is a form of general power of attorney.

(b) *General:* an agent who has authority to represent his principal in all business of a certain kind, *e.g.* to manage a branch bank.

Such an agent has implied authority to represent his principal in all matters incidental to the business in question. And a third party dealing with the agent is not affected by any secret restrictions on the agent's authority: *Watteau* v. *Fenwick* (1893), *see s.* **32** *below.*

(c) *Special:* an agent appointed for a particular purpose, not part of his normal business activities, and who is therefore given only limited powers, *e.g.* where a bank manager is asked by a friend to act as agent in the sale of the friend's house.

(d) *Del credere:* an agent employed to sell goods, who promises to make sure that clients introduced by him to his principal will pay for the goods sold. (Note: this is not a contract of guarantee and does not need to be evidenced in writing.)

3. Express appointment. Where the agent is employed to execute a deed on behalf of his principal his appointment must be by deed, and the agency is called a Power of Attorney, *e.g.* where A is appointed to execute a conveyance of land.

In most other cases the agent's appointment can be in any form.

4. Implied agency. An agency may be implied from certain relationships, *e.g.* partnership. Thus where a dealer acts as middleman between a hire-purchase finance company and the hirer of goods, there is now an implied agency between the company and the dealer to the extent that the company must accept liability for representations made by the dealer: *H.P. Act*, 1965, *see s.* **48**, below.

Similarly the law implies an agency in favour of a wife living with her husband, whereby she is entitled to pledge his credit for the purchase of necessaries suitable to their standard of living. *The presumption of a wife's agency can be rebutted* by showing that:

(a) the husband had *expressly warned* the tradesman not to supply goods on credit to his wife; or

(b) the husband had *expressly forbidden the wife* to pledge his credit, even though this prohibition was unknown to the trader (but where the wife has previously dealt with that trader and the husband had accepted liability in the past, the trader is entitled to express notification of revocation of the agency, otherwise agency by estoppel may arise);

(c) that his wife had a *sufficient allowance* to cover necessaries without pledging the husband's credit; or,

(d) that the wife was already *sufficiently supplied* with the goods in question, or that they were unreasonable having regard to the husband's income at that time.

5. Agency by estoppel. Where P allows third parties to believe that A is acting as his authorised agent, he will be estopped from denying the agency (even if in fact he had no authority at all) if such third parties rely on it to their detriment.

This rule applies even where no agency was ever intended by the principal.

Similarly a husband, partner or master, who allows his wife, co-partner or servant to act as his agent cannot evade liability on the agent's contracts even after revocation of the agency unless he has expressly notified third parties with whom the agent has habitually been dealing: *Scarf* v. *Jardine* (1882).

6. Agency by ratification. Where (i) *a duly appointed agent exceeds his authority*, or (ii) *a person having no authority purports to act as agent*, the principal incurs no liability on the contract supposedly made on his behalf.

But in such cases the principal may expressly or impliedly ratify the agent's transaction and so accept liability.

Ratification is only possible where:

(a) *The agent claimed expressly* to be contracting as agent, and named his principal: *Keighley Maxsted* v. *Durant* (1901).

(b) *The principal must have had full contractual capacity* both (i) at the time of ratification, and (ii) at the time the agent made the contract.

   Thus a company after its incorporation cannot ratify a contract supposedly made on its behalf before incorporation, since it did not exist and therefore had no contractual capacity when the contract was made: ✷ *Kelner* v. *Baxter* (1866).

   Nor in such a case can the agent enforce the contract in his own name, if he contracted expressly as agent: *Newborne* v. *Sensolid (G.B.) Ltd.* (1954).

(c) At the time of ratification *the principal must have full knowledge* of all material facts, or must have agreed to dispense with it: *Marsh* v. *Joseph* (1897).

   NOTE: Where ratification takes place it is retrospective, *i.e.* it dates back to the time when the contract was made by the agent. Thus ratification might defeat an attempted repudiation by the third party, made after the date of contracting and on the discovery by the third party of the agent's lack of authority: *Bolton Partners* v. *Lambert* (1889).

7. Agency of necessity.

(a) *A deserted wife* lacking means of support for herself and her children can pledge her husband's credit for necessaries, provided she has not been given an adequate allowance: *Biberfield* v. *Berens* (1952).

(b) *Commercial agency of necessity* may arise in favour of a carrier, shipmaster, etc., providing the person claiming it can prove:

   (i) *That it was impossible to get instructions* from the principal, *e.g.* because communication was impossible: *Springer* v. *G. W. Railway* (1921).

   (ii) That there was a *real and definite commercial necessity. e.g.* where the master of a ship sells a cargo to prevent it rotting.

   (iii) *That he acted honestly* in the interests of his principal while lacking any instructions.

   (These rules probably mean that a commercial agency of necessity will only be implied in favour of a person who is already a duly appointed agent for the principal, and who must exceed his instructions in an emergency. It is doubtful whether a person not already an agent could claim an agency of necessity.)

SECTION 30.　TERMINATION OF AGENCY

1. By act of parties. An agency may be terminated by mutual agreement like any other contract, but in addition the principal may at any time revoke the agent's authority and so prevent him making binding contracts with third parties (though revocation, if unjustified, may leave the agent with a right of action for breach of contract against the principal).

Revocation is not possible in these circumstances:

(a) Where the authority is *"coupled with an interest,"* i.e. where the agent was appointed to enable him to secure some benefit already owed to him by the principal: *Smart* v. *Saunders* (1848).

(b) *A power of attorney* (agency created under seal) if given for consideration is irrevocable, even by the death of the principal. And if a power of attorney is given for a limited time, whether supported by consideration or not, it is irrevocable within one year of creation: *L.P.A.*, 1925, *s*. 126, 127.

(c) Where revocation would involve *personal loss to the agent*, the principal may be estopped from revoking without the consent of the agent: *Seymour* v. *Bridges* (1885).

(d) The principal cannot revoke in such a way as to *damage the interests of innocent third parties*, e.g. by breaking contracts the agent has already made with them.

2. By operation of law. Agency is automatically terminated in the following cases:

(a) *By death of principal or agent*, save in some exceptional cases.

(b) *By bankruptcy or insanity of principal or agent*, save in exceptional cases:

> EXAMPLE: X employed T as solicitor to sue Y. T commenced the action and brought the case to court. Unknown to T, X had gone insane in the meanwhile. HELD: T's agency was automatically terminated, and he was therefore liable to Y for damages for breach of warranty of authority: ✳ *Yonge* v. *Toynbee* (1910).

(c) *By frustration: see s.* **25.**

(d) *By intervening illegality.*

(e) *By the agent accomplishing his mission.*

(f) *By effluxion of time*, where the agency was created for a limited time.

SECTION 31. DUTIES OF PRINCIPAL AND AGENT

1. Duties of agent.

(a) *To exercise due care and diligence* on the principal's behalf, plus any special skill he professes to have: *Keppel* v. *Wheeler* (1927).

(b) *To disclose promptly to the principal* any material information he may receive in execution of his task.

(c) *Not to disclose confidential information* entrusted to him by his principal.

(d) *Not to delegate performance* of his duties (*delegatus non potest delegare:* "a delegate cannot delegate"). But this prohibition is not strictly applied, and the agent may usually delegate performance where required by (i) commercial usage or (ii) necessity, or (iii) where expressly or implied authorised by the principal: *De Bussche* v. *Alt* (1878).

(e) *Not to let his interest conflict with his duty, e.g.* not to compete with his principal: *Armstrong* v. *Jackson* (1917).

(f) *Not to make any secret profit.* If, beyond his commission, he receives any extra profit in the course of his duties he must disclose this to the principal.

If he fails to do so: (i) the principal can sue him for the amount kept secret; (ii) the principal can refuse to pay the agent his commission, and can terminate the agency without notice; (iii) the principal can sue the agent and the third party for damages to compensate him for any loss he has sustained: ✱ *Salford Corporation* v. *Lever* (1891).

2. Duties of principal.

(a) *To pay any agreed commission* or remuneration and not to prevent or hinder the agent from earning this: *Rhodes* v. *Forwood* (1876).

The agent has a lien over goods belonging to the principal enabling him to retain such goods until his commission is paid.

When commission becomes payable depends on the contract between principal and agent, *e.g.* when the agent is employed to sell goods or land, his commission may become payable:

(i) when he introduces a client (whether sale results or not); or

(ii) on completion of the sale, and payment of the price. (The signing of an agreement "subject to contract" does not amount to completion: *Luxor Ltd.* v. *Cooper* (1941).)

(b) *To indemnify the agent* against liabilities properly incurred in the discharge of his duties: *Christoforides* v. *Terry* (1924).

3. Vicarious liability. A master may be liable for wrongs (torts) committed by his agent. The extent of this indirect or vicarious liability depends on whether the agent is:

    (a) *An independent contractor, i.e.* an outsider employed to do certain work and told *what* to do but left free to decide how he will do it.

The principal is only liable for his torts if (*a*) he expressly or impliedly commissioned the tort, or (*b*) he delegated to the contractor performance of a legal duty and the contractor is negligent.

    (b) *A servant, i.e.* a person employed as an integral part of the principal's business, who is told both *what* to do and *how* to do it: *Mersey Docks etc.* v. *Coggins* (1947).

The principal is liable for all torts committed by a servant *in the course of his employment, i.e.* where the servant does improperly what he is employed to do properly.

NOTE:

    (i) *Course of employment.* What acts are part of the course of employment, or reasonably incidental thereto, is a *question of fact* in each case.

        Thus a solicitor was held liable where one of his staff gave fraudulent advice to a client of the firm, despite the solicitor's claim that giving *fraudulent* advice could not be regarded as part of the course of employment: *Lloyd* v. *Grace, Smith & Co.* (1912).

        But a bus company was held not liable for the negligent driving of a bus conductor who had temporarily taken over the wheel, since this was not what he was employed to do: *Ricketts* v. *Tilling* (1915).

    (ii) *Express prohibition.* The master is vicariously liable if the servant is doing improperly what he is employed to do properly, even if the master has expressly forbidden the particular wrongful act.

        Thus a bus company was held liable for an accident caused by bus drivers racing to bus stops, despite the fact that the company had expressly prohibited such racing: *Limpus* v. *L.G.O.C.* (1862).

SECTION 32. THE AUTHORITY OF THE AGENT

1. Real and ostensible authority. Extent of the agent's authority depends (i) on his contract with his principal, or (ii) on the law, where this implies a particular authority for particular kinds of agency.

This implied, or ostensible authority, may exceed the agent's actual authority from his principal, and may therefore render the principal liable on contracts made by the agent beyond the limits of his actual authority.

EXAMPLE: The manager of a public house was forbidden to order tobaccos by his principal, but did so. HELD: The principal was liable to pay the seller, since a manager of a public house would usually have authority to make orders of this kind, and the seller could therefore rely on the agent's ostensible authority in the absence of express knowledge of the limitation imposed by the principal: *Watteau* v. *Fenwick* (1893).

2. Breach of warranty of authority. Every person professing to act as agent for another impliedly warrants that he has authority to make binding contracts on behalf of his principal.

If therefore an agent lacks the authority he professes to have he is liable to an action for damages for breach of the implied warranty of authority, brought by the person with whom he has been dealing: ✳ *Collen* v. *Wright* (1857).

The agent is still liable for damages, even if he was acting in good faith, genuinely believing he had the authority he claimed, *e.g.* where his authority has been terminated without his knowledge by the death of his principal: *Yonge* v. *Toynbee* (1910).

But he is not liable if his lack of authority was known to the third party at the time of making the contract, or if the third party agreed to exclude the liability for breach of warranty: *Lilly* v. *Smales* (1892).

(Where a dishonest agent deliberately claims authority he knows he does not possess, he is also liable to an action for *fraud* by the third party whom he has deceived.)

3. Relations between principal and third parties. Generally, once he has made a contract on behalf of his principal the agent drops out of the transaction and *privity of contract* exists between the principal and the third party: *see s.* **27.**

But the results of an agent's contract differ slightly depending on whether (*a*) he has disclosed the fact of his agency, or (*b*) he has concealed the fact that he is merely an agent for another person.

Each of these possibilities is dealt with separately below.

4. Agent acting for named principal. Here the agent generally incurs neither rights nor liabilities under the contract, and drops out as soon as it is made: *Gadd* v. *Houghton* (1876).

EXCEPTIONS:

(a) *Where the agent agrees* to accept personal liability.
(b) *Where the agent signs a deed* he is personally liable thereon and the principal incurs no liability unless the agent was himself appointed by deed (a power of attorney)—in which case the agent drops out and the principal is liable in the ordinary way.
(c) *Where the agent signs a bill of exchange* in his own name, he is personally liable thereon. (To avoid this he should make it perfectly clear that he is signing merely as agent, *e.g.* by signing "for and on behalf of" a named principal. A director signing a cheque on behalf of his company should always take this precaution.)
(d) *Where trade custom* makes the agent personally liable, *e.g.* in some exceptional situations where he is contracting on behalf of an overseas principal: *Miller, Gibb & Co.* v. *Smith & Tyrer* (1917).

5. Agent acting for undisclosed principal. This covers two possible situations: (a) *where the agent discloses the fact that he is merely an agent*, but conceals the identity of his principal, and (b) *where he conceals the agency altogether*, and appears to be acting on his own behalf.

(a) *Agency revealed: principal concealed.* Here the agent drops out in the normal way, providing he makes it clear when contracting that he does so merely as agent. If he fails to do so he is personally liable on the contract. (The exceptions stated under 4 above apply to this situation.)
(b) *Agency concealed altogether: the Doctrine of the Undisclosed Principal.* Here the third party can enforce the contract against the agent or, when he discovers his identity and existence, against the principal.

The third party thus has an option whether to compel the agent to accept personal liability, or to shift liability to the principal as soon as his identity is revealed.

BUT NOTE:

(i) *He cannot enforce the contract against both* agent and principal. If he sues one he cannot later sue the other.
(ii) *He may be estopped* from suing the principal at all if he allows the principal to think he has settled matters satisfactorily with the agent, *e.g.* by unreasonable delay in taking action against the principal after his identity is revealed: *Heald* v. *Kenworthy* (1855).

SECTION 33. SPECIAL CLASSES OF AGENT

1. Factors. A factor is a *mercantile agent* employed to sell goods for a commission "in the ordinary course of his business," *i.e.* a professional buying and selling agent: *Factors Act*, 1889. (A factor differs from a broker in that he has possession of the goods to be sold, while a broker usually does not.)

If a factor has possession of goods with the consent of the owner for some purpose other than sale but contrary to his instructions does sell the goods, the purchaser obtains a good title (providing he did not know of the limitation on the factor's authority. In such cases the principal is legally estopped from denying that the purpose of the factor's possession was sale:
★ *Factors Act, s.* 2. A factor has a lien over goods in his possession and power to pledge them for security.

2. Brokers. A broker is a commercial agent employed to make contracts between his principal and others for a commission usually called brokerage. (An agent employed to make non-commercial contracts is therefore not a broker, *e.g.* a contract to hire a singer for a charity concert.)

Unlike factors brokers do not have possession of goods for sale, and cannot therefore sell in their own name. They have no lien over goods and no power to lodge them for security.

A broker is primarily agent for the seller of goods, but on making a contract with a purchaser he becomes agent for the purchaser also.

3. Auctioneers: *see s.* **47.**

4. Position of banks. The relationship between bank and customer is primarily that of debtor and creditor, with the bank usually the debtor (as long as the customer's account is in credit).

In addition there is a complex implied contract between a bank and its customers, which imposes many duties on the bank similar to those of an ordinary agent: *Joachimsson* v. *Swiss Bank Corporation* (1921).

"The limits of a banker's business cannot be laid down as a matter of law;" *Banbury* v. *Bank of Montreal* (1918), but the following general rules apply:

(a) The bank is legally bound to honour its customer's cheques up to the limit of his credit (or agreed loan facilities), but not beyond. Thus if the account is £100 in credit and the customer draws a cheque for £100 10s. 0d., the bank is theoretically entitled to refuse payment (it cannot legally pay part of a cheque).

(b) The bank has an implied right to charge *reasonable commission* for its services (and interest on loans).

(c) *The bank must not disclose* its customer's affairs, save under compulsion of law, *e.g.* under a court order.

(d) Unlike most agents, the bank has a *general lien* over any of the customer's securities in its possession, *e.g.* shares, title deeds, insurance policies, etc.

(e) *Advice on investment* is a service offered expressly by most banks. Where offered, there is an *implied duty* to exercise care in providing advice, and the bank could be liable in negligence if one of its managers gave negligent advice and so caused damage to the customer: *Woods* v. *Martins Bank* (1958).

(f) A bank is entitled to dispose as it pleases of *moneys deposited* by a customer provided it pays his cheques on demand (during business hours) or through a clearing house.

(g) A bank must abide by any *express mandate* of the customer, and by any express agreement made with him.

(h) The bank is entitled to require that the customer shall exercise *reasonable care in drawing cheques*. If the bank pays a forged cheque and the forgery was facilitated by the customer's carelessness, the loss falls on the customer and not on the bank: *London Joint Stock Bank* v. *Macmillan & Arthur* (1918).

PARTNERSHIPS

SECTION 34. NATURE AND FORMATION OF PARTNERSHIPS

1. Definition of partnership. "Partnership is the relation which subsists between persons carrying on a business in common with a view of profit"; *Partnership Act*, 1890, *s.* 1.

Registered, statutory and chartered companies are specifically excluded from this definition (note also that a non-profit making association cannot be a partnership).

Capacity to form a partnership is governed by the ordinary rules of contractual capacity: *see ss.* **13** and **14**. An infant who remains a partner after becoming twenty-one becomes liable for the firm's debts incurred after his 21st birthday: *Goode* v. *Harrison* (1821).

2. Tests for establishing partnerships: P.A., s. 2.

(a) *Co-ownership* of property does not of itself create a partnership in the property, even though the co-owners share profits.

(b) *Sharing of gross returns* of a business does not of itself indicate a partnership, even if coupled with co-ownership of the property or business.

(c) *Share of profits* is presumptive evidence of partnership, but the presumption can be rebutted by showing that the purpose of sharing was for some other reason, *e.g.*,

(i) *Payment of a debt* by instalments out of profits.

(ii) *Remuneration* to a servant or agent of the business.

(iii) *Payment of an annuity* of portion to a widow or child of a deceased partner in the business.

(iv) *Payment of interest* (varying with profits) on a loan advanced for use in the business.

(v) *Payment to the seller of the goodwill of a business* (where the consideration is a share of profits).

However if the business goes bankrupt, the recipient of moneys under (iv) and (v) above is a deferred creditor in the bankruptcy: *see s.* **81.**

NOTE: Whether a partnership exists therefore depends on the circumstances in each case and the intention of the parties. *Sharing losses* is stronger evidence of partnership than sharing profits, but is still not conclusive: *Walker* v. *Hirsch* (1884). If *executors* of a will carry on the testator's business as instructed in the will, they do not automatically become partners: *Re Fisher & Sons* (1912).

3. The firm name. If the partners trade under a firm's name which does not consist of their own true names without any addition, such firm name must be registered, *e.g.* where A, B, & C trade under the name of X & Co.: ✳ *Registration of Business Names Act*, 1916.

In such cases they must register each partner's (i) christian and surnames, and any former names, and present and former nationality, (ii) usual address, (iii) any other business occupation.

Registration must be effected within 14 days of commencement of business, and within 14 days of any subsequent alteration in the required particulars. Registered firms must also publish the names and nationalities of partners in catalogues, circulars, letters, etc.

Default in registration renders the firm's contracts void (and each partner is liable to a £50 fine). The court has a discretion to validate such contracts retrospectively if satisfied (*a*) that the default was accidental, or (*b*) that ratification would be just and equitable: *re Shaw* (1927).

4. Illegal associations. An association may be illegal because:

(*a*) Its *objects* are illegal;
(*b*) Its *membership* exceeds the statutory limits (*i.e.* 20 in banking and most other partnerships, or more in some firms of solicitors, accountants and stockbrokers: *Companies Act*, 1967);
(*c*) It is an association *forbidden* by law, *e.g.* a professional partnership between a solicitor and an unqualified person.

The effects of illegality are that (i) the members cannot enforce any rights or obligations among themselves (ii) the members cannot enforce any contract against any innocent outsider, and (iii) the illegality cannot be raised as a defence in any action brought against them by an innocent outsider.

SECTION 35. DEALINGS WITH OUTSIDERS

1. Agency of partners. Each general partner is an *implied agent* for the firm, and can make his co-partners liable on debts incurred by him on behalf of the firm: *P.A. s.* 5. But he has *no implied authority* to bind the firm in any matter outside the scope of the firm's business: *s.* 7.

A person dealing with a partner is not affected by any *secret restriction* on the partner's agency, unless he knows of it or does not believe him to be a partner: *s.* 8.

Liability of partners for debts and other contractual obligations is *joint*: *s.* 9 (contrast liability in tort). Thus a creditor can sue all the partners jointly, or any one of them for the whole debt. But he has only *one right of action*, and if he obtains judgment for the whole debt against one (even if the judgment is unsatisfied) he cannot later launch proceedings against the others, since he is taken to have waived his rights against them: ★ Rule in *Kendall* v. *Hamilton* (1897).

2. Extent of implied agency.

(a) *A partner can bind the firm by the following transactions:*

  (i) *By selling* the firm's goods: *Dore* v. *Wilkinson* (1817).
  (ii) *By purchasing goods* for the firm: *Bond* v. *Gibson* (1808).
  (iii) *By accepting payment* of debts due to the firm: *Porter* v. *Taylor* (1817).
  (iv) By engaging or discharging *employees*: *Birkham* v. *Drake* (1841).

(b) *In a trading partnership*, he has the following additional powers:

  (i) *To borrow* money on the firm's credit: *Lane* v. *Williams* (1692).
  (ii) *To sign bills of exchange* on behalf of the firm; *Bills of Exchange Act*, 1882.
  (iii) *To employ a solicitor* on behalf of the firm: *Tomlinson* v. *Broadsmith* (1896).

NOTE: There is *no implied authority* (i) to execute deeds—this requires express authorisation by power of attorney: *see s.* 29; (ii) to submit disputes to arbitration; and (iii) to give a guarantee in the firm's name, unless the giving of guarantees is within the usual business of the firm.

3. Liability of incoming and outgoing partners.

(a) *Incoming partners.* A new partner is not liable (unless otherwise agreed) for debts incurred before he joined the firm: *P.A. s.* 17 (1).

(b) *Outgoing partners.* A retiring partner is *not liable* for debts incurred after he retired, but is liable for debts incurred before his retirement: *s.* 17 (2). (Release from this liability is by means of a novation under which the remaining partners are substituted for the retiring partner in respect of his liability to the creditors, with the latters' consent.)

But an *outgoing partner remains liable* if he has allowed creditors to believe him to be continuing in the firm: *s.* 36. To protect himself from this liability, he must (a) give express notice of his retirement to persons who were dealing with the firm before his retirement, (b) notify persons who trade with the firm in the future by advertising his retirement in the *London Gazette*: *s* 36 (2).

(c) *Death or bankruptcy.* The estate of a deceased or bankrupt partner is not liable for partnership debts incurred after death or bankruptcy: *s.* 36 (3).

(d) *Dormant partners.* A general partner not known to be a member of the firm to creditors seeking to enforce a partnership debt, is not liable for debts contracted after his retirement from active participation.

(e) *Holding out.* A person not a partner who holds himself out, or allows others to hold him out, as being a partner in a firm is liable to persons who rely on such representations as though he were in fact a partner, *i.e.* he becomes a partner by estoppel: *s.* 14.

(f) *A continuing guarantee* given to a firm is terminated as to future transactions by any change in the membership of the firm: *s.* 18. This section does not apply where (i) there is an agreement to the contrary (ii) the guarantee relates to past transactions, or (iii) the guarantee is given *by* the firm: see Guarantees, *Chapter XIX.*

4. Nature of firm's liability.

(a) Partners are *jointly liable* for the firm's *contracts*, unless otherwise agreed: ∗ *P.A. s.* 9 (the liability may be *joint and several* if the partners expressly so agree).

(b) Partners are *jointly and severally* liable for *torts* committed on behalf of the firm: ∗ *s.* 12.

(c) *The estate of a deceased partner* is severally liable for the firm's debts incurred during his lifetime, subject to the prior payment of his own separate debts: *s.* 9.

NOTE: *Difference between joint and joint and several liability.*

(i) *In joint liability,* the plaintiff has only one right of action and he may use this either in suing the firm jointly, or in suing any individual partner separately. But if he sues one alone he waives his right of action against the others, and cannot later sue them even though he obtains judgment against the one sued but is unable to get his money because of that partner's insolvency: ✷ *Kendall* v. *Hamilton* (1879).

(ii) *In joint and several liability,* the plaintiff has several causes of action. He can sue all partners together, or can sue them separately (in successive actions if necessary).

(iii) *As between the partners themselves,* whether the liability is joint or joint and several, they must contribute equally to the damages paid.

5. Notices and admissions.

(a) *Any admission or representation* by a partner in the course of business and about the firm's affairs is evidence against the firm: *P.A.*, *s.* 15.

(b) *Notice given bona fide to any active partner* concerning business matters, operates as notice to the firm: *s.* 16.

SECTION 36. RIGHTS AND DUTIES OF PARTNERS

1. Partnership articles. A partnership may arise by express agreement, or by implication, *i.e.* where persons conduct a business in common with a view of profit: *P.A.*, *s.* 1.

Where a partnership is formed by express agreement (the "partnership articles"), the rights and duties of the partners among themselves are regulated by that agreement. Where a partnership arises by implication, or wherever the articles (if any) are silent, the rights and duties of the partners are governed by the *Partnership Act*, 1890.

NOTE: Once formed, a partnership is a relationship requiring the utmost good faith and each partner must disclose to his colleagues all material information coming to his notice: *see s.* 16.

2. Rights and duties: P.A., s. 24. Unless otherwise agreed, the following rules apply:

(a) *Equal shares.* Partners are entitled to share equally in capital and profits, and must contribute equally towards losses (agreement to the contrary may be inferred from past dealings).

(b) *Indemnity.* The firm must indemnify a partner against liabilities properly incurred (i) in the ordinary course of business, or (ii) in anything necessarily done for the preservation of the business.

(c) *Interest on advances.* A partner is entitled to interest at 5% on money (other than capital) advanced to the business (but he is not entitled, before the ascertainment of profits, to interest on capital).

(d) *Management.* Every partner is entitled to participate in management of the business.

(e) *No remuneration.* A partner is not entitled to any remuneration for his services (unless expressly agreed).

(f) *New partners* can only be introduced with the consent of *all* existing partners (notice that there is no implied power to expel partners: *see* 3 *below*).

(g) *Disputes as to ordinary matters* may be settled by majority (but change of business requires unanimous agreement).

(h) *Partnership books* are to be kept at the firm's principal place of business and every partner is entitled to inspect them and copy them whenever he thinks fit.

3. Expulsion of partners. A partner can only be expelled from the firm if a power to do so has been conferred by *express agreement* between the partners: *P.A. s.* 25. Such power must be executed in good faith and in the interests of the firm, otherwise the expulsion is void: *Blisset* v. *Daniel* (1853).

4. Duties of partners. Apart from any duties imposed by the partnership articles, the following statutory duties are implied:

(a) *Uberrima fides.* Partners must render true accounts and full information on partnership matters to their colleagues: *s.* 28.

(b) *To account* for any benefits derived from the partnership business without the consent of the other partners, *i.e.* a partner must not make "secret profits" (cf. agents: see *s.* **31**).

(c) *Not to compete* with the firm, without the consent of the other partners. Any profits made by such unauthorised competition can be claimed by the firm: *s.* 30.

5. Partnership property. All partnership property must be held and applied exclusively for the purposes of the firm and in accordance with the partnership articles (if any): *s.* 20 (1).

Whether property is partnership property or not is a question of fact in each case. "Partnership property" includes:

   (a) *Property originally brought into the partnership stock: s.* 20 (1).
   (b) *Property acquired on account of the firm,* for the purpose of and in the course of the partnership business: *s.* 20 (1).
   (c) *Property purchased with the firm's money* (unless otherwise agreed): *s.* 21.

   (Thus the mere fact that partners are co-owners of land and share its profits does not make it automatically partnership property, unless it falls into one of the above categories: *s.* 20 (3).)

   As between partners, *partnership land* is treated as personal property: *s.* 22. Land is conveyed to the partners (or to four of them, if there are more than four) as trustees for sale.

6. Execution against a partner. A creditor who obtains judgment against an individual partner cannot seize partnership property in execution of the judgment: *s.* 23. His remedy is to appoint a *receiver* of the debtor partner's share of profits.

By *s.* 33 (2) if a receiver is so appointed, or a partner's share is otherwise charged with payment of his private debts, this entitles the other partners to *dissolve* the partnership.

7. Assignment of a partner's share. A partner's share in the business is the proportion of the existing assets to which he would be entitled if all the firm's assets were sold and proceeds distributed after discharge of all the firm's debts.

A partner may assign his share (by way of sale, gift, mortgage, etc.) but the assignee *does not thereby become a member* of the firm, can take no part in management or inspect books, etc., unless the other partners agree: *s.* 31.

Thus the assignor remains a partner, though his assignee becomes entitled to his share of profits and of the assets in the event of any distribution. The firm's creditors can therefore sue the assignor for the firm's debts, but he can (unless otherwise agreed) claim indemnity from the assignee: *Dodson* v. *Downey* (1901).

SECTION 37. DISSOLUTION OF PARTNERSHIP

The effect of dissolution is to terminate the partnership relation, and to entitle the partners (unless otherwise agreed) to share the assets after payment of the firm's debts. Dissolution may occur in the ways listed below.

1. By agreement.

(a) Under the partnership *articles*, if they provide a method.
(b) *By express and unanimous agreement* at any time (overriding the articles).

2. By operation of law.

(a) *Expiration.* If entered into for a *fixed term* or for a *single venture*, the firm is dissolved on expiration of the fixed term or termination of the venture. (If however the partnership is continued beyond the term originally agreed, the rights and duties of the partners remain the same: *s.* 26.)
(b) *Notice.* If entered into for an *undefined term*, any partner may determine the partnership at any time by notice to the others: *s.* 26. (If the partnership was originally constituted by deed, the notice must be in writing: *s.* 26 (2).)

The partnership is then dissolved (i) from the date stated in the notice, or (ii) if not stated, then from the date of communication of the notice to the other partners: *s.* 32.

3. By death or bankruptcy (unless otherwise agreed): *s.* 33
(1). Also if a partner allows his share to be charged with payment of his debts this entitles the others to dissolve the partnership if they wish: *s.* 33 (2).

4. By supervening illegality, *i.e.* if some event occurs which makes it unlawful for the business to be carried on: *s.* 34.

5. By court order: s. 35. The court may order dissolution on the application of any partner in the following cases:

(a) *Mental incapacity* of any partner: *Mental Health Act,* 1959, *s.* 103.
(b) *Permanent incapacity* of a partner (other than the applicant).

(c) *Conduct prejudicial* to the business (by any partner other than the applicant).

(d) *Breach of the partnership agreement* (by any other than the applicant). This includes conduct which make it impracticable for the other partners to carry on.

(e) Where the business can only be *carried on at a loss*.

(f) Where, *in the opinion of the court*, it is *just and equitable, e.g.* where there are only two partners and they are at loggerheads: *re Yenidje Tobacco Co. Ltd.* (1916).

6. Notice of dissolution. To avoid incurring liability after dissolution (*e.g.* by estoppel) a partner may publish notice of dissolution and can compel his co-partners to join him: *s.* 37.

7. Effect of dissolution. The authority of partners to bind the firm continues so long as is necessary to wind up the business, provided that the firm is in no case bound by the acts of a partner who has been bankrupted: *s.* 38.

Also each partner has an *equitable lien* (*see s.* **73**) over the firm's assets entitling him to have them applied in payment of the firm's debts, and in payment of whatever is due to partners; this lien can be enforced by injunction forbidding unfair distribution: *s.* 39.

8. Return of premium: s. 40. To buy entry into an existing firm, a new member sometimes has to pay a premium (in consideration of existing goodwill) in addition to any investment of capital.

On dissolution, he is entitled to demand the return of a proportion of the premium if the partnership was for a fixed term and was dissolved before the expiry of that term, unless dissolution was caused by (i) agreement, or (ii) misconduct by the party seeking return of the premium, or (iii) death of a partner: *s.* 40.

The portion returned will usually be in the same ratio to the whole premium as the unexpired term bears to the whole term: *Attwood* v. *Maude* (1868).

9. Dissolution through misrepresentation: s. 41. Where a partnership agreement is rescinded on the grounds of fraud or misrepresentation by any partner, the partner entitled to rescission can also demand the following:

(a) *A lien* on the firm's assets (after payment of debts) for any money he had invested.
(b) *Subrogation, i.e.* a right to stand in the place of any of the firm's creditors for any payment made by him to discharge the firm's debts.
(c) *To be indemnified* by the person guilty of the fraud or misrepresentation against all the firm's debts and liabilities.

10. Profits made after dissolution: s. 42. If a partner dies or retires, and the other partners carry on the business after the dissolution, without any final settlement of accounts, the outgoing partner or his estate can (unless otherwise agreed) claim:

(*a*) Such share of profits after dissolution as is attributable to the use of his share of the assets (after due allowance for the labour and skill of the continuing partners), or
(*b*) Interest at 5% on the share of the assets. This claim is not exercisable where the articles give continuing partners an option to purchase a deceased or retiring partner's share, and they duly exercise that option.

11. Settling accounts: ✸ s. 44. Unless otherwise agreed, the following rules apply:

(a) *Losses* (including deficiencies of capital) are paid first out of profits, next out of capital and lastly (if necessary) by the partners individually in the proportion in which they are entitled to share profits.
(b) *The assets* (including sums contributed to make up losses or deficiencies of capital) are then *applied* in the following manner:

   (i) In paying outside creditors.
  (ii) In repaying advances made by partners (distinct from investment of capital).
 (iii) In repaying capital to partners.
 (iv) The residue, if any, is divided among the partners in the proportions in which profits are divisible.

NOTE: Where after paying (i) and (ii) above there is insufficient to repay capital to all the partners in full, deficiencies are shared in the same way as profits: *Nowell* v. *Nowell* (1869).

But under the *Rule in* ✸ *Garner* v. *Murray*, if such deficiency is *attributable to the insolvency of one of the partners*, it must (unless otherwise agreed) be borne by the other partners in the proportion of their *last agreed capitals* (and not in the proportion in which they share profits or losses).

Thus G, M, & W were partners investing unequal capitals. On dissolution (after paying outside creditors) their balance sheet showed:

Liabilities		*Assets*		
G. (capital)	£2500	Cash		£1891
M. (capital)	£ 314	W (indebted)	£263	
		Deficiency	£660	
				£ 923
	£2814			£2814

HELD: (i) The firm's loss of £660 must be shared by the partners equally, and (ii) W's total deficit (£263 + one third of £660 = £483) must be shared between G and M in proportion to their last agreed capitals, *i.e.* £2500 and £314 respectively: *Garner* v. *Murray* (1906).

12. Goodwill. This is a partnership asset and means the good reputation and business connections of a firm developed over the years: *Trego* v. *Hunt* (1896).

Unless otherwise agreed in the articles, upon dissolution the goodwill must be sold and the proceeds of sale distributed as capital. Where dissolution is caused by death, the estate of the deceased partner is entitled to share in the proceeds of sale: *re David & Mathews* (1899).

If the goodwill is not sold and there is no agreement as to its disposal, any partner can carry on the business (even using the firm's name), providing that by so doing he does not expose former partners to liability; *Burchell* v. *Wilde* (1908).

But if by agreement the goodwill is assigned to any person, he can (a) restrain partners from soliciting old customers of the firm, or (b) using the firm's name (but not from setting up a merely competing business): * *Bourne* v. *Wicker* (1927).

13. Sale of goodwill. Where goodwill is sold (either to a partner or to an outsider) the value is divisible among the partners in the same manner as they share profits and losses (unless otherwise agreed).

(a) *Purchaser's rights* (unless otherwise agreed): (i) He may represent himself as continuing the former business of the vendors. (ii) He has exclusive rights to the firm's name: *Churton* v. *Douglas* (1859); (iii) He has the sole right to solicit former customers of the business bought: *Trego* v.

Hunt (1896), except where the vendor did not sell voluntarily, *e.g.* where a bankrupt's trustee sells his business, the bankrupt can recommence business after his discharge and can then solicit any former customers; *Walker* v. *Mottram* (1881).

(b) *Vendor's rights.* He is entitled to open a competing business, unless restrained by a covenant in the contract of sale: *see Restraints of Trade, s.* **21.**

SECTION 38. LIMITED PARTNERSHIPS

1. Limited Partnership Act, 1907. This allows a partnership to claim limited liability for some of its members. Limited partnerships are not common, since it is easier and more advantageous to operate a limited registered company.

2. Characteristics of limited partnerships.

(a) *Number of partners.* There must not be more than twenty members (ten in the case of banking), of whom at least one must be a general partner: *Limited Partnership Act,* 1907, *s.* 4 (2).

(b) *General and limited partners:* a general partner is fully liable for all debts and obligations of the firm as in an ordinary partnership, and is entitled to participate in management.

A limited partner (i) contributes a *stipulated amount* to the firm's capital, and is *not liable* for the firm's debts beyond that amount (which cannot be withdrawn from the business, except on dissolution), (ii) *cannot participate in management* (and if he does so he loses his limitation of liability), (iii) has *no agency* for the firm, and (iv) is entitled to inspect *accounts,* etc.: *ss.* 4, 6.

(c) *Registration:* a limited partnership must register (i) the firm's name, (ii) the nature of the business, (iii) the principal place of business, (iv) the full names of each partner, (v) any fixed term for which the partnership is created, (vi) a statement that the liability of some of the partners is limited, (vii) the sum contributed by each limited partner (in default of registration the firm cannot claim limited liability: *s.* 5).

(d) *Majority decisions:* in any ordinary partnership the votes of all partners count, but in a limited partnership only the votes of general (unlimited) partners count, unless otherwise agreed.

(e) *New partners:* in an ordinary firm admission of new members generally requires consent of existing partners: *P.A., s.* 24.

In a limited partnership, unless otherwise agreed (i) a new partner can be admitted *without consent* of any limited partner, and (ii) a limited partner may assign his share to another person (with consent of the general partners, but without the consent of other limited partners): *s.* 6.

(f) *No dissolution by notice:* a limited partner cannot dissolve the firm by notice: *s.* 6 (5).

(g) *Death, bankruptcy, or lunacy* of a limited partner does not automatically dissolve the partnership: *s.* 6 (2).

(h) *Winding-up:* if a limited partnership is dissolved, the firm's affairs are wound up by the general partners alone, unless the court orders to the contrary: *s.* 6 (3).

(i) *General partner becoming limited partner:* if by agreement a general partner becomes a limited partner, such change in status must be notified in the *London Gazette* and the change confers no limitation of liability until notified: *s.* 10 (1).

AGENCY AND PARTNERSHIP

1. Explain how an agency may arise (a) by implication, (b) by estoppel, (c) by necessity. (**29. 4, 5, 7.**)

2. In what circumstances may a person ratify a contract made on his behalf but without his authority? (**29. 6.**)

3. A, an infant, hires X as his agent to buy a house. X contracts to buy the house before discovering that A is an infant. A few days later A reaches his 21st birthday and purports to ratify the contract made by X. Is the ratification effective? (**29. 6; 14.**)

4. "Generally a principal can revoke his agent's appointment at any time." Discuss. (**30. 1.**)

5. What are the chief rights and duties of an agent, in regard to his principal? (**31.**)

6. Explain briefly: (a) ostensible authority of an agent, (b) breach of implied warranty of authority by an agent, (c) the doctrine of the undisclosed principal. (**32. 1, 2, 5.**)

7. In what circumstances may an agent be personally liable on a contract he has made on behalf of his principal? (**32. 4.**)

8. Distinguish between factors and brokers, and explain the normal limits of their authority. (**33. 1, 2.**)

9. "The limits of a banker's business cannot be laid down as a matter of law." Discuss. (**33. 4.**)

10. Define a partnership and state the tests outlined by the Partnership Act for deciding whether a partnership exists or not. (**34. 1, 2.**)

11. Explain what is meant by an illegal association. In what circumstances must a business association register a trade name? (**34. 3, 4.**)

12. To what extent can a partner be regarded as having implied authority to act as agent for his firm? (**35. 1, 2.**)

13. In what circumstances may a retired partner continue liable for the firm's debts after his retirement? (**35. 3.**)

14. Explain what is meant by saying that the liability of partners is generally either joint, or joint and several. (**35. 4.**)

15. "The rights and duties of partners depend on agreement, express or implied, between themselves." How far do you agree? What are the usual rights and duties of partners? (**36. 1–4.**)

16. Explain what is meant by: (a) partnership property, (b) execution against a partner's share, and (c) goodwill. (**36. 5, 6; 37. 12.**)

17. In what circumstances may a partner assign his share in a firm, and what is the effect of such assignment? (**36. 7.**)

18. Explain briefly the circumstances in which a partnership may be dissolved. What is the effect of dissolution? (**37. 1–6.**)

19. On dissolution of a partnership how, in the absence of contrary agreement, are accounts settled? (**37. 11.**)

20. Distinguish between, and explain briefly, the rules in (a) *Nowell* v. *Nowell* (1869), and (b) *Garner* v. *Murray* (1904). (**37. 11.**)

21. A and B, partners, sold their business to X two years ago, for an inclusive price to cover goodwill. X now learns that A, trading under his own name, has opened a competing business and is writing to old customers of the A & B firm, saying: "Please note that A, formerly of A & B, has now opened new premises at 333 New Street." Explain the legal position. (**37. 12, 13; 21. 6.**)

22. What is a limited partnership? How is such a partnership formed, and how does it differ from an ordinary partnership? (**38.**)

SPECIMEN QUESTIONS

1. A, acting without authority, enters as agent for B into a contract with X. B refuses to ratify the contract, as a result of which X suffers loss. State whether X can sue B or A for damages and, if so, on what grounds.

How are X's rights affected if: (a) A's authority had been terminated without A's knowledge? (b) X knew of A's lack of authority? *A.C.C.A., Intermediate, June* 1961. (**30. 2; 32. 2.**)

2. Mention the circumstances in which a trading partnership or a professional partnership may be formed. Refer to the rules whereby it may be decided whether or not a partnership is in existence.

Examine the following cases:

(a) A and B are the joint owners of a lorry which they let out on hire to builders.

(b) M assigned his bakery business to three trustees C, D, and E, for the benefit of his creditors; and C, D, and E carried on the business and paid off the creditors out of the profits made.

(c) F and G, executors of T's will, carried on T's business as directed in the will.

(d) In 1960 P took into partnership R, then aged 20; and before R attained the age of 21 the partnership incurred debts. R is now aged 22, and is still a partner. *C.I.S., Final, Dec.* 1962. (**34. 1, 2.**)

3. Distinguish between the authority possessed by a general agent and that possessed by a special agent.

Explain the position of each of the following agents:

    (a) an auctioneer;
    (b) a factor;
    (c) a broker;
    (d) a del credere agent.

In what circumstances and to whom is an agent liable for breach of warranty of authority? *C.I.S., Final, June* 1961. (**29**. 1, 2; **32**. 1–3; **33**. 1, 2; **47**. 2.)

4. State the duties of an agent to his principal, and those of a principal to his agent.

In what circumstances is a principal liable to a third party for the tortious acts of his agent?

T, the owner of residential property, consulted S, a solicitor, in connection with a mortgage transaction. M, the solicitor's conveyancing manager, induced T to execute a conveyance of the property in his favour. M then sold the property and misappropriated the proceeds of sale. Is S liable for M's misappropriation? Give reasons. *C.I.S., Final, Dec.* 1961. (**31**. 1–3.)

5. (a) How may an agency be terminated? Discuss whether there are any circumstances in which an agent's authority is irrevocable.

(b) Q. Co., an American firm, has appointed A to be its British sales agent for five years in charge of the sale of its products in Britain. After two years, Q. Co. informs A that it is cancelling his authority with immediate effect. Discuss whether this revocation of authority is legally binding on A. *C.I.S., June* 1967. (**30**. 1.)

6. (a) What is meant by the term "partnership property"? (b) A, B, and C are partners in a grocery business. A wishes to retire from business and has assigned his share in the firm to his son, X. B and C now refuse to allow X to join them in managing the firm's business, and insist that A remains liable for the firm's debts. Explain the legal position. *A.C.C.A., December* 1967. (**36**. 5, 7; **35**. 3.)

7. In what circumstances may a principal be bound by contracts made by his agent in excess of the agent's actual authority? *A.C.C.A., June* 1967. (**29**. 5; **32**. 1.)

8. (a) On what grounds may a partnership be dissolved by the court?

(b) In order to obtain membership of a partnership A paid the firm a premium of £1000. The firm was dissolved shortly afterwards. Can A recover any part of his premium? *A.C.C.A., June* 1967. (**37**. 5, 8.)

PART THREE

MERCANTILE AGREEMENTS

SALE OF GOODS AND HIRE PURCHASE

THE law relating to sale of goods is laid down by the Sale of Goods Act, 1893, an act which codified the law then existing. The body of law contained in this statute has however been considerably added to by judicial decisions since the Act was passed.

The law relating to hire purchase is laid down by the Hire Purchase Acts, 1938–65.

SECTION 39. THE CONTRACT FOR SALE OF GOODS

1. Sale of Goods Act, 1893, s. 1. This defines the contract as one "whereby the seller (i) *transfers*, or (ii) *agrees to transfer* the property in goods to a buyer for a money consideration called the price" (the word property here means rights of ownership).

Two kinds of contract are dealt with in the definition: (i) a sale and transfer of property, *i.e.* an executed contract, and (ii) an agreement to sell and transfer in the future, *i.e.* an executory contract.

2. Meaning of "goods." Goods means all chattels and tangible things in possession (chattels personal), but not things in action and money. *Note* that the word "goods" cannot be used in the singular; you cannot speak of selling a good, but only of an item of goods or an article.

"Goods" also means:

(a) *Industrial growing crops*, once they have been severed from the land. (Until severance they are classed as part of the land itself and are not goods.)

(b) *Ships.*

(c) *Future goods*, *i.e.* goods to be made or acquired by the seller after making the contract: *S.G.A.*, *s.* 62. (A sale of such goods operates as an executory contract, *i.e.* an agreement to sell in the future: *s.* 5.)

3. An agreement to sell. Means a contract to transfer property in goods (*a*) at some future time, or (*b*) subject to some condition being fulfilled.

EXAMPLE: S agreed to sell a horse to B if B should be satisfied with it after an 8 day trial. After 3 days the horse died (without any fault on the part of B). HELD: B was not liable to pay the purchase price, since ownership would not pass to him for another 5 days. Consequently the contract was discharged by frustration: *Elphick* v. *Barnes* (1880).

4. Sales and Agreements to sell compared.

SALE	AGREEMENT TO SELL
1. *An executed contract*, operating as an actual transfer of the ownership.	1. *An executory contract* to transfer ownership at a later date.
2. *If the buyer defaults*, the seller can sue him for the price.	2. *If the buyer defaults*, the seller can only sue for unliquidated damages for breach of contract.
3. *If the seller defaults*, the buyer can sue for damages and claim delivery of the goods.	3. *If the seller defaults*, the buyer can only sue for damages.
4. Since ownership passes to the buyer, he bears *the risk* of loss or deterioration.	4. Since ownership does not pass to the buyer, *the risk* of loss or deterioration remains with the seller.

5. Contracts for work and materials. The *S.G.A.* does not apply to these contracts, in which the purchaser is buying the skill of a craftsman and not merely the goods to be produced by him. Whether a particular contract is one for the sale of goods or for the supply of work and materials is sometimes a difficult question of fact.

The test is: Is the essential object of the agreement the provision of goods or the exercise of skill?

EXAMPLE: A dental mechanic, employed to make false teeth, was *held* to be making a contract for sale of goods: *Lee* v. *Griffin* (1861). But employment of an artist to paint a portrait is a contract for supply of work and materials, since the artist's skill is the main constituent of the contract: ✱ *Robinson* v *Graves* (1935).

In contracts for work and materials there is an implied condition that the work will be carefully and properly carried out, and that the materials used shall be reasonably suitable to the purchaser's requirements, provided these are made known at the time of contracting.

EXAMPLE: A woman at a hairdresser's was injured by a hair-dye to which she was allergic. She had not told the hairdresser of her allergy. HELD: The hairdresser was not liable: *Ingham* v. *Emes* (1955).

6. Contract of barter. The *S.G.A.* lays down that a contract for the sale of goods is one in which the consideration is *payable in money*. Consequently the act does not apply to barters or exchanges.

But a contract of part-barter, or *part-exchange*, where part of the consideration is paid in money, is within the *S.G.A.*: *Simpson* v. *Connolly* (1953).

7. Conditional bills of sale. The *S.G.A.* does not apply to mortgages in the form of sales of chattels with a provision for resale on repayment of the price or loan. These are governed by the *Bills of Sale Acts*, 1878–82, *see s.* **72**.

8. Capacity to contract. Capacity is co-extensive with ordinary contractual capacity, *but note* the special liability imposed on infants, lunatics and drunkards to pay a reasonable price for necessaries: *S.G.A.*, *s.* 2, *and see* Infants, *s.* **14**.

9. Form of contract. Any form suffices, written or oral: *S.G.A.* *s.* 3. (Formerly by *S.G.A.* *s.* 4. contracts to sell goods worth more than £10 had to be evidenced in writing, but this section was repealed by the *L.R.* (*Enforcement of Contracts*) *Act*, 1954.)

10. Price.

(a) *Fixed by parties.* The price may be fixed (i) at the time of contracting by the parties themselves, or (ii) may be left to be determined in the course of dealings between the parties, or (iii) may be left to be fixed in some way stipulated in the contract, or (iv) may be left to be fixed by some third party.

(b) *Fixed by a third party.* Where the contract states that the price is to be fixed by a third party, and he fails to do so, the contract is void: *s.* 9.

But if the purchaser has by then taken the benefit of the goods, he must pay a reasonable price for them.

If the third party's failure to fix the price is due to the fault of one of the parties, that party is liable to an action for damages: *s.* 9 (2).

(c) *Where no price fixed in any* of the ways listed in (a) or (b) above, the purchaser must pay a reasonable price.

SECTION 40. CONDITIONS AND WARRANTIES

1. Conditions and warranties. There is no definition of the former in the *S.G.A.*, but *s.* 62 makes clear that the word warranty is to have its normal contractual meaning. It is therefore assumed that the word condition also bears the conventional meaning: *see s.* 9.

2. Terms implied by the S.G.A. The Act implies several very important conditions and warranties in contracts governed by the Act (unless expressly excluded). These are analysed in detail in *s.* 41 below.

3. Assessment of terms. Whether a particular term is a condition or warranty is a *question of fact* in each case, and the terminology used by the parties is not necessarily binding on the courts.

The importance of the distinction lies in that breach of warranty entitles the injured party to sue for damages for breach of contract, but not to treat the contract as at an end. *A breach of condition* (a main term) entitles the injured party, either (*a*) to treat the contract as at an end (and to sue for any compensation due to him in a *quantum meruit* action: *see s.* 26), or (*b*) to treat the breach as though it were merely a breach of warranty, go on with the contract and sue for damages for breach: *Wallis* v. *Pratt* (1911).

NOTE: Stipulations as to *time of payment* are not to be regarded as conditions of the contract unless expressly so agreed:

S.G.A., *s.* 10. (But contrast *time for performance*: in mercantile contracts this is usually regarded by the courts as a condition: *Reuter* v. *Scala* (1879).)

4. Ex post facto warranties. This means conditions which, after breach, are treated as breaches of warranties: *see s.* **9.**

In sales of goods the buyer can treat any breach of condition as breach of an *ex post facto* warranty: *s.* 11 (1) (*a*).

NOTE: In some cases (unless otherwise agreed) the buyer *must* treat a breach of condition as breach of an *ex post facto* warranty where:

(a) *The contract is for the sale of specific goods* and the property in them has passed to him, or
(b) *The contract is non-severable* and the buyer has accepted any part of the goods: ✱ *s.* 11 (1) (*c*).
("*Specific goods*" means goods identified and agreed upon at the time the contract is made: *s.* 62. *A "non-severable" contract* means one in which the goods are delivered in one lot which is not easily divisible, *e.g.* a ton of coal.)

5. Conditions and warranties, express or implied. Terms in a contract of sale of goods may be express or implied (by statute, trade usage, or the course of dealing between the parties), *see s.* **9.**

Where express terms are *added* to the contract after it is made, they must be supported by additional consideration otherwise they are not binding.

Terms implied by the *S.G.A.* may be *negatived* (i) by express terms in the contract, or (ii) by trade usage.

6. Terms and mere representations. Terms of the contract must be distinguished from mere representations made by a party during the preliminary negotiations. The distinction presents a difficult *question of fact* in each case, *e.g.* if in selling a used car A describes it as having done not more than 20,000 miles, is this a term of the contract or merely a representation?

The distinction used to be important because of the *different remedies* available for misrepresentation and for breach of contract: see *ss.* **16** and **26.** Now, however, the *Misrepresentation Act*, 1967, allows a plaintiff to obtain damages even in cases of innocent misrepresentation (where negligence is present) and the distinction between mere representations and warranties is much reduced in importance.

E

7. Dangerous goods. A person selling dangerous goods must warn the buyer of the danger, if he knows of it himself. If he fails to do so (*a*) he is liable for breach of contract to the person with whom he contracted; (*b*) he is liable for the tort of negligence to any person to whom the purchaser transmits the goods: *Donoghue* v. *Stevenson* (1932).

> EXAMPLE: A sold C a tin of disinfectant knowing that it could be dangerous if opened without special care, but failed to warn C. C's sight was damaged by the powder. HELD: A was liable in damages: *Clarke* v. *Army & Navy Co-operative Soc., Ltd.* (1903).

SECTION 41. TERMS IMPLIED BY THE SALE OF GOODS ACT

1. Seller's right to sell: ✳ s. 12 (1), (condition). The seller impliedly undertakes that he has the right to sell the goods (or, in an agreement to sell, that he will have the right to sell at the time the property is to pass to the purchaser).

EXAMPLES:

(*a*) Unknown to either party, goods sold were so labelled that if the buyer re-sold them (as was intended) he would infringe a trade-mark; HELD: Breach of this condition: *Niblett* v. *Confectioners Materials Co. Ltd.* (1920).

(*b*) S sold a stolen car to B, who after 4 months had to return it to the true owner. HELD: B could recover the price from S, whether S knew the car was stolen or not: *Rowland* v. *Divall* (1923).

2. Sales by sample: ✳ s. 15, (condition). That in a sale by sample:

(*a*) Bulk shall *correspond* with sample in quality; and

(*b*) The buyer shall have reasonable *opportunity to compare* bulk with sample, and

(*c*) The goods shall be *free of any defect rendering them unmerchantable*, and which would not be apparent on reasonable examination of the sample.

NOTE:

(i) *Where part only* of the goods are not up to sample, the buyer must still accept or reject all (unless the contract is severable, *i.e.* in instalments, in which case each instalment may be treated separately).

(ii) *Mere display of a sample during negotiations* does not make the contract a sale by sample. There must be definite agreement to this effect. Whether or not it is a term of the contract is a question of fact in each case.

(iii) Where in a sale by sample goods are sold *"with all faults and imperfections,"* the seller may be relieved from liability under (c) above but may still be liable under (a) and/or (b): *Champanhac Ltd.* v. *Waller Ltd.* (1945).

(iv) *"Merchantable"* merely means that goods must be readily saleable in their actual condition, having regard to the prevailing standards for such goods: *Bristol Tramways* v. *Fiat Motors Ltd.* (1910), and *see* 4 *below.*

3. Correspondence with description: ✶ s. 13, (condition). That in a sale by description the goods shall correspond with the description and with the sample: *s.* 13.

NOTE:

(i) *What is a sale by description?* This means that the buyer relies for his information on the description of the goods given by the seller, *e.g.* in the contract or in preliminary negotiations. Thus where he buys goods which he has not seen, it must be a sale by description. And it may be a sale by description even if he has seen the goods, if he relies on the seller's description and there is some inaccuracy in that description which is not apparent: *Thornet & Fehr* v. *Beers & Son* (1919).

(ii) This section is construed *strictly in favour of the buyer,* and covers almost any representation as to the nature, origin or identity of the goods, *e.g.* the methods of packing the goods: *Moore & Co.* v. *Landauer & Co.* (1921).

(iii) *A discrepancy between description and actuality* such as could not have been seen on *reasonable examination* is a breach of this condition, *e.g.* the buyer examined lace described as seventeenth century and after purchase discovered it was actually eighteenth century. HELD: The discrepancy was not discernible on examination, and he was entitled to rescind the contract: *Nicholson & Venn* v. *Smith Marriot* (1947).

(iv) *Where the description of the goods is an express term* of the contract, another term expressly excluding "all conditions and warranties implied by law" will not protect the seller, *e.g.* B bought a "new Singer car" from S, and the contract excluded all implied terms. The car was not new. HELD: B could reject the car: *Andrews Bros (Bournemouth) Ltd.* v. *Singer & Co.* (1934).

4. Merchantable quality: ✻ **s. 14** (2), (condition). Goods must be of merchantable quality if:

(a) they are *bought by description*,

(b) *from a dealer* in goods of that description.

NOTE:

(i) *Merchantable quality* means that the goods must be such as would be acceptable to a reasonable person, having regard to prevailing conditions. They are not merchantable if they have defects with makes them unfitted for ordinary use, or are such that a reasonable person knowing of their condition would not buy them.

(ii) *If the goods are defective*, it is no defence to the seller to show that the defect could be easily repaired: ✻ *Grant* v. *Australian Knitting Mills, Ltd.* (1936).

(iii) *The condition is excluded* as regards defects which the buyer should have discovered when he examined the goods (if in fact he did examine them): *s.* 14 (2).

Note that s. 34 gives a general right to examine goods before accepting them, and if the buyer waives this right (even though given an opportunity of examination by the seller), he cannot later rely on *s.* 14 (2): *Thornett & Fehr* v. *Beers & Sons* (1919).

5. Fitness for particular purpose: ✻ **s. 14** (1), (condition). Goods must be reasonably fit for the purpose for which they are required if:

(*a*) the buyer expressly or impliedly *makes known* the intended purpose, so as to show that he relies on the seller's skill and judgment, and

(*b*) the goods are *of a description* which it is in the course of the seller's business to supply (whether he be the manufacturer or not).

There is *no* such condition if the goods are bought under a *patent or trade name: s.* 14 (1).

NOTE:

(i) *It is sufficient* if the seller should have realised the intended purpose, even though the buyer did not specifically tell him, *e.g.* a bottle of milk should be reasonably fit for human consumption: ✻ *Frost* v. *Aylsbury Dairies Ltd.* (1905), and if the buyer asks for a hot-water bottle, since the purpose is obvious, the condition will apply: *Preist* v. *Last* (1903).

Thus G (aged 6) bought a catapult from P and was

injured by its defective condition. HELD: G could recover damages for breach of *ex post fact* warranty from P under *s*. 14 (1) (unfitness for purpose) and under *s*. 14 (2) (merchantable quality). (Also P could recover damages from his supplier under *s*. 15 (sale by sample), since he had bought by sample and the defect was not apparent on reasonable examination of the sample): ✷ *Godley* v. *Perry* (1960).

(ii) *The buyer may be relying on the seller's skill* even if the contract is one under which the seller is to *manufacture* the goods to the buyer's specifications: *Cammell Laird Ltd.* v. *Manganese Bronze Ltd.* (1934).

(iii) Although the condition is excluded in purchases under *patent or trade names*, this exclusion will not apply if the buyer only takes the goods because they are recommended by the seller as being suitable for the purpose intended, *e.g.* where B asked S, a dealer, for a comfortable car for touring and S recommended a Bugatti, which B found unsuitable, it was HELD that B could rely on *s*. 14 (1), even though the sale was under a trade name: *Baldry* v. *Marshall* (1925).

(iv) *Though goods may satisfy s*. 14 (1) the buyer may still be able to sue for breach of *s*. 14 (2) if they are not of merchantable quality. This is so even if they are sold under a trade name: *Bristol Tramways* v. *Fiat Motors Ltd.* (1910).

6. Quiet possession: ✷ s. 12 (2), (warranty). The buyer can sue for damages if his enjoyment of the goods is disturbed by reason of defects in the seller's title.

7. Freedom from encumbrances: ✷ s. 12 (3), (warranty). The buyer can sue for damages if the seller did not reveal that the goods were subject to any charge or encumbrance in favour of a third party, *e.g.* where the goods were mortgaged.

There is no right of action if the seller disclosed the charge or encumbrance when contracting.

8. Exclusion of implied terms. The above implied terms can be excluded *by express agreement:* ✷ *s*. 14 (4). But such an exclusionary clause will be construed strictly, and in any case the seller will not be able to avail himself of the exclusion if he has broken the contract in some other way: *Karsales (Harrow) Ltd.* v. *Wallis* (1956).

EXAMPLE: An auction catalogue wrongly described a heifer as "unserved" and this was orally confirmed by the auctioneer. The printed conditions of sale stated that all liability for misdescription was excluded. HELD: The express warranties given by the auctioneer overrode the exclusionary clause, and the buyer could claim damages for misdescription: *Couchman* v. *Hill* (1947).

SECTION 42. PASSING OF OWNERSHIP AND RISK

1. Passing of ownership. The transfer of the legal property in the goods is important for assessing *who bears the risk* of loss or deterioration, etc.

The position depends (*a*) on whether the contract is a sale or an agreement to sell (*see s.* **39** *above*), and (*b*) on whether the goods are specific and ascertained, or unascertained: *see below*.

2. Specific and ascertained goods.

(a) *Specific goods* mean goods identified and agreed upon at the time of making the contract: *s.* 62.

Goods are not specific merely because the source of supply has been agreed, *e.g.* "500 tons of coal from stack No.2."

(b) *Ascertained goods* mean goods identified and agreed upon after the making of the contract.

(c) *Unascertained goods* mean goods not yet identified and agreed upon, but merely described, *e.g.* the coal in (a) above.

3. When the property passes.

(a) *Specific and ascertained goods:* The property in them passes whenever *the parties intend* it to pass. The intention of the parties may be (i) stated in the contract or (ii) left to be ascertained by the court from the circumstances: *see* 4 *below*.

(b) *Unascertained goods:* The property passes only when they become ascertained, *i.e.* no property can pass in unascertained goods.

4. Tests of intention. Where the contract does not state when the property is to pass, the court will apply the following tests to ascertain the intentions of the parties:

(a) *Unconditional contract* for sale of specific goods in a deliverable condition: the property passes when the contract is made (even if delivery is postponed): *s.* 18 (1).

  The risk then passes to the buyer, even though the seller retains a lien for unpaid purchase money: *s.* 20.

(b) *Sale of specific goods not in a deliverable state:* the property does not pass until (i) the seller puts them into a deliverable state, and (ii) the buyer is notified thereof: *s.* 18 (2).

(c) *Sale of specific goods in a deliverable state*, but requiring some additional act such as *weighing, measuring, testing, etc.*, to fix the price: the property does not pass until (i) the seller has done the required act, and (ii) the buyer is notified thereof: *s.* 18 (3).

(d) *Goods delivered on approval or on sale or return, etc.:* the property does not pass until (i) the buyer signifies acceptance, or adopts the goods (*e.g.* by using them), or (ii) the buyer retains the goods for an unreasonable time or beyond any agreed time limit. What is a reasonable time is a question of fact in each case: *s.* 18 (4).

(e) *Contract for sale of unascertained or future goods:* the property passes when (i) the seller unconditionally appropriates goods of the required description to the contract, (ii) puts them in a deliverable state, and (iii) notifies the buyer: *s.* 18 (5).

  (*Appropriation by the seller* includes delivery to the buyer or to a carrier on behalf of the buyer, provided the seller has not reserved a right of disposal: *s.* 18 (5). If a right of disposal is reserved, property does not pass until the seller's conditions are satisfied: *s.* 19 (1). Where the goods are shipped on a Bill of Lading to the order of the seller or his agent, it is presumed that a right of disposal is reserved: *s.* 19 (2).)

5. Perishing of specific goods.

(a) *If before the contract is made*, the contract is void: *s.* 6 (and see *Couturier* v. *Hastie* (1857), *s.* **15**). This is a simple case of common mistake as to the existence of the subject-matter of the contract.

(b) *If after the contract is made*, and before the property passes to the buyer; the contract is void: *s.* 7. (But if the destruction was due to the fault of either party, the contract would not be void: instead the innocent party could sue for breach of contract.)

(c) If after the contract is made, and *after the property has passed* to the buyer: the buyer bears the loss and must pay for the goods.

"Perished" means destroyed or so changed or deteriorated as to defeat the purpose of the contract. But mere deterioration does not amount to perishing unless it causes the goods to become valueless: *Horn* v. *Minister of Food* (1948).

6. Passing of risk. Unless otherwise agreed, the risk will pass to the buyer only when the property in the goods passes to him.

Note that passing of risk is *independent of possession, e.g.* if the property in the goods has passed to the buyer, the risk falls on him even though the seller has not yet delivered the goods.

NOTE:

(*a*) Where performance of the contract is delayed by the fault of one party, the risk of loss or damage falls on that party: *Stern Ltd.* v. *Vickers Ltd.* (1923).

(*b*) Where delivery involves a sea journey, the goods remain at the seller's risk unless he gives the buyer reasonable notice (so that he can insure the goods): *s.* 32 (3).

(*c*) Where delivery is to a distant place, and the seller agrees to deliver at his own risk, the buyer must nevertheless accept the risk of any necessary deterioration incidental to the long journey: *s.* 33.

SECTION 43. NEMO DAT QUOD NON HABET

There is a general rule of law that *nemo dat quod non habet* ("no one can give what he has not got"). As applied to the sale of goods, the rule means that a seller of goods *cannot give a better title* to the purchaser than he himself possesses. Thus a purchaser who buys stolen goods from a thief can get no valid title to them, since the thief has no title: *see s.* **41.** 1. (Sales by a hirer of goods under a H.P. agreement are dealt with in *s.* **48** below.)

The Sale of Goods Act, 1893, lays down *important exceptions* to this general rule and these are stated below.

1. Estoppel. Where the true owner is estopped from denying the actual seller's right to sell the purchaser will get a good title.

EXAMPLE: A allowed some of his property wrongfully to be detained by S, and also allowed B to think that S was entitled to the property. S sold the goods to B . HELD: B got a good title. as A was estopped from denying S's right to sell: *Pickering* v, *Sears* (1837).

2. Orders for sale. Where a person not the owner sells goods (*a*) under a court order, or (*b*) under a legal power of sale, *e.g.* the power of sale given to a legal mortgagee, the purchaser gets a good title.

EXAMPLE: A deposits goods with B for B to repair them, and then fails to collect and pay for the repaired goods. B has a statutory power to sell the goods: *Disposal of Uncollected Goods Act*, and *see s.* **59.**

3. Factors Act, 1889, s. 2. The purchaser will get a good title if he buys in good faith from a factor, with whom the owner deposited the goods (even though the factor may have no actual authority to sell).

A factor is a *mercantile agent* whose ordinary business is the buying and selling of goods in his possession: *Factors Act*, 1889, *s.* 1, *see* **33.** 1 above.

4. Sale of Goods Act, 1893, s. 25.

(a) *Seller in possession after sale.* If the buyer of goods allows the seller to remain in possession of them (or in possession of documents of title thereto) the seller can resell the goods to a second purchaser who will get a good title. The seller can then be sued in damages by the first buyer: *s.* 25 (1).

(b) *Buyer in possession after sale.* If the seller allows the buyer to get possession of goods (or documents of title thereto) before paying for them the buyer can sell the goods and pass a good title: *s.* 25 (2). (The seller can then only sue the original buyer for damages.)

5. Writs of execution. If a person fails to pay a debt when ordered by the court, a writ may be issued empowering the sheriff to seize his chattels and to sell them in satisfaction of the debt. The sheriff then has power to give a good title, although he is not the owner of the goods sold.

6. Sale under voidable title. The purchaser from a seller whose own title is voidable will get a good title, provided (*a*) he had *no knowledge of any defect* in the seller's title and (*b*) the seller's title had not been avoided at the time of the sale.

EXAMPLE: A rogue obtained jewels on credit from P by fraud and sold them to B before P discovered the fraud. HELD: P could avoid the rogue's title to the jewels on the grounds of fraud, but since he had not done so before B bought the jewels B got a good title: *Phillips* v. *Brooks* (1919), *see s.* **15.**

It appears that where the other party cannot be found, avoidance is effective as soon as the victim exhibits clear intention to avoid, *e.g.* by reporting the fraud to the police: *Car & Universal Finance Co.* v. *Caldwell* (1965).

7. Market overt. The purchaser normally gets a good title if he buys in a market overt (open market).

The term "market overt" covers (a) all shops in the City of London, and (b) elsewhere, all markets established by statute, charter or custom as open markets.

A bona fide purchaser for value without notice of any defect in the seller's title will get a good title, provided:

(a) The sale is in accordance with the customs of the particular market.
(b) The sale took place in public, *e.g.* in the public part of a shop.
(c) The market dealer was the seller, not the purchaser.
(d) The goods were openly displayed, and were of a class the seller normally deals in.
(e) The sale took place in the normal opening hours of the market.

NOTE: The market overt provisions *do not protect a purchaser where:*

(i) The goods sold are horses.
(ii) The transaction took place in Scotland.
(iii) The goods sold belong to the Crown.
(iv) The seller's title was voidable and has been avoided.
(v) The sale took place in a private part of the shop or stall, *e.g.* behind a curtain.
(vi) The goods were stolen and the thief has been convicted (the arrest of the thief is not enough; he must have been convicted).

SECTION 44. PERFORMANCE OF THE CONTRACT

1. Delivery. It is the duty of the seller to deliver the goods, and of the buyer to accept and pay for them: *s.* 27. Unless otherwise agreed payment and delivery are normally *concurrent: s.* 28.

Delivery means voluntary transfer of possession from one person to another. It may be *actual or constructive, e.g.* by handing over documents of title, or authority for the buyer to obtain the goods from some person in whose possession they are: *Central Newbury Car Auctions* v. *Unity Finance* (1957).

Delivery may also be by the seller agreeing to hold the goods as agent for the buyer: this is known as *attornment.*

2. Time and place of delivery.

(a) *Time for delivery.* Where the seller is to send the goods to the buyer but no time is fixed, they must be sent within a reasonable time and delivery must be at a reasonable hour: *s.* 29 (2).

The seller usually bears the expense of putting the goods into a deliverable condition, and he must take reasonable care to see that they reach the right person: *s.* 29 (5).

(b) *Place of delivery* (unless otherwise agreed) is the seller's place of business, or if he has none then his residence: *s.* 29 (1).

If the sale is of specific goods known by both parties to be lodged at some other place, then delivery is to be made at that place: *s.* 29 (1).

3. Delivery to a carrier. Where the seller is to send the goods, delivery to a carrier (as agent for the buyer) whether named by the buyer or not, is prima facie proper delivery to the buyer: *s.* 32 (1).

In such cases the seller must make a reasonable contract with the carrier, otherwise the buyer is entitled to refuse to be bound: *s.* 32 (2).

4. Delivery of wrong quantities: s. 30.

(a) *If less than ordered* the buyer may reject the lot; if he accepts the lesser quantity he must pay a proportionately reduced price.

(b) *If more than ordered,* the buyer may reject the lot, or may accept the agreed quantity only (if this is possible). He must then pay a proportionate price.

(c) *If goods ordered are mixed* with goods not ordered, the buyer may accept those ordered and reject the others (if it is possible to separate them, otherwise he must accept or reject the lot).

5. Delivery by instalments. Delivery is presumed to be in one transaction, unless it was expressly agreed that it should be by instalments.

If instalments are to be paid for separately on delivery, it is a question of fact whether failure to deliver one instalment justifies repudiation of the whole contract: *s.* 31.

The test is: Is the breach regarding one instalment sufficiently fundamental to injure the contract as a whole? It is relevant to consider the likelihood of the breach being repeated.

6. Acceptance by the buyer.

(a) *The buyer is entitled to examine* goods not previously seen, before accepting them: *s.* 34. Generally the place of delivery is the place of examination, unless otherwise agreed.

(b) *The buyer accepts* (i) when he so informs the seller, or (ii) when he does some act of ownership, *e.g.* sells the goods, or (iii) keeps the goods an unreasonable time without notifying the seller that he wishes to reject them: *s.* 35.

(c) *If the buyer rejects the goods,* when entitled to do so, he is not bound to return them to the seller, but only to notify the seller of rejection so as to enable the latter to collect them: *s.* 36.

(d) *If the buyer's rejection amounts to repudiation* of the contract the seller has an immediate right of action. The same applies when the buyer keeps the goods for an unreasonable length of time *without* making up his mind.

In such a case the seller's damages will be measured as the amount of loss caused by the wrongful retention: *Long* v. *Lloyd* (1958).

7. Delivery by sea. In contracts for the carriage of goods sold by sea, various special terms are usual. These may be expressly agreed between the parties, but more often they rely on one of the established customary agreements with the implied terms that these contain.

The most common of these standard agreements are *f.o.b.*, *c.i.f.*, and *ex-ship* contracts: see below.

8. F.O.B. (free on board). Under such a contract, the seller's duties (unless otherwise agreed) are:

(*a*) To deliver the goods to a named port of shipment.

(*b*) To put the goods on board ship at his own expense.

(*c*) To negotiate a reasonable Bill of Lading or other contract of carriage, and forward it to the buyer (who pays the freight).

(*d*) To notify the buyer of shipment, so as to enable him to insure the goods at sea. (If the seller fails to do this the goods will travel at his risk; otherwise the goods will be at the buyer's risk.)

Once the goods are shipped the property in them (and usually the risk) passes to the buyer. If the seller is prevented from putting the goods on board, *e.g.*, by a strike, the property and risk remain with him: *Colley* v. *Overseas Exporters* (1921).

9. C.I.F. (cost, insurance, freight). Here the seller's duties go further than in an f.o.b. contract, and are:

(*a*) To deliver the goods to the port of shipment at his own expense, and to see them safely on board.

(*b*) To insure the goods during transit.

(*c*) To negotiate a suitable bill of lading or other contract of carriage and to forward this to the buyer to enable him to claim the goods on arrival at the port of destination. (Purchase money is not normally paid until the documents of title reach the buyer.)

Once the goods are delivered to the ship the *risk* passes to the buyer (and should be covered by his insurance). The property in the goods passes to the buyer when the goods are shipped, unless the seller reserves a right of disposal in which case property does not pass until the price is paid.

The buyer is entitled to reject (*a*) the documents of title, and/or (*b*) the goods. Acceptance of one does not bind him to accept the other. But the buyer must pay the price when he receives the documents of title, even though he has not yet examined the goods. (It is also the buyer's responsibility to pay unloading charges, and transport from the port of destination to any further inland destination.)

10. Ex ship. Here the seller is bound to arrange the shipment of the goods to the port of destination, and to such further inland destination as the buyer may stipulate. The buyer is not bound to pay for the goods until they are unloaded from the ship and all freightage charges paid. The goods travel at the seller's risk, but he is not bound to insure them (though of course he usually does).

SECTION 45. RIGHTS OF AN UNPAID SELLER AGAINST THE GOODS

1. Unpaid seller. The term includes any person who is in the *osition of seller*, though not himself the owner, *e.g.* a factor.

The seller is *unpaid* as long as any part of the purchase price is outstanding.

Payment by a *negotiable instrument* is conditional only, *i.e.* is not effective until the negotiable instrument has been honoured. *See s.* 22, 5.

2. Differing situations. The seller may have to contend with two different legal situations, (*a*) where the property has not passed to the buyer, and (*b*) where the property has passed the buyer. His rights differ in these two cases.

3. Property not passed to buyer. Here the seller may (*a*) withhold delivery if the price is unpaid or not tendered, or if the buyer is insolvent, or (*b*) if part of the goods have been delivered, he may withhold the remainder: *s.* 39.

4. Property passed to buyer. Here the seller has the following rights:

    (a) *Lien:* see 5 below.

    (b) *Stoppage in transit:* see 8 below.

    (c) *Re-sale:* see 12 below.

5. Lien: s. 41. The seller's lien is a right to *retain possession* of goods until payment or tender of payment.

A lien arises when:

    (a) goods have been sold without any agreement as to credit, or

    (b) goods have been sold on credit, but the period of credit has expired, or

    (c) goods have been sold on credit and the buyer has become insolvent (whether the period of credit has expired or not).

6. Lien is lost when:

    (a) goods have been delivered to a *carrier* for transmission to the buyer, without the seller reserving a right of disposal, or

(b) the buyer or his agent lawfully *obtains possession* of the goods, or

(c) the seller *waives* his lien: *s.* 43.

7. The seller may exercise a lien:

(a) When in possession merely as agent for the buyer.

(b) Where part delivery has taken place. (The lien extends over the remainder of the goods.)

(c) If the seller breaks his contract while the buyer is solvent, he will still be entitled to claim a lien if the buyer subsequently becomes insolvent.

8. Stoppage in transit: s. 44. This means a right to *stop the goods* when they are on their way to the buyer (and after they have left the possession of the seller).

The right arises when:

(a) the goods are in transit (*see* 9 *below*), and

(b) the buyer becomes insolvent. (The buyer is *insolvent* if he has ceased to pay his debts as they fall due or in the ordinary course of business: *s.* 62.)

9. Meaning of transit. Goods are in transit until the buyer accepts them, *i.e.* if in the hands of a carrier prior to delivery, or if rejected by the buyer when delivered: *s.* 45.

NOTE: Where goods are in the possession of a *carrier*, the position depends on whether he is agent for the seller or for the buyer (a question of fact in each case). If he is *agent for the seller*, then the goods are still in the possession of the seller and his right is one of lien, not stoppage. If he is *agent for the buyer* transit is over, and the seller has no right of stoppage. (The carrier may become agent for the buyer either by appointment as such, or by notifying the buyer that he holds the goods on his behalf, *i.e.* that they await collection.)

Transit ceases when the goods reach their ultimate destination, but not some intermediate destination (unless further instructions are conveyed to the carrier to send them on, in which case transit has ceased).

10. How stoppage is effected. This is done by the seller (a) *taking possession* of the goods or documents of title thereto, or (b) *giving notice* to the carrier of his exercise of the right of stoppage.

If the seller *wrongfully* stops the goods, *e.g.* where the buyer is solvent, he is liable for damages for the *tort of conversion* if the property has passed to the buyer, or for damages for breach of contract if the property has not yet passed to the buyer.

If a carrier wrongfully delivers stopped goods to the buyer, he is liable for damages to the seller. And if he wrongfully obeys the seller's instructions to stop transit, he is liable for damages to the buyer.

11. Transit ceases when:

(*a*) Goods reach their destination and possession is delivered to the buyer or his agent.

(*b*) The buyer or his agent obtains delivery before they reach their destination.

(*c*) A carrier wrongfully refuses to deliver the goods to the buyer of his agent.

(*d*) The goods have reached their destination and the carrier has notified the buyer that he holds them as his agent.

(*e*) Goods are delivered to the master of the buyer's ship, or of a ship which the buyer has chartered.

NOTE: Sale by the buyer does not affect the seller's right of stoppage, unless the seller has assented thereto.

12. Resale: s. 48.

The contract is not necessarily rescinded by the exercise by the seller of his rights of lien or stoppage, nor does the seller automatically thereby acquire a right to resell the goods to another purchaser.

The seller has a right of resale after exercise of his rights of lien or stoppage in transit where:

(a) *the goods are perishable*, or

(b) *the price has not been paid* within a reasonable time after notice given by the seller of his intention to resell, or

(c) a right of resale was *expressly reserved* by the seller in the contract.

In addition to the above, the seller may also have a right of action for damages for breach of contract.

SECTION 46. ACTIONS FOR BREACH OF CONTRACT

1. By the seller: s. 49. He has the following rights of action:

(a) *For the price.*

   (i) Where the property in the goods has passed to the buyer and he has failed to pay for them.

   (ii) Where the price is payable on a certain day and has not been paid, the seller can sue for the price notwithstanding that the property has not passed to the buyer or the goods have not yet been appropriated to the contract.

(b) *Damages for non-acceptance.* This action lies where the buyer has refused to accept the goods and the property has not passed to him: *s.* 49 (3).

   The measure of damages is the estimated loss directly and naturally resulting to the seller: *s.* 50 (2). Where there is an available market for the goods, the measure of damages will therefore normally be the difference between the contract price and the market price at the date of breach: *s.* 50 (3). Where there is no available market, the seller is entitled to damages for loss of his bargain: *Thompson* v. *Robinson* (1955).

2. By the buyer.

(a) *For non-delivery.* The buyer can recover damages calculated in the same manner as in 1 above: *s.* 50 (2), *s.* 51.

(b) *For recovery of price,* where this has been paid and the goods have not been delivered.

(c) *For specific performance,* where the contract is for sale of specific or ascertained goods. But such an order is discretionary, and the court may award damages instead: *s.* 52.

(d) *For tort* (detinue or conversion) if the property has passed to the buyer and the seller has wrongfully detained or disposed of the goods.

(e) *For breach of condition* the buyer can reject the goods, or, if he choses, accept them and sue for damages for breach of an *ex post facto* warranty: *see s.* **9.**

(f) *For breach* of warranty, the buyer can only sue for damages; he cannot reject the goods.

SECTION 47. AUCTION SALES

1. Auction sales. An auction is a sale at which the auctioneer (as agent for the seller) invites persons present to bid (offer) for goods sold.

The bidder is the offeror, and can withdraw his bid at any time before the auctioneer accepts it, usually by knocking with a hammer.

The general rules laid down by the Sale of Goods Act apply to sales of goods by auction; therefore if the sale is of specific goods the property in them will pass to the buyer as soon as the hammer falls, *i.e.* as soon as the contract is made.

Each lot put up for sale becomes the subject of a separate contract.

2. Position of auctioneer. Auctioneers require to be licensed annually: *the Auctioneers Act, 1845.*

(a) *Agent for the seller.* He is primarily agent for the seller, but on accepting a bid he becomes also agent for the buyer. Thus his signature on a memorandum of sale would be binding on both seller and buyer: *Cohen* v. *Roche* (1927).

NOTE: He has a lien on the goods for his charges and has a right of action for the price against a buyer who has taken delivery and has failed to pay. He has implied authority to receive payment in cash, but no implied authority to sell on credit.

(b) *Auctioneer's warranties.* Independently of any liability as agent, he impliedly warrants on his own behalf:

(i) That he has authority to sell the goods.
(ii) That he knows of no defect in the seller's title.
(iii) That he will give possession upon payment of the price, and that the purchaser's possession will not be disturbed by the seller or by himself.

    (*He does not warrant* the seller's title in a sale of specific goods, unless he fails to make it clear he is merely acting as agent: *Benton* v. *Campbell, Parker & Co. Ltd.* (1925).)

3. Auctions with and without reserve.

(a) *Auction with reserve.* This means any auction which is announced as being (i) subject to a reserve price being reached, and/or (ii) subject to the seller himself reserving a right to bid.

If a reserve price has been announced and the auction-eer inadvertently accepts a bid at a lower price, the buyer cannot enforce the sale.

(b) *Auctions without reserve.* These are the normal auctions, and in such sales the seller cannot legally bid, either personally or through an agent. If he does so, the buyer can treat the sale as fraudulent.

4. Bidding rings. It is a *criminal offence* for any dealer to make an agreement supported by consideration to abstain from bidding at any sale which he attends: *Auctions (Bidding Agreements) Act,* 1927, *s.* 1. (A "dealer" is any person who makes it his business to attend auctions for the purpose of buying goods for resale.)

If a dealer is convicted under this enactment, the buyer can claim damages for fraud against any person who is a party to the agreement (and providing the buyer is innocent of any complicity). Also the seller can avoid the sale, unless the goods were bought by an innocent purchaser.

5. Mock Auctions Act, 1961. It is a criminal offence to pro-mote or conduct a "mock auction," *i.e.* an auction at which:

(a) articles are sold to a bidder (i) for a sum lower than his highest bid, or (ii) where part of the price is refunded; or
(b) the right to bid is restricted to persons who have already agreed to buy one or more other articles; or
(c) any article is offered as a gift by way of inducement.

SECTION 48. HIRE PURCHASE ACTS

1. The Hire Purchase Acts, 1938–65. The 1965 Act con-solidates the law relating to hire purchase and similar trans-actions. The Act covers:

(a) *Hire purchase*—where a person hires goods for a specified period (by monthly or weekly instalments) and has an option to purchase the goods hired at the expiry of the period of hire (usually with the last scheduled payment). During the period of hire, he is a mere bailee of the goods: *see* Bailment, *s.* **59** below.
(b) *Credit sale*—where goods are sold to a purchaser (who ob-tains both possession and title) for more than £30 payable by five or more instalments. (Where the price is less than £30, the *H.P. Act* 1965 does not apply.)

(c) *Conditional sale*—where a person agrees to buy goods and
obtains immediate possession, but the transfer of title is
postponed until the fulfilment of a condition, *e.g.* the
completion of stated instalments of purchase price.

2. Statutory requirements. The Acts provide that all of the
above agreements must be made subject to the following
requirements:

(a) *Statement of cash price*. Before the contract is made the
owner (or seller) must notify the hirer (or purchaser) in
writing of the *cash price* of the goods, *e.g.* by drawing his
attention to a price catalogue or price-tab.
(b) *Written contract*. The contract is unenforceable by the owner
(seller) unless in writing, signed by the hirer (buyer) and by
or on behalf of the owner (seller).

In hire-purchase and conditional sale agreements, the
contract must state:

(i) The total hire-purchase price (or conditional sale
purchase price), the amount of each instalment and
when payable.
(ii) A list of the goods comprised;
(iii) A notification of the hirer's (or buyer's) rights.

3. Statutory right of cancellation. Where the hirer/buyer
signs any of the three classes of agreement covered by the
Acts *at a place other than appropriate trade premises*, he has a
statutory right (which cannot be negated by agreement) to
cancel the contract *within four days* of receiving his (statutory)
copy of the agreement.

"Appropriate trade premises" means a place at which the
owner (or seller) normally carries on business, or a place where
similar goods are normally sold. (Thus the right of cancellation
primarily protects those who hire or buy goods at their own
homes from door-to-door salesmen.)

4. Implied terms. In *hire purchase* and *conditional sale*
agreements the following terms are compulsory (*i.e.* unlike
similar implied terms in agreements covered by the *Sale of
Goods Act*, they cannot be excluded):

(a) *Condition* that the goods are of *merchantable quality*: *H.P.
Act*, 1965, *s.* 17 (2). This condition does not apply where:

(i) the goods are *expressly hired* as *second-hand*: *s.* 18, or,
(ii) *the hirer has examined the goods*, and the defects com-

plained of should have been apparent on examination: *s*. 17 (2) and (3).

(b) *Condition* that the goods shall be *reasonably fit* for their *intended purpose*, *provided* that the hirer/buyer has made known the purpose for which they are required: *s*. 17 (4).

(c) *Condition* that where the goods are hired/sold *by sample*, bulk shall correspond with sample and that the hirer/buyer shall have reasonable opportunity of comparison: *s*. 19 (1).

(d) *Condition* that where goods are let or sold *by description* they shall correspond with the description: *s*. 19 (2).

(e) *Condition* that where goods are hired/sold by *sample and description*, they shall *correspond both* with the sample and the description: *s*. 19 (2).

(f) *Condition* that the owner/seller has the *right to sell* the goods (whenever the property is to pass): *s*. 17 (1).

(g) *Warranty* that the hirer/buyer shall have *quiet possession*: *s*. 17 (1).

(h) *Warranty* that the goods shall be *free of charges or encumbrances* (whenever the property is due to pass): *s*. 17 (1).

NOTE: *Credit sales* are still covered by the *S.G.A.*, 1893, and the implied terms in such agreements (while being almost identical with the above) can be excluded by express agreement: *S.G.A.*, *s*. 14 (4).

5. Dealer as agent. In many hire purchase transactions there are in fact three parties involved. Thus A wishes to buy a car and arranges to take one stocked by B, a dealer, who offers to arrange hire purchase through C, a finance company. The resulting hire purchase contract will be between A (the hirer) and C (the owner, who will have bought the car for cash from B).

Formerly there was a danger (particularly with second-hand cars) that B might induce A to enter into the hire-purchase agreement by misrepresentation. After discovering the misrepresentation A would naturally wish to sue either B, the dealer, or C, the owner. He would then find (i) that he had no contractual relationship with B, a mere outsider to the hire-purchase contract, and could not sue him, and (ii) the hire-purchase contract would contain a clause expressly exempting C from liability for any misrepresentations made by B.

To combat this situation the courts, during the 1950s, pronounced that there might arise, in suitable cases, a "collateral contract" between A and B entitling A to sue B for his misrepresentation; but A still had no remedy in contract against C because of the exemption clause.

The *H.P. Act*, 1965, has now strengthened the hirer's position by enacting that in such cases representations made by a dealer (in *all* agreements covered by the Act) shall be deemed to have been made by him as agent for the owner or seller (C): *s.* 16.

The overall effect of the courts' rulings and the 1965 Act are as follows:

(a) *At common law:* A has a right to sue B for misrepresentation or breach of the collateral contract *i.e.* a contract whereby A agrees to hire (or buy) the car from C, in return for A arranging the hire purchase or conditional or credit sale: *Andrews* v. *Hopkinson* (1956), *see* p. 21 above.

(b) *Under the H.P. Act 1965:* A has a right to sue the owner/seller (C) for misrepresentation made by his statutory agent (B).

6. Right to end the agreement. The hirer or conditional-purchaser can determine the agreement *at any time before the final instalment is paid* by giving *written notice* to the owner/seller or his agent: *s.* 27 (1). But he must complete payment of at least *one-half of the price*: *s.* 28.

Thus if the hirer has paid less than a half at the date of termination, he can be compelled to make up the difference; if he has paid more than a half, he cannot recover any of the money he has paid.

7. Application of the H.P. Acts. The Acts apply to contracts (as specified in 1 above) where the total price payable by the hirer/purchaser does not exceed £2000: *H.P. Act*, 1965, *ss.* 2 (2) and (3). With credit sales there is a minimum of £30: *see* 1 above.

NOTE: If the hirer/purchaser is a corporation it is not protected by the Acts: *H.P. Act*, 1965, *s.* 3.

8. Hire Purchase Act, 1964. This Act protects a person who buys a motor vehicle from a person who has possession of the vehicle (but not ownership) under a hire purchase or conditional sale agreement, *e.g.* A obtains a car on H.P. from C and then (illegally) sells it to X—the 1964 Act protects X's title to the car (*cf. S.G.A.*, *s.* 25 at p. 125 above).

9. Advertisements (Hire Purchase) Act, 1957. Under this Act all hire purchase advertisements must contain the following information:

(a) The amount of the deposit (if any) *or* the deposit expressed as a fraction of a larger stated sum.

(b) The amount and number of instalments, and the times payable.

(c) Instalments payable before delivery of the goods (if any).

(d) The cash price of the goods.

(e) The true rate of interest.

SPECIMEN QUESTIONS

1. (a) Describe carefully the rights of an unpaid seller under a contract for the sale of goods.

(b) B bought from S 100 bales of cotton ex S.S. *Hercules* which was at the time on her way to London. When the ship arrived in London B handed a cheque for the price of the cotton to S's London agent and received delivery orders on the warehouse where the cotton was stored. B endorsed the delivery orders to T and received payment from him. The cheque which B had issued was dishonoured and S, through his London agent, refuses now to allow T to remove the cotton from the warehouse. Advise the parties. *C.I.S., Final,* 1963. (**45.** 1–12; **22.** 5.)

2. When does the property pass when goods are sent on sale or return?

A sent goods to B on sale or return and included in the contract a term that the goods should remain the seller's property until settled for or charged. B pawned the goods to C.

Can A recover the goods from C? Would the position be the same if B had been a Mercantile Agent? *A.C.C.A., Intermediate, Dec.* 1963. (**42.** 4; **33,** 4.)

3. (a) State in general terms what is meant by a "right of stoppage *in transitu.*"

(b) How is stoppage *in transitu* effected? *C.A., Final, May* 1964. (**45.** 8–10.)

4. (a) How does a contract for the sale of goods differ from a contract for work and materials?

(b) A contracted to build a racing car for B, to B's specifications. When delivered the car proved to be roadworthy but was unsuitable for racing. B now wishes to return the car and recover his money. Explain the legal position *A.C.C.A., June* 1967. (**39.** 5; **41.** 5.)

5. Where a contract for the sale of goods does not expressly cover the passing of the property in the goods, what statutory rules are applied to ascertain the intentions of the parties? *A.C.C.A., December* 1967. (**42.** 4.)

CARRIAGE OF GOODS

CARRIAGE of goods, whether by land, sea, or air, is usually conducted by persons who make carrying their business and who fall within the category of "common carriers."

SECTION 49. COMMON CARRIERS

1. Common carriers. A common carrier is one who offers for hire to transport from place to place, either by land, air, or water, the goods of anyone wishing to employ him.

The law traditionally imposes special duties on common carriers, above and beyond those imposed on people who casually, for hire or otherwise, carry goods.

2. Position of common carriers. The carrier is *bound to carry all goods* offered to him at a *fair price* (which may be demanded in advance), *unless* (i) he has no space, (ii) the goods are of a kind he does not profess to carry, or (iii) the destination is not on his normal route.

If he unjustifiably refuses to carry goods he may be *prosecuted* and/or *sued* for damages.

(Many carriers evade classification as common carriers by reserving in advance the right to refuse to carry any goods at will. Thus A offered to carry various types of goods, while reserving the right to reject any, and to charge varying rates according to the kind of goods carried, the destination, etc. HELD: He was not a common carrier: ✱ *Belfast Ropework Co. Ltd.* v. *Bushell* (1918).)

3. Duties of carriers. It is the duty of *any* carrier (whether common or not):

(a) *To deliver at the place directed.* This is discharged by delivery at the right place, not necessarily to any particular person.
(b) *To deliver within a reasonable time,* allowing extension of time for unforeseeable delays such as unexpected strikes: *Sims* v. *Midland Rly.* (1913).

(c) *To obey the instructions of the consignor* as to alterations of delivery, etc.

(d) *Not to deviate* unnecessarily from his agreed route.

The carrier's rights are: (i) to demand reasonable payment (in advance, if desired), (ii) to refuse goods not properly packed, and (iii) to claim a lien on the goods carried for his charges.

4. Liability of common carrier. He is an *insurer* for the safety of the goods he carries, from the moment they are received by him until they are delivered. He is therefore *liable for all damage* to the goods, whether occasioned by negligence or not, *except* where the damage is caused by:

(a) *Act of God:* an act of nature of such extraordinary description or degree that no reasonable person could be expected to guard against or foresee it, *e.g.* lightning, freak winds, earthquake, etc.

(b) *Queen's enemies:* the forces of a state with which this country is at war, *e.g.* capture of the carrier's ship by an enemy warship, but not damage by rioters, rebels, etc., since they are not the forces of an enemy state.

(c) *Inherent vice in the goods carried:* some latent defect in the goods themselves, over which no one has control and against which the carrier cannot guard, *e.g.* disease in animals not visible when consigned, but not mere normal unruliness or stupidity.

(d) *Negligence of the consignor:* Although the carrier is bound to insure the safety of the goods, he is not liable for harm caused directly by the negligence of the consignor, *e.g.* through bad packing.

5. Measure of damages. This will be (*a*) the value of the goods, assessed at destination on the date of scheduled delivery, or (*b*) loss attributable to delay or depreciation, etc.

Provided that the carrier must not be made liable for damage other than (*a*) flows naturally and directly from his breach of duty, plus (*b*) such additional damage as he should reasonably have foreseen at the time of making the contract: *Hadley* v. *Baxendale* (1854), and *see s.* **26**.

6. Modification of carrier's liability. Save where prohibited by statute, common carriers may vary their legal liability by contract; but the courts interpret exemptionary clauses strictly, and as far as possible to the disadvantage of the carrier: *see s.* **9**. (Exemption clauses by private carriers are less strictly interpreted and may even protect the carrier against liability for theft by his servants: *John Carter Ltd.* v. *H. Hanson Haulage (Leeds) Ltd.* (1965).)

7. Liability of consignor. The consignor must notify the carrier if goods are *dangerous, e.g.* explosives or combustibles. He is also deemed to *warrant the fitness* of goods to be carried, and is liable for damages for breach of warranty even if ignorant of an unfitness which causes harm to the carrier.

SECTION 50. CARRIAGE BY LAND

1. Two principal statutes. The Carriers Act, 1830, and the Transport Act, 1962, are the principal statutes governing carriage by land. Otherwise, the applicable rules are those of common law, stated in the preceding section.

2. Carriers Act, 1830. This applies only to *common carriers.* The main provisions of the Act are:

  (a) *The carrier is under no liability* for loss or damage to packages containing *certain articles*, worth all told more than £10, *unless* at the time of consignment the consignor notified the carrier of the true value and contents of the package. (The carrier may then charge a higher fee for the increased risk. The carrier must post notice of such extra charges at his office; otherwise he is not allowed to charge them. When such higher fee is charged, the consignor may demand a receipt for any payment made.)

    Articles covered include: gold, silver, gems, watches, bills and securities, paintings and engravings, title deeds and some other documents, glass, china, furs, etc.

  (b) *A notice alone* cannot limit or reduce the carrier's liability: there must be express agreement to that effect.

  (c) *The Act gives no protection* to the carrier for loss or damage caused by the crime of the carrier's servants, or the carrier's own negligence. (But the burden of proof is on the consignor.)

  (d) A carrier is only liable for the *real value* (of which he may require proof), *i.e.* he need not accept the consignor's assessment.

3. The Transport Act, 1962. This applies to British Railways, British Waterways, London Transport, etc. which are not to be regarded as common carriers by rail or inland waterway. Under the Act the controlling boards of these bodies have power to fix charges and conditions of carriage.

Railway transport is governed by two main types of agreement:

(a) *Board's risk conditions.* The Board is *liable* for any loss, misdelivery or damage, unless it can prove Act of God, seizure under legal process, default of consignor (*e.g.* bad packing, or inherent vice in goods), or wastage through normal conditions.

It may also evade liability for *casualty* if it can prove it has exercised reasonable care, or there has been fraud by the consignor.

The Board is also usually liable for loss caused by *deviation* from the scheduled route causing delay unless it can prove that the deviation was not caused by any negligence.

The Board's *liability is limited* to (*a*) £800 per ton in case of total loss, or (*b*) a proportion of £800 in case of partial loss.

(b) *Owner's risk conditions.* The Board's liability is lower, so are the carriage charges. The Board is *not liable* for loss, damage, deviation, misdelivery, delay or detention, save where such is proved to have been caused by wilful misconduct of the Board's servants, including gross negligence.

Negligence is presumed where loss arises through non-delivery of the whole consignment.

NOTE: *Damageable goods improperly packed.* The Board may refuse such goods, and where it agrees to carry them it is only liable if (*a*) there is wilful misconduct, or (*b*) damage would have occurred even though the goods had been properly packed, and (*c*) the Board would have been liable under Board's risk conditions.

4. Termination of rail transit. Transit ceases when (*a*) the goods are *delivered*, or (*b*) the sender exercises his right of *stoppage in transit: see s.* **45**, or (*c*) where it is agreed to take goods to a *particular depot* to await collection—here transit ceases one day after notice of arrival.

5. Notice of claims must be served on the Board within 3 *days* of termination of transit, and any *claim* must be made within 7 *days*. (If the claim is for non-delivery, the times are extended to 14 days and 28 days from commencement of transit.)

6. Passengers' luggage. To make the Board liable, the passenger must prove (*a*) that the Railway *assumed control* of the luggage, and (b) that the luggage was *"personal luggage,"* i.e. for the personal use of the passenger.

Assumption of control is a question of fact in each case. Putting luggage in the guard's van is indicative of assumption of control, but the fact that the passenger took the luggage into the compartment with him does not of itself rule out the possibility that the railway has assumed control.

7. Railway passengers. The Board is *not a common carrier of passengers* and therefore (a) may refuse any passenger, and (b) does not insure passengers' safety.

The Board can lay down any limitation on contractual or other liability for the safety of passengers, save that it *cannot* impose conditions which (i) negative liability for death or injury, or (ii) prescribe a time limit for the enforcement of claims therefor.

8. Carriage by road. Where a passenger is carried by road transport, in public service vehicles, the contract cannot negative in any way claims for bodily injury or death of the passenger: *Road Traffic Act*, 1960, s. 151.

Ordinary common carriers are under the usual liabilities of common carriers: *see s.* **49** *above.* Private carriers are liable only for negligence, or as otherwise agreed.

Carriage of goods by road is free of all statutory restrictions.

9. Carriage by air. *The Carriage by Air Act,* 1932 (as amended) governs international carriage between the United Kingdom and countries which are parties to the various international conventions dealing with carriage by air.

Under the Act the carrier is *liable* for loss of goods or injury to passengers, *unless* he can establish one of the specified defences, *e.g.*

(a) that all reasonable precautions were taken for safety of goods;
(b) that loss or injury was due to negligent pilotage or navigation.

Maximum liability (i) for death or injury is 125,000 francs, and (ii) for loss or damage to goods is 250 francs per kilo (unless agreed otherwise). The maximum liability for goods may be increased by Order in Council, up to 25,000 francs per kilo.

The Carriage by Air Order, 1952, applies similar rules to carriage by air within the United Kingdom, *i.e.* "non-international" carriage.

SECTION 51. CARRIAGE BY SEA

1. Carriage by sea. The owner of a ship may be a common carrier, and as such (if not protected by contract) is an insurer of goods carried, subject to the usual general defences, *e.g.* Act of God: *see s.* **49** *above.*

Carriage by sea is arranged under a contract called a *contract of affreightment*, either in the form of a *charterparty* or a *bill of lading.*

2. Bills of lading. Usually the shipper arranges with the owner or master of the ship the amount of *freight* (the carriage charge) and the terms of carriage. He gets a receipt for the goods consigned (the *mate's receipt*) on delivery to the ship, and a *bill of lading* signed by the master when the goods are actually put on board.

The bill of lading *contains* the terms of the contract, and must be stamped (6*d.*). The bill usually states that the goods were received in good order and condition (if such was the case), the weights and measures of the goods (if known) and the conditions of carriage.

3. Charterparties. Sometimes a shipper hires a ship for his own sole purposes, *i.e. charters* it. Under such a *charterparty* he may take over control of the ship and crew, in which case master and crew become his servants. Such a contract is not really a contract of carriage so much as a lease of the ship.

More usually the shipper charters the ship for a definite voyage, agreeing to take all its freightage space for the voyage or series of voyages, and the master and crew remain the servants of the owners.

4. Implied undertakings by shipowners.

(a) *That the ship is seaworthy, i.e.* is fit for the particular voyage contemplated. This is an *absolute warranty,* and breach of it renders the owners liable irrespective of any question of fault or negligence on their part, unless liability is modified by the contract.

Bad stowage may amount to unseaworthiness if it endangers safety of the ship (not merely the safety of the cargo): *Elder Dempster* v. *Zochonis & Co.* (1924).

If the shipper discovers unseaworthiness before the voyage commences, he may repudiate the contract.

(NOTE: The warranty is not absolute in bills of lading governed by the *Carriage by Sea Act*, 1924.)

(b) *That the ship will be ready* (i) to load cargo and (ii) to sail, on the agreed date. (If delay is fundamental, the shipper may repudiate the contract; otherwise he can only sue for damages.)

(c) *That the ship will not deviate unnecessarily.* Deviation to save *life* is permissible, but deviation to save *property* is not (except in bills of lading governed by the *Carriage of Goods by Sea Act*, 1924).

Most contracts contain a *deviation clause* allowing the ship to call at agreed ports in any order, and to make other necessary and pre-agreed deviations. But such clauses are strictly construed.

5. Liability of shipowners: *The Merchant Shipping Acts*, 1894–1958, provide that regarding British ships, no owner, charterer, manager, or operator, etc., shall be liable for damage for which he is not personally or jointly responsible in the following cases:

(a) *Loss or damage by fire* (even though caused by unseaworthiness).

(b) *Loss caused by robbery* of such articles as jewels, watches, gold, silver, etc., unless the true value was declared by the consignor at the time of contracting.

(c) *Where loss of life or bodily injury* is caused to passengers, or damage to goods (or to persons other than passengers), by negligence or default in navigation, the damages payable by the owners are limited to (i) 3,100 gold francs per ton of the ship's weight for injury to persons, and (ii) 1,000 gold francs for injury to goods.

(d) *The dangerous nature of any goods* must be notified to the shipowner, who may refuse to carry dangerous goods, or charge additional sums, etc.

6. Freight. The shipowner's *carriage charges* are called freight and usually become *payable* only when (i) he has delivered the goods, or (ii) is prevented from delivering them by some fault of the consignor. Unless otherwise agreed, the person responsible for paying freight is the consignor.

Freight may take the following forms:

(a) *Advance freight*, payable before the goods will be delivered. If through no fault of the ship-owner the goods are lost (*e.g.* through one of the *excepted perils*: *see s.* **49**, 4), liability to pay freight remains.

(b) *Lump sum freight*, *i.e.* a sum payable by a charterer for the use of the ship. If the ship is ready on the agreed date but no cargo is loaded, the charterer still becomes liable to pay the freight.

(c) *Pro rata freight*, *i.e.* a reduced sum payable where (by agreement) the cargo is delivered at some port other than that originally agreed.

(d) *Dead freight*, *i.e.* a sum payable by way of compensation for loss of revenue where a charterer fails in a promise to provide a *full and complete* cargo: *see s.* **53**, 5.

7. General and particular average. Three types of proprietary interest are risked in sea voyages: the ship (owner's interest), the freight (charterer's interest), and the cargo (cargo owner's interest). Loss sustained by any one interest must usually be borne by that interest alone, and is called a *particular average loss*, *e.g.* cost of damage to the ship, falling on the owner alone.

But if one interest suffers loss by reason of damage or expense incurred on behalf of the whole venture (*i.e.* on behalf of all three interests), such loss must be averaged out over all three interests, and the other two must contribute compensation to the interest which has sustained loss, *i.e.* a *general average* assessment is made. (*See also* Marine Insurance: *s.* **58**.)

General average contributions can only be claimed where:

(*a*) The danger was *common to all*, and was real danger, *e.g.* not a false alarm.

(*b*) The party claiming contribution must not have caused the danger.

(*c*) The interest against which contribution is claimed must have been saved.

SECTION 52. BILLS OF LADING

1. Bill of lading: A document signed by the master, the shipowner, or his agent, specifying the goods shipped and setting out the terms of carriage.

Such document is a *receipt, evidence of contract, and a document of title* to the goods. A bill of lading is not a negotiable instrument, but does entitle the holder to delivery of the goods; and property in the goods passes to the transferee of a bill on indorsement of the bill to him.

2. Carriage of Goods by Sea Act, 1924. This Act (based on the international Hague Rules) governs all bills of lading for the carriage of goods from any port in Great Britain or Northern Ireland.

The Act provides that:

(a) *There is no absolute warranty as to seaworthiness: s.* 2. (Compare Bills not covered by the Act: *s.* 46, 4, *above*.)

(b) *If a bill is subject to the Act, it must so state* (this is called the "Paramount Clause").

(c) *Bills governed by the Act must contain* (i) particulars of identification of the goods (by "leading marks" stamped upon them), (ii) the number of pieces shipped, (iii) the condition of the goods as they appear on inspection (such statement being prima facie evidence of their receipt in the stated condition).

The shipper is taken to guarantee the accuracy of particulars he furnishes to the carrier, and must indemnify him for any loss occasioned by inaccuracy: *Brown Jenkinson & Co.* v. *P. Dalton Ltd.* (1957).

(d) *Statements as to apparent condition* of goods refer only to *external appearance* (therefore to make a shipowner liable it must be proved that the internal condition of the goods was sound when shipped, or that damage was caused by some external act of the shipowner of his agents).

Such statements *estop* the shipowner from denying the external condition of the goods was as stated in the bill.

(e) A bill of lading is prima facie *evidence of receipt* by the carrier of the stated goods, but the master's signature does not estop the owner from proving (i) that the goods were not in fact shipped, or (ii) that the owner's agent acted without authority—where this happens the agent himself may be liable to breach of warranty of authority: *V/o Rasnoimport* v. *Guthrie and Co. Ltd.* (1966).

(f) *The Act implies that the shipowner will* (i) use reasonable diligence to make the ship seaworthy, (ii) properly man and equip it, (iii) provide adequate hold storage, refrigeration plant, etc., and (iv) use reasonable care in loading and unloading, or that his agents will do so. (The burden of proving compliance with these requirements is on the shipowner.)

(g) *Excepted perils.* The shipowner is not liable for damage due to (i) negligence or default by the master, crew, etc., in navigating or managing the ship *at sea* (not in dock), (ii) fire, (iii) accidents of navigation, (iv) Act of God, (v) war, (vi) strikes and lock-outs, (vii) riots and civil commotion, (viii) saving life or property at sea, (ix) wastage due to inherent vice in the goods, (x) inadequate packing, or other fault of the consignor, (xi) latent defects not discoverable by careful inspection.

These exemptions *only apply provided* that loss is not occasioned by the negligence or default of the carrier or his servants or agents, including stevedores: *Leesh River Tea Co. Ltd.* v. *British India S.N. Co. Ltd.* (1966).

(h) *The Act does not apply to* (i) coastal shipping in British waters, or from one British port to another, (ii) shipping of special goods outside the normal course of sea trade, for which special terms may be agreed, (iii) charterparties.

(i) *The carrier cannot contract out of liability* under the Act, but he is not liable for damage to goods exceeding £100 in value per unit, unless otherwise agreed (in practice the *British Maritime Law Association Agreement* (1950) raises liability to £200 in most cases).

SECTION 53. CHARTERPARTIES

1. Charterparties. A charterparty is a contract whereby a charterer hires a ship for the carriage of cargo on a particular voyage (a *voyage charter*) or for a period of time (a *time charter*). Possession of the ship and control of the crew usually remain with the owner, but occasionally the ship is completely leased to the charterer (a *charter by demise*), and he may provide his own crew.

A charterparty differs from a bill of lading in that it deals with the whole ship, while a Bill does not.

2. Form of charterparty. They must be *in writing* and usually contain:

(a) *A statement of the ship's tonnage* (so that its cargo capacity can be assessed). A substantial inaccuracy in tonnage gives rise to a right of action for breach of *warranty.*

(b) *A statement of the ship's whereabouts,* which is a *condition* of the contract and if untrue entitles the charter to repudiate the contract: *Behn* v. *Burness* (1863).

A charterparty may also contain a *paramount clause, i.e.*

F

one which stipulates that the liability of the shipowner shall be limited in the manner provided by bills of lading covered by the *Carriage of Goods by Sea Act*, 1924.

3. Usual terms. In a voyage charter the following terms are usually included:

(a) *An undertaking by the owner* that on the agreed date the ship will be seaworthy, fully provisioned and ready to sail when loaded, to the agreed port of destination.

(b) *An "excepted perils" clause*, protecting the owner from liability for loss caused by Act of God or the Queen's enemies, restraint of princes (interference by a foreign state), *barratry* (wilful default by the master, mutiny by the crew, etc.) and perils of the sea, *e.g.* natural disasters, storms, icebergs, etc.

(c) *An undertaking by the charterer* to complete loading and unloading within a certain number of days (called *lay days*) and to pay compensation (called *demurrage*) for undue delay.

     Sometimes the charterparty also provides that if the charterer completes loading and unloading more quickly than agreed, the freight charge shall be reduced; the reduction is called *dispatch money*.

4. Shipowner's implied undertakings. The following undertakings by shipowners are implied by law in all charterparties:

(a) That the ship will be *seaworthy*.

(b) That it will be *ready to load and sail* on the agreed dates (substantial delay may amount to breach of condition; trifling delay is merely breach of warranty).

(c) That the ship will *not deviate* from its route except for good cause, or as agreed in the contract.

     Good cause usually means where necessitated by (i) the safety of the ship, or (ii) for the purpose of saving life (not merely property).

5. Full and complete cargo. A charterparty sometimes binds the charterer to provide the ship with a full and complete cargo, *i.e.* as much as the ship can safely carry (excluding deck loading, unless otherwise agreed). If a particular quantity of cargo is agreed (usually measured in tons), the charterer discharges his obligation if he provides approximately that quantity, even though he fails to take all available space.

If the charterer fails to provide the agreed full and complete cargo, the shipowner (unless otherwise agreed) can:

(a) charge the charterer *dead freight, i.e.* damages for loss of revenue for the unoccupied space, or

(b) *deviate* from his route to collect supplementary cargo.

6. Cesser and lien clauses. These are usually inserted and provide:

(a) *Cesser clause:* the charterer's liability under the charter-party is to cease as soon as the agreed cargo is loaded.

(b) *Lien clause:* the master and owners are given a lien on the cargo for the unpaid freight and for demurrage charges.

SPECIMEN QUESTIONS

1. State the forms which a contract of affreightment may take, and mention what undertakings by the shipowner or carrier are implied in every contract of affreightment.

Explain what is meant by "deviation" and state the effect thereof. In what circumstances is deviation allowable by statute or otherwise? *C.I.S., Final, Dec.* 1961. (**51.** 1–4.)

2. (a) Who is a "common carrier" and how does his position in law differ from that of a "private carrier"?

(b) Miss E contracted with G, a local removal man, that he move her furniture from London to Brighton. One of the conditions of the contract was that G would not be responsible for loss or damage by fire. During transit one of the removal men carelessly dropped a cigarette in the van. The van caught fire and Miss E's furniture was lost. Consider with reasons whether Miss E will be able to recover damages from G. *C.I.S., Final, Dec.* 1963. (**49.** 1–6.)

3. State the circumstances in which the common law liability of a common carrier by land may be modified in respect of the goods which he accepts for carriage.

Explain the position where the carrier refuses to give the consignor a receipt for a parcel of watches in respect of which an increased charge for carriage has been paid. *C.I.S., Final, June* 1961. (**49.** 2–4, 6; **50.** 2.)

CHAPTER XI

INSURANCE

SECTION 54. NATURE OF INSURANCE

1. Nature of insurance. A contract of insurance is one which has as its object indemnification of the insured against loss, or the payment of a sum of money to the insured or his nominees on the happening of a stated event.

The document of contract is usually called a *policy*, and the person seeking to be insured is the *proposer*.

2. Insurance not a wager. Distinguish carefully between an insurance contract (which is valid and enforceable) and a wager (which is void: *see s.* **19**).

(a) *A wager* is a contract to pay money on the ascertainment of some uncertain future event. What renders this void is that the parties have nothing to lose, apart from the money staked on the wager, *e.g.* a wager on the outcome of a horse race.

(b) *An insurance contract* is a contract to provide compensation to the insured in the event of him suffering some apprehended harm to some *insurable interest*, *e.g.* his property, or his health. Here the insured would suffer harm (to property or health) irrespective of the contract, and the contract is simply an attempt to provide him with compensation if the apprehended danger materialises.

(*If the insured had no "insurable interest,"* the contract would be a wager and therefore void.)

3. Insurance is uberrimae fidei. The parties to any insurance contract must make *full disclosure of all material facts* at the time of contracting, otherwise the contract will be voidable by the other party.

This duty falls primarily on the proposer, who must disclose to the insurer all facts which might influence a prudent insurer whether to accept the risk or not, or whether to charge a higher premium. Thus a motorist proposing an accident insurance must disclose any previous motor accidents, and a householder proposing burglary insurance must disclose the true value of the property to be insured.

Failure to disclose such material facts (and any alterations in them subsequent to the making of the contract) entitles the insurer to avoid the contract. The insurer may even require the proposer to warrant the truth of immaterial matters, and breach of such warranty will then also render the contract voidable. *Roselodge Ltd.* v. *Castle* (1966), see **57.** 1. below.

4. Double insurance. If the insured takes out simultaneous policies against the same risk, so providing insurance beyond the extent of his potential loss, he can still *recover only the amount of his actual loss*.

Thus if X's house is worth £5000 and he takes out two fire policies (each for £5000) with two different insurers, he still cannot recover more than the amount of his real loss if the house is destroyed by fire, *i.e.* a maximum of £5000. But he can choose which insurer to call upon, and the insurer who pays out on the policy is then entitled to contribution from the other.

SECTION 55. LIFE INSURANCE

1. The contract of life insurance. This is a contract under which the insurer promises to pay a stated sum upon the death of the person whose life is insured.

The consideration for the insurer's promise is the payment by, or on behalf of, the insured of certain sums called premiums.

NOTE:

(a) *Insurable interest.* The contract is *void* unless the proposer has an *insurable interest* in the life insured: *Life Assurance Act,* 1774, *s.* 1.

A person has an insurable interest in his own life, and the following have insurable interests in each other's lives: (i) husband and wife, (ii) employer and employee, (iii) creditor and debtor (and guarantor).

But there is *no insurable interest between* parents and children, brothers and sisters, etc., unless the person seeking the insurance is financially dependent on the person whose life is insured.

(b) *The name of the person who is to receive the moneys payable* under the policy, must be inserted in it: *L.A.A., s.* 2.

A policy taken out by a husband or wife, and designated as being for the benefit of his or her spouse, creates a trust of the moneys payable, so that the moneys payable are not liable to death duties on the death of the insured: *Married Women's Property Act*, 1882, *s.* 11.

(c) *Suicide of insured.* If the insured commits suicide while sane the sum assured by the policy is irrecoverable: *Beresford* v. *Royal Insurance* (1938). (Any provision to the contrary in the policy is void.)

    If the insured commits suicide while of unsound mind, the policy moneys are recoverable (unless the contract provides otherwise).

2. Assignment of life policies. A life policy may be assigned either by (*a*) delivery and indorsement of the policy, or by (*b*) delivery with an accompanying instrument of assignment.

Written notice of the assignment must be given to the insurer, who must acknowledge receipt thereof: ✻ *Policies of Assurance Act*, 1867, *s.* 3. Where there are *competing claims*, the date of receipt by the insurer of the notice of assignment regulates all questions of priority of the competing claims: *P.A.A.*, 1867, *s.* 6.

As with other assignments of choses in action, the assignee takes his assignment *subject to equities* arising before receipt of notice by the insurer. The assignee can sue in his own name to enforce the policy.

    NOTE: It appears that a person may take out a policy on his own life, and then assign it to another who has no insurable interest, without invalidating the policy. Thus the assignee of a policy, who has no insurable interest, may still be able to enforce it: for this reason life policies can be assigned as securities—see below.

3. Assignment by way of mortgage. A life policy can be used as security for a loan (*e.g.* by a bank). The methods by which this can be achieved are as follows:

(a) *Legal assignment* to the creditor (who must then give the notice to the insurer required by the P.A.A. 1867).

    NOTE: (i) The assignment must be under *seal*, stamped 5*s.* per cent of the advance; (ii) The assignee can sue in his own name; (iii) The insurer holds the policy moneys for the benefit of the assignee; and (iv) The assignee gains priority from the date of registration.

(b) *Equitable assignment* to the creditor, by deposit of the policy plus a memorandum of the reasons for deposit. Stamp duty of 2*s.* per cent of the advance is payable.

On redemption of a legal mortgage of a policy, the mortgagee *reassigns* the policy to the mortgagor (and stamp duty of 1*s.* per cent is payable on the deed of reassignment). When an equitable mortgage is redeemed, no formal reassignment is necessary: the lender merely cancels the memorandum of deposit and returns the policy, and no stamp duty is payable.

4. Life policies as securities. They have several advantages and disadvantages as securities.

(a) *Advantages:* (i) Methods of mortgaging are *simple*; (ii) The surrender *value* of the policy is increased by each payment of premium, so that the value of the security will appreciate as long as premiums are paid; (iii) The policy can be *realised* immediately (if, for instance, the insured fails to pay his premiums when due) by surrender to the insurer; (iv) *Death* of the insured makes the moneys assured immediately available.

(b) *Disadvantages:* (i) The mortgagee is to some extent at the mercy of the person paying the premiums, and his default may *invalidate* the policy; (ii) The insurer may be able to *avoid the policy* if the proposer failed to disclose all material facts; (iii) *Suicide* of the insured may invalidate the policy; (iv) The policy may contain provision for avoidance by the insurer on breach of various *covenants* by the insured.

SECTION 56. FIRE INSURANCE

1. The contract. A contract of fire insurance is one providing for indemnification of the insured up to a certain amount in the event of injury or loss by fire, caused to a specified property during a specified time.

The insured can only recover for *actual loss: Castellain* v. *Preston* (1883).

The proposer must have an *insurable interest* in the property insured: *Life Assurance Act*, 1774, *s.* 1. Owners, tenants, trustees, and mortgagees have insurable interests, but a shareholder in a company has no insurable interest in the property of the company.

NOTE: To discourage people setting fire to their own property in order to get insurance money, the *Fire Prevention* (*Metropolis*) *Act*, 1774, *s.* 83, provides that any person interested in the property (such as a tenant, mortgagee, etc.) can compel the insured to use the money in repairing and reinstating the damaged premises.

2. Average clauses. A fire policy often contains an *average clause* which *provides* that the insured can only recover *such proportion of the loss caused by fire as the value of the policy bears to the value of the property insured.*

Thus, if property worth £5000 is insured for only £2500 and fire damage is caused to the extent of £2500, the insurer can refuse to pay more than half this amount.

3. Subrogation. On payment of all moneys due under the policy, the insurer is entitled to be subrogated to the rights of the insured, *i.e.* to pursue any remedies available to the insured in contract or tort in respect of the loss. Thus if the fire was caused by the negligence of X, the insurer (after paying out on the policy) could sue X for his negligence.

If the assured forestalls this right of subrogation by discharging or waiving any claim against such third parties, the insurer is likewise discharged from liability under the policy to the same extent: *Phoenix Assurance Co.* v. *Spooner* (1905).

Subrogation is only available where the insurer has paid the whole claim of the assured, and any action can only be brought in the name of the assured.

4. Excepted perils. Risks covered include loss by fire (even though caused by the assured's own negligence, but not if caused by his wilful default), and loss occasioned by a fire brigade in putting out the fire.

Excepted perils include riot, civil commotion, war, explosion, and sometimes Act of God.

A policy will not cover consequential loss (such as loss of profits of a business), unless expressly so agreed.

SECTION 57. ACCIDENT, BURGLARY, AND OTHER FORMS OF INSURANCE

1. The contract. The same general rules apply as with life and fire insurance. Note that burglary insurance is a form of indemnity insurance (*i.e.* compensation for actual loss), while accident insurance is often lump sum insurance (*i.e.* stipulating for the payment of a lump sum on the occurrence of a specified event).

Policies in this class usually provide that notice of the

burglary, accident, etc., must be given to the insurer within a specified time, failing which the insurer may be discharged from liability: *Re Williams & Thomas* (1902).

EXAMPLE: Diamond merchants insured their wares but failed to disclose a fact they considered immaterial, *i.e.* that their sales manager had been convicted of smuggling diamonds in the U.S.A. eight years previously. Later they were robbed of diamonds and claimed under the policy. HELD: Even though the manager was not involved in the robbery, his conviction was a material fact and should have been disclosed in the proposal—the claim was dismissed: *Roselodge Ltd.* v. *Castle* (1966).

2. Burglary insurance. The policy usually provides cover against house-breaking and theft from the premises insured as well as against burglary (house-breaking by night). Cover is restricted to the premises agreed.

3. Accident policies. These usually provide for the payment of a lump sum in the event of death by accident, and of smaller sums in other eventualities. Provision may also be made for payment of weekly sums during disability, sickness, etc.

The policy usually covers only accidents (or sickness) to the insured alone, though other persons may be included if so desired.

(a) *Accidents to the insured.* Cover is for personal injury or death, caused by chance or by the negligent or intentional act of any third person, *e.g.* assault. It will not cover injuries deliberately self-inflicted.

(b) *Accidents to third parties, e.g.* to passengers in the insured person's car, or a visitor to his premises, etc. Such cover gives the injured person a right to sue the insurer for the sum assured if (i) the insured becomes bankrupt, or makes any composition with his creditors, or (ii) is a company which goes into liquidation. Otherwise only the insured can sue: *Third Parties (Rights against insurers) Act,* 1930.

NOTE: All motorists must be insured against injury to third parties. A person injured by a car who obtains judgment against the motorist can recover the damages awarded in that action from the motorist's insurer: *Road Traffic Act,* 1960, *ss.* 207, 208. In such policies, restrictions on the insurer's liability because of the age or condition of the assured or of the car, or of the load carried, are void.

SECTION 58. MARINE INSURANCE

1. The contract. This is a contract whereby the insurer (underwriter) promises to indemnify the insured against loss caused by maritime perils: ✳ *Marine Insurance Act*, 1906, *s.* 1.

Maritime perils mean perils at sea, but the policy may be extended to cover inland navigation: *M.I.A.*, 1906, *s.* 2.

2. Insurable interest. The insured must have an insurable interest in the vessel, or in the maritime venture *at the time of the loss: s.* 5.

Persons having insurable interests include mortgagees of a ship, lenders of money on security of the ship and/or freight ("bottomry"), or on the security of the cargo ("respondentia"), the master and crew to the extent of their wages, the owners of the ship, cargo, etc.; the underwriter himself (who can thus re-insure against his own risk as insurer).

3. Duty of disclosure. The contract, like all insurance contracts, is *uberrimae fidei* and full disclosure must be made of facts which materially affect the risk.

Matters need not be disclosed if: (*a*) they diminish the risk, or (*b*) are waived, or (*c*) may be deemed to be known in the ordinary course of trade.

Where the contract is made by an agent, he must disclose all facts which are known (or should be known) to his principal.

4. Kinds of policy.

(a) *Voyage policies*, to insure for a voyage from one place to another, *i.e.* a particular voyage.

(b) *Time policies*, which provide cover for a stated period. (This must not be longer than 12 months, subject to any renewals at the end of the 12 months.)

(c) *Mixed policies, i.e.* a combination of Voyage and Time cover.

(d) *Valued policies*, where the value insured is specified.

(e) *Unvalued policies*, where the value insured is not specified but is left open for assessment in accordance with customary usage if the occasion arises.

(f) *Floating policies*, where the name of the ship is left blank so that the policy is available for any ship owned by the insurer.

(g) *Open cover.* This is not an actual insurance policy, but a contract to issue a policy at a given time or on the occurrence of a particular event.

(h) *Re-insurance,* where the underwriter himself insures against his own liability under a marine insurance policy.

5. Measure of indemnity. The assured can only recover for *actual loss.* If the loss is *total,* he is entitled to the maximum sum assured by the policy whatever that may be.

In the case of *partial loss* the position is:

(a) *Partial loss to ship.* The insured can recover the cost of repairs, or the amount of depreciation if the ship is not repaired.

(b) *Partial loss of goods.* The insured can recover the value of the goods lost, or if the policy is a *valued policy* the loss calculated as a proportion of the total amount assured.

6. Warranties. In marine insurance the word *warranty* is largely used in the same sense as the word *condition* in ordinary contracts, and means that the assured undertakes absolutely that something shall be done, or some requirement fulfilled, or affirms or denies the existence of particular facts.

Such a warranty *must be exactly complied with*, otherwise the policy will be avoided: *M.I.A.,* 1906, *s.* 33.

Warranties may be expressed or implied by the *Marine Insurance Act,* 1906.

7. Implied warranties.

(a) *In a voyage policy* (i) that the ship shall be seaworthy at the start of the voyage: *s.* 39, (ii) that the ship is normally fit to carry any goods insured: *s.* 40.

(b) *Generally,* (i) that the adventure is legal: *s.* 41, (ii) if cover is granted for the ship in port, that she shall be reasonably fit to meet the hazards of the port: *s.* 39.

(There are *no implied warranties* covering (i) the nationality of the ship, or the seaworthiness of a ship covered by a time policy, or (ii) that goods insured are seaworthy.)

8. Premiums. These must normally be paid before the policy is issued, and are returnable as and when agreed, or where the policy is void for any reason, or where in an unvalued policy the venture has been over-insured: *s.* 84.

9. Risks covered. These include all the normal risks of sea journeys, loss from fire, pirates or thieves, barratry (wilful misconduct by master or crew), and collision (up to three-quarters of the damage sustained).

The insurers are only bound to compensate for direct loss, and consequential loss (*e.g.* loss of profits) requires express cover.

10. Loss may be total or partial. Total loss may be either:

(a) *actual*, as where the property covered is destroyed or is so changed as to have changed its character entirely, or where the assured is deprived of its use. (Actual loss may be presumed if a ship is missing for an unreasonable time, and no information can be obtained as to its whereabouts);

(b) *constructive*, where the property covered is reasonably abandoned in circumstances which make it appear that total loss is inevitable, *e.g.* where the crew leaves a sinking ship, of which no more is heard.

(Where there is *constructive total loss*, the insured may treat it as *partial loss* if he wishes, or may relinquish his property to the insurer who may salvage it if possible. In the latter case he must give *notice of abandonment* to the insurer, and acceptance of such notice is *conclusive evidence* that the insurer admits liability.)

11. General average loss. Where a general average loss has occurred, the assured may recover the total value assured from the insurer who may then (by subrogation) recover his due contribution from the other parties liability.

(For meaning of general average, see *Carriage of Goods*, s. 51, 7.)

12. Assignment of policy. Unless prohibited by the contract, a marine policy can be assigned by indorsement: *s.* 50. The assignment is subject to equities in the normal way. It may be made either before or after loss.

13. Discharge of insurer. In a voyage policy the insurer is automatically discharged if the ship (*a*) sails from a port other than specified in the policy, or (*b*) deviates unreasonably from the scheduled route (in which case discharge dates from the time of deviation).

Deviation is excused (i) where authorised by the policy, or

(ii) where for the purpose of saving life (not property), or (iii) where necessary to obtain medical aid for any person aboard the ship, or (iv) where necessary for the safety of the ship, or (v) otherwise where caused by circumstances beyond the control of the master or his employer.

SPECIMEN QUESTIONS

1. Explain the expression "insurable interest" in connection with a contract of marine insurance; and state what persons possess an insurable interest in such a contract.

What duty of disclosure rests on the assured? *C.I.S., Final, Dec.* 1962. (**58.** 1–3.)

2. (*a*) What is the nature of a contract created by a fire insurance policy?

(*b*) A is insured with several companies in respect of the same property to an amount exceeding the value of the property. In the event of a loss through fire what are the rights of A and the insurance companies? *C.A., Final, May* 1962. (**54.** 1, 4; **56.** 1, 3.)

3. Adam made a proposal to an insurance company for an insurance on his life for £5000. On the proposal form he answered various questions truthfully and disclosed all relevant facts. A few days later, but before the proposal was definitely accepted, Adam was taken ill with pneumonia. Subsequently the company accepted the proposal and the first premium was paid. Two days later Adam died of pneumonia and the company learned for the first time of his illness. Is the company liable to pay the £5000? *C.A., Final, Nov.* 1962. (**16.** 3, 10; **54.** 3; **55.** 1.)

4. (*a*) What is meant by a warranty in a contract of marine insurance? How does it differ from a warranty in a contract for the sale of goods?

(*b*) What warranties are implied in a contract of marine insurance? *C.I.S., Final, Dec.* 1964. (**58.** 6, 7.)

BAILMENT

SECTION 59. NATURE AND KINDS OF BAILMENT

1. Definition of bailment. A bailment is a delivery of goods by one person to another for some limited purpose, on condition that when the purpose has been accomplished the goods shall be returned.

The bailment may be *simple* or *exclusive*. In an exclusive bailment the bailee (the person to whom the goods are bailed) can during the continuance of the bailment retain the goods against anyone, including the bailor, *e.g.* a pledge or pawn of goods: see **72** below. In a simple bailment the bailee can defend his possession against anyone, *except* the bailor.

2. Duties of bailee.

(a) *To take reasonable care of the goods* bailed to him. What is reasonable depends on the type of bailment. If the bailee has been paid for his services (a bailment for reward), his duty is higher than if he received no payment (gratuitous bailment).

(b) *To return the goods* in accordance with the contract. If he fails to do so, he is liable for loss or damage notwithstanding the exercise of reasonable care: *Shaw* v. *Symmons* (1917).

(Contracts of bailment frequently contain a clause restricting the duty of care or excluding it, but if the bailee returns the goods to the wrong person he has no protection from such a clause: ✱ *Alexander* v. *Rly. Executive* (1951), and *see 4 below*.)

NOTE:

(i) *The burden of proving* exercise of reasonable care is on the bailee. Therefore if he has lost the goods or they are damaged when returned, it is for the bailee to prove that loss or damage was *not* due to his negligence.

162

(ii) *If goods are lost or damaged* while in his custody, and the bailee cannot show how this happened, he is liable: *Houghland* v. *R. R. Low Ltd.*

(iii) If goods are lost while in his custody it is *not enough* for the bailee to show that he was reasonably careful to protect them; he must show also that he made reasonable efforts to recover them: *Codman* v. *Hill* (1919).

(iv) The bailee is liable for the *negligence or dishonesty of his servants*, if he did not use reasonable care in selecting them, *e.g.* where he entrusts goods bailed to a known thief: *Williams* v. *Curzon Syndicate Ltd.* (1919). But he is not generally liable for wrongs committed by his independent contractors; or by servants if he can show he was reasonably careful in his selection of them.

(v) If the bailee professes a *particular skill*, he is liable if he fails to exercise that skill, even if the bailment is gratuitous: *Wilson* v. *Brett* (1843).

(vi) *The bailee is not liable* for loss or damage occasioned by Act of God (inevitable and unforseeable accident), robbery with violence, or war.

(vii) *Where there is no express contract* between the parties, the duties of the bailee arise from the law of tort: *Chesworth* v. *Farrar* (1966).

3. Duty of bailor. If the goods are bailed for a particular purpose of which the bailor knows, *e.g.* hire of a car, he is under a *duty to disclose any defect* rendering the goods unsuitable for that purpose.

He impliedly warrants the fitness of the goods hired, and owes a duty of reasonable care, *i.e.* he is not liable as regards defects of which he had no knowledge or reasonable opportunity of knowledge.

(In other types of bailment the bailor generally owes no duty of care, except a duty to warn the bailee if goods are dangerous, *e.g.* where explosives are deposited in a cloakroom.)

4. Particular contracts. The bailee may by express terms seek to *exclude liability* for negligence, particularly in bailments for reward. Such terms must be clear and unambiguous and are generally construed against the bailee as far as possible, under the *contra proferentem* rule: *Morris* v. *C. W. Martin & Sons Ltd.* (1965).

Thus the bailee loses the protections of such exemption clauses if he breaks the contract in some other way, *e.g.* by delivering goods to the wrong person: *Alexander* v. *Rly. Executive* (1951), unless the misdelivery was merely negligent: *see s.* **7, 3**.

EXAMPLES:

(*a*) If the bailment is a *contract for personal service*, the bailee loses the protection of exemption clauses if he breaks his contract by delegating performance to another, *e.g.* where a laundry accepted articles "at owner's risk entirely" and then delivered them for cleaning to another firm which lost them: *Davies* v. *Collins* (1945).

(*b*) The bailee is liable if he *deviates* from the contract, and cannot then rely on exemption clauses, *e.g.* where he undertakes to store goods at a certain warehouse but in fact warehouses them elsewhere and they are lost: *Lilley* v. *Doubleday* (1881).

(*c*) The bailee also loses the benefit of exemption clauses if he or his agent *misrepresents* the effect of the clauses: *Curtis* v. *Chemical Cleaning & Dyeing Co.* (1951).

5. Bailee's power of sale. A bailee cannot sell or otherwise dispose of goods bailed unless:

(*a*) the contract so provides, or
(*b*) a right of sale is conferred by statute.

Otherwise if he sells goods bailed he is liable for damages for the tort of conversion, *i.e.* converting to his own use and disposition goods to which another is entitled.

A *statutory power of sale* of uncollected goods is given by the *Innkeepers Act* (1878), *The Pawnbrokers Acts*, and *The Disposal of Uncollected Goods Act*, (1952).

✶ *The Disposal of Uncollected Goods Act* applies in favour of a bailee who accepts goods in the course of his business to work upon them, *e.g.* a repairer.

In order for the Act to apply (i) a notice of its provisions must be displayed at the bailee's premises, and (ii) a notice that acceptance of goods by the bailee is subject to the provisions of the Act.

Then, after notice that the goods are ready for collection, if the bailor fails both to pay for and take delivery of the goods, the bailee can (after 12 months) serve notice by registered post of his intention to sell the goods. If his charges remain unsatisfied after a further 14 days, he can sell the goods either by public auction or privately at a price not lower than he has previously notified the bailor. The bailee may then deduct his costs from the sale price and must hold the balance (if any) for the bailor for 6 years, after which the balance belongs to the bailee.

6. Types of bailment.

(a) *Deposit* (*depositum*), means goods are deposited for *safe custody*, *e.g.* in a cloakroom. The bailee cannot use the goods and must (subject to any terms of the contract) exercise reasonable care of them while in his possession. He must return them to the bailor, and no exemptionary clause will protect him if he delivers them to the wrong person: *Alexander* v. *Railway Exec.*

(b) *Loan for use* (*commodatum*). The bailee is entitled to use the goods loaned and is not liable for *fair wear and tear*, unless he deviates from the conditions of the loan.

(c) *Hire* (*locatio rei*). Here the *bailor impliedly warrants* the fitness of the goods bailed for the purpose hired. The bailee must take reasonable care of the goods and use them in accordance with the terms of the contract. He is not liable for loss by robbery, accidental fire occasioned without negligence, etc. In a hire for reward the owner cannot usually reclaim the goods save in accordance with the terms of the contract, *i.e.* the bailment is exclusive.

Hiring is *automatically determined* (even in hire purchase contracts) if the hirer attempts to sell the goods: *Helby* v. *Mathews* (1895). (For hire purchase generally *see s.* **48.**)

(d) *Innkeepers.* They are bailees of their guests luggage in certain circumstances: *see ss.* 7, 8 *below.*

(e) *Deposit for work to be done* (*location operis faciendi*), *e.g.* deposit for repair or alteration. The bailee must take care of the goods and hand them to the true owner or his agent when requested, but he has a lien over the goods for his charges and need not return them until his charges are paid.

(f) *Pawn or pledge* (*vadium*) of chattels as security for a loan: see Chapter XV, *s.* **72.**

7. Innkeepers and guests. A hotel or innkeeper is one who holds himself out as ready to receive all travellers who: (i) are willing to pay a *reasonable price* for accommodation offered, and (ii) come in a condition *fit to be received*: *Hotel Proprietors Act*, 1956, *s.* 1.

An innkeeper *must* accept all travellers provided he has enough room and they are willing to pay and are in a reasonably fit condition to be received. Failure to accept *bona fide* travellers renders him liable to an action for damages: *Browne* v. *Brandt* (1902), and possibly to prosecution.

Any person is a traveller who calls for a meal or a drink: *Williams* v. *Linnitt* (1952). But he is only entitled to protection for his luggage if he stays to take sleeping accommodation.

8. Innkeeper's liability. The inn or hotel keeper is an *insurer of his guest's luggage* (but not of their pet animals, cars, etc.), and can only *evade liability* for loss or damage by showing that it was caused by: (i) Act of God, (ii) war, (iii) guest's own negligence (though leaving luggage in an unlocked room is not usually such negligence: *Brewster* v. *Denman* (1945)), or (iv) inherent vice in the goods themselves.

By the * *Hotel Proprietors Act*, 1956, the innkeeper's liability is restricted to £50 for any one article or a total of £100 for any one guest, unless:

(a) Loss or damage was caused by the *wilful default* or negligence of the innkeeper or his servants, or

(b) The goods were expressly *deposited* with the innkeeper for safe custody in some place specially provided, *e.g.* the hotel safe.

A *notice* of these restrictions on liability must be given to the guest before or at the time of registering (when the contract is made), and a notice placed in the room is therefore inadequate: *Olley* v. *Marlborough Court Hotel* (1949).

Such notice must be prominently displayed at or near the reception office and/or in the main hall of the hotel. If not so displayed the innkeeper loses the protection of the Act.

9. Innkeeper's lien. The innkeeper has a *right to retain all* a guest's luggage for non-payment of his charges. This lien does not extend to things over which the innkeeper owes no duty of care, *e.g.* the guest's car or pet animals.

The lien is lost if the guest is allowed to remove the goods; there is no power to detain the guest himself.

By the *Innkeepers' Act*, 1878, the hotelier is given a statutory right to sell such goods as are subject to his lien, and reimburse himself for his charges out of the proceeds of sale. The right to sell becomes exercisable when the goods have been retained for six weeks; and one month's notice of the sale must be given to the guest to give him a final chance to pay the bill.

10. Involuntary bailment. A person may become a bailee involuntarily, *e.g.* where goods are sent to him by mistake, or without being ordered. The legal position of such a bailee is uncertain.

EXAMPLE: Author sent an unsolicited manuscript to a theatrical producer, who lost it. HELD: The producer was under no duty as to its safe-keeping: *Howard* v. *Harris* (1840).

It appears that an involuntary bailee can incur no liability for negligence, but he might be liable for *conversion* if he intentionally or negligently converted the goods to his own use: *Elvin & Powell* v. *Plummer Roddis* (1933). But it is still unsettled as to what is the position of a person who receives unordered goods, for instance from a book or record club. Must he keep them safely until called for, or must he notify the sender that he does not want them, or can he simply put them out in the street? No definite answer can be given, but the safe course would appear to be to notify the sender that the goods are unwanted and await collection.

SPECIMEN QUESTIONS

1. To what extent is the borrower of goods loaned to him for use under a duty to take care of the goods?

B deposited a motor van with a firm of garage proprietors for sale on commission upon the terms of a printed document which stated that "customers vehicles are driven by our staff at customers' sole risk." While the van was being demonstrated to a prospective buyer, it was damaged through the negligence of one of the staff. Discuss the legal position. *C.I.S., Final, Dec.* 1962. (**59.** 2, 4, 6.)

2. Explain the nature of a bailment. Mention three forms which bailment may take, and explain the nature of the consideration which will support a contract of bailment.

B contracted to warehouse D's furniture at B's depository in Chelsea, but B warehoused a part of the furniture at a depository in Fulham. The furniture warehouse at Fulham was destroyed by fire. Discuss the legal position. *C.I.S., Final, June* 1961. (**59.** 1, 6; **12.** 4.)

ARBITRATION AND AWARDS

SECTION 60. ARBITRATION

1. Reference to arbitration. Arbitration in mercantile disputes is now mainly governed by the * *Arbitration Act*, 1950. A dispute may be referred to arbitration in the following ways:

(a) *By Order of the Court.* The Rules of the Supreme Court provide that the court may refer settlement of disputes to official referees, Masters of the Court, registrars, district registrars, etc. The reference may relate to a specified issue (*e.g.* the costs in an action before the court), or to the whole dispute.

Reference by the court usually occurs in cases where some special technical or local knowledge is required, and all the parties consent to the dispute going before a specially qualified arbitrator.

(b) *By certain statutes* which may provide that disputes arising under such statute are to be settled by arbitration. The statute may then lay down special rules for the conduct of the arbitration (otherwise the *Arbitration Act*, 1950, will normally apply).

(c) *By consent of the parties*, out of court, *e.g.* under an arbitration clause in a contract. An arbitration agreement is "a *written* agreement to submit present or future differences to arbitration, whether an arbitrator is named therein or not": *A.A.*, 1950, *s.* 32. Oral agreements are valid but are not covered by the Act.

(Contrast a *Valuation*, which is made *before* any dispute arises and in order to forestall disagreement.)

2. Arbitration agreements. If in a contract there is an arbitration clause, the court may stay any proceedings respecting the agreement and refer the dispute to arbitration: *A.A.*, *s.* 4.

The court may stay proceedings if:

(a) The dispute is within the scope of the arbitration clause.
(b) The applicant has not in any way consented to proceedings being brought before the court, *e.g.* by filing a defence.

(c) The applicant is willing to do anything necessary to assist arbitration.

(d) The contract stipulates that no right of action is to accrue under the contract until the arbitration procedure described therein has been resorted to: *Scott* v. *Avery* (1856).

(e) There is no reason in the interests of justice to refuse the application.

NOTE: *Reasons for refusing the application* (*A.A.*, *s.* 24) include (i) suspected bias of the arbitrator, *e.g.* where he is an associate or relative of one of the parties to the dispute, (ii) the fact that allegations of fraud are being made against one of the parties to the dispute, (iii) the fact that the dispute involves a point of law and is therefore best left to the court.

3. Construction of arbitration agreements. The Act implies the following clauses in arbitration agreements, unless expressly excluded by the parties:

(a) *Reference is to a single arbitrator*, unless otherwise stated. (If reference is to two arbitrators, they must appoint an umpire to decide between them, by a casting vote.)

(b) Parties to arbitration must submit to *examination on oath*, must produce necessary documents if ordered, etc. Witnesses may also have to submit to examination on oath.

(c) The arbitrator's *award is final* and binding, but he can always make an interim award, pending final decision.

(d) Arbitrators can *apportion costs*, and any provision in the agreement that any party must pay his own costs however the arbitration is decided, is void.

(e) Arbitrators can order *specific performance*, except in contracts relating to land.

(f) The parties may *alter the arbitration agreement* by mutual consent, but the arbitrator cannot. (The court may rectify the agreement at any time, but not so as to introduce new matter: as to rectification, *see s.* **15**, 8.)

(g) *The time* for making the awards may be fixed by the agreement; if not, then a reasonable time is implied, and can be extended by the courts.

(h) The arbitration clause can now be enforced against an *assignee* of the contract: *Shayler* v. *Woolf* (1946).

(i) *Death or bankruptcy* of any party to the agreement do not affect the validity of the agreement or the arbitrator's appointment.

(j) An arbitration agreement may be *revoked by the court* if (i) the arbitrator shows bias, or (ii) there is any question of fraud involved in the dispute.

SECTION 61. CONDUCT OF PROCEEDINGS

1. The arbitrator. Any person can be an arbitrator, even though personally interested in the subject-matter of the dispute.

Reference to an arbitrator is presumed to mean a single arbitrator, unless otherwise stated. If a dispute is referred to a single arbitrator and none is appointed (or the one appointed refuses to act), and the parties fail to agree on a replacement, any party can serve 7 says notice demanding appointment. If then no appointment is made, he can appeal to the court: *A.A., s.* 10; *Tritonia Shipping Inc.* v. *South Nelson Forest Products Corpn.* (1966).

> If reference is to two arbitrators and one is not appointed, the appointor of the other arbitrator can serve similar 7 days notice and on expiry of the notice can make his own appointment (subject to the court's power to invalidate such appointment).
>
> If reference is to three arbitrators, an award by two of them is binding.
>
> An arbitrator's authority is irrevocable (unless otherwise agreed). But the court may revoke his appointment, or remove him, or nullify the arbitration agreement entirely. Grounds for removal would include misconduct, bias, fraud, or failure to act with reasonable speed: *s.* 23. When removing an arbitrator, the court may appoint a replacement: *s.* 25.
>
> An arbitrator in a commercial dispute is presumed to be entitled to reasonable remuneration, unless otherwise agreed. And he has a lien for his fees on the subject-matter of the award.

2. Conduct of proceedings.

(*a*) The arbitration *agreement may provide rules* for governing proceedings, *e.g.* the customs of a particular trade.

(*b*) The arbitrator is entitled to call for *examination on oath*, discovery of documents, presentation of pleadings in writing, etc., unless otherwise agreed.

(*c*) At the hearing the arbitrator may *exclude persons* other than the parties.

(*d*) The arbitrator fixes the *time and place of the hearing* and must notify the parties. If any party *fails to attend*, the arbitrator can proceed in his absence but must first give reasonable notice of his intention to do so.

(*e*) The arbitrator must *hear both sides*, and obey the ordinary rules of evidence. Improper rejection of evidence is grounds for setting the award aside, but not if it was caused by mere honest mistake as to its value: *Falkingham* v. *Victorian Rly. Commissioners* (1900).

(*f*) *Attendance of witnesses* can be compelled by writ of *sub poena* issued by the High Court, at the arbitrator's request. Any witness giving false evidence on oath is guilty of the crime of perjury: *Perjury Act, s.* 1.

(*g*) In commercial cases where an *umpire* is appointed, arbitrators may appear before him and give evidence as witnesses: *Bourgeois* v. *Weddell & Co.* (1924).

(*h*) The arbitrator can state his award in the form of a *"special case"* for the opinion of the court, and can be ordered to do so if the court thinks fit: *s.* 9. The special case may state a question of law for the court's decision, or may relate to the award itself. A clause in the arbitration agreement prohibiting the stating of a special case is void: *Czarnikov* v. *Roth, Schmidt & Co.* (1922). The court does not construe special cases rigidly, and may draw inferences from the facts: *Universal Cargo Carriers Corpn.* v. *Citati* (1958). Statement of the special case renders the arbitrator *functus officio* and terminates his jurisdiction.

3. The award.

(*a*) The arbitrator can make his award at *any time*, unless otherwise stated in the agreement. If a time is fixed by the *Arbitration Act* or any other statute, the court generally has power to extend the time limit.

(*b*) The award may be *verbal or in writing*, or in such form as the agreement expressly requires.

(*c*) An award of money (unless otherwise agreed) *carries interest* like a judgment debt, and the arbitrator has the same powers as a High Court judge to award interest on any debt.

(*d*) *Costs* are generally in the discretion of the arbitrator, which must be fairly exercised but need not be supported by reasons: *Berry* v. *Stopher* (1959).

4. Requisites of a valid award.

(*a*) It must be *certain* in meaning (though the court may assist interpretation where necessary, and may rectify mistakes in expression).

(*b*) It must be *final* (though this does not prohibit the making of interim awards, pending final decision of the dispute).

(*c*) It must be *possible and reasonable*.

(*d*) It must *settle all the points referred* to arbitration, but must not deal with matters outside the reference.

(If part of the award is valid and part void, the court may apply the Doctrine of Severance to separate the good from the bad and enforce the valid parts.)

5. Remission to arbitrator. The award is final, but the court has power to remit any matter back to the arbitrator for reconsideration any time within 3 months of the award being made: *s.* 22.

Grounds for remission are (*a*) defect in the award, sufficient to justify setting it aside, (*b*) serious omission through inadvertence, (*c*) formal defect, (*d*) mistake by the arbitrator, (*e*) technical misconduct by the arbitrator, (*f*) discovery of new and material evidence.

6. Setting awards aside. An award may be set aside because of (*a*) *misconduct* of the arbitrator, (*b*) *uncertainty* or lack of finality in the award, (*c*) *illegality* of the contract on which the award was made.

(In a reference by consent of the parties, mistake is rarely grounds for setting aside the award unless it is a mistake of law.)

7. Enforcement of awards. Enforcement is as follows: (*a*) in the same manner as a judgment of a court, (*b*) by action in the court to enforce the award, (*c*) by court order for specific performance.

Some foreign awards are enforceable in the same way as a foreign judgment, under the *Convention on the Execution of Arbitration Awards* (1927). But a foreign award is not enforceable at all unless it is final, and is valid by English law.

Arbitration agreements are subject to the *Limitation Act*, 1939, and rights of reference or enforcement of any award may lapse thereunder: *see s.* 24.

SPECIMEN QUESTIONS

1. (*a*) In what ways may a reference to arbitration be made? What is the effect of an oral submission?

(*b*) What are the main advantages and disadvantages of arbitration? *C.I.S., Final, Dec.* 1963. (60. 1–3.)

2. Define an arbitration agreement, and state to what arbitration agreements the *Arbitration Act*, 1950, applies.

Where one party to an arbitration agreement commences legal proceedings concerning the subject-matter of the agreement, mention the circumstances in which the court may stay the proceedings.

R rendered services to a sanitary authority under an agreement whereby disputes were to be referred to the authority's surveyor. Disputes arose which would probably lead to a conflict of interest between E and the surveyor. If E commences proceedings against the authority, ought the court in your opinion to stay the proceedings? *C.I.S., Final, June* 1961. **(60. 1, 2.)**

3. A contract provided for any dispute between the parties to it to be referred to arbitration. A dispute has arisen and been properly referred to a single arbitrator, who has made a valid award.

(*a*) Can either party appeal against the award?

(*b*) How can the award be enforced? *C.A., Final, May* 1962. **(61. 4–6.)**

4. State FIVE of the provisions which, unless a contrary intention is expressed, are included in every arbitration agreement. *C.A., Final, May* 1964. **(60. 3.)**

5. State the conditions upon which an award obtained in an arbitration conducted in a foreign country may be enforced in England. *C.A., Final, Nov.* 1961. **(61. 7; 10. 2.)**

6. A contract between a British subject and a French Company provided that disputes arising under it should be determined by arbitration in France. An arbitration held in France has resulted in an award being made in favour of the British party to the contract, and he desires to enforce the award in England. Can he do so, and if so, subject to what conditions? *C.A., May* 1967. **(61. 7, 4.)**

PROGRESS TEST 3

MERCANTILE AGREEMENTS

1. Distinguish between an agreement to sell, and a contract for the sale of goods. How do such contracts differ from contracts for the supply of work and materials? (**39.** 1, 3–5.)

2. In what circumstances must the injured party treat a breach of condition in a contract for the sale of goods as though it were a breach of warranty? (**40.** 4.)

3. Summarise briefly the conditions and warranties implied by the *Sale of Goods Act*, and explain how such terms can be excluded from contracts covered by the Act. (**41.**)

4. Explain the meaning of the following phrases in connection with the sale of goods: (*a*) sale by sample; (*b*) sale by description; (*c*) merchantable quality. (**41.** 2–4.)

5. "Generally in a sale of goods there is no term implied that goods shall be of any particular quality or that they shall be fit for any particular purpose." How far do you agree? (**41.** 4, 5.)

6. A enter B's shop and asks for soap. B, who runs a general store, sells him soap intended for washing poodles. A uses the soap to wash his own hair and as a result goes bald. Has A any remedy under the *Sale of Goods Act*? (**41.** 5.)

7. A buys a car from B in reliance on B's assertion that the car has not done more than 20,000 miles. At the time of purchase A signs a contract which states: "This contract overrides and excludes all conditions and warranties implied by the *Sale of Goods Act*, and all representations made by the seller." A now finds that the car has done 100,000 miles. What is his legal position? (**41.** 8.)

8. Distinguish between specific, ascertained and unascertained goods and explain why the distinction is important. (**42.** 1–6.)

9. When, if ever, may a purchaser of goods get a better title than was possessed by the person from whom he bought the goods? (**43.**)

10. Explain briefly the rules laid down by the Sale of Goods Act regarding: (*a*) delivery of wrong quantities, (*b*) delivery by instalments, and (*c*) time and place of delivery. (**44.** 2, 4, 5.)

11. Summarise the duties of the seller in f.o.b., c.i.f. and ex ship contracts and explain the meaning of these technical terms. (**44.** 8–10.)

174

12. What are the rights of an unpaid seller, and what does this term mean? **(45.)**

13. What is the position of an auctioneer as agent for the seller and the buyer of property? **(47. 2.)**

14. "Hire-purchase is much more hire than purchase." Discuss. **(48. 1.)**

15. What conditions and warranties are implied by the Hire-purchase Acts and to what contracts do these Acts apply? **(48. 1–4.)**

16. A is persuaded to take a car on hire-purchase through the misrepresentation of B, the dealer. The car is sold by B to a finance company, which then lets the car to A on hire-purchase. Later A discovers the misrepresentation, and wishes to know whether he can sue B for damages. Explain the legal position. **(48. 5.)**

17. What is a common carrier, and what are his duties and liabilities at Common Law? How far can such duties and liabilities be modified by contract? **(49. 1–6.)**

18. Explain briefly the main provisions of: (a) The Carriers Act, 1830, and (b) The Transport Act, 1962. **(50. 2, 3.)**

19. How far is a railway company liable for the safety of (a) passengers, and (b) passengers' luggage? **(50. 6, 7.)**

20. Explain briefly the meaning and significance of the following: (a) bill of lading, (b) charterparty, (c) freight, (d) demurrage, (e) general average. **(51. 2, 3, 6, 7.)**

21. State briefly the main provisions of the *Carriage of Goods by Sea Act*, 1924, with regard to bills of lading. **(52. 2.)**

22. Write short explanatory notes on the following: (a) voyage charter, (b) paramount clause in a charterparty, (c) full and complete cargo. **(53. 1, 2, 5.)**

23. How does an insurance contract differ from a wager. What is meant by "insurable interest" (a) in life insurance, and (b) marine insurance? **(54. 1, 2; 55. 1; 58. 2.)**

24. State the main provisions of the Policies of Assurance Act, 1867, with regard to the assignment of life insurance policies. Explain how such a policy can be used as security for a loan. **(55. 2, 3.)**

25. Explain the significance of the average clause in a fire insurance policy. In what circumstances can the insurer claim subrogation to the rights of the insured? **(56. 2, 3.)**

26. What is meant by a warranty in a marine insurance contract, and what warranties are implied under the Marine Insurance Act, 1906? **(58. 6, 7.)**

27. In connection with marine insurance, explain the following terms: (a) bottomry, (b) respondentia, (c) constructive total loss, (d) general average loss. **(58. 2, 10, 11.)**

28. Explain briefly the following: (a) depositum, (b) *locatio rei*, (c) Disposal of Uncollected Goods Act, 1952, (d) innkeepers' lien. **(59. 5, 6, 9.)**

29. What are the duties of a bailee? How far is a bailee liable for loss occasioned by the negligence of his employees? **(59. 2.)**

30. Explain the main provisions of the *Hotel Proprietors' Act*, 1956. **(59. 7, 8.)**

31. How may reference to an arbitrator occur? **(60. 1.)**

32. In what circumstances may the court stay proceedings, and refer a dispute to arbitration under an arbitration agreement? **(60. 2.)**

33. What are the principal powers of an arbitrator under the Arbitration Act, 1950? How may an arbitration award be enforced? **(60. 3; 61. 1–3, 7.)**

NEGOTIABLE INSTRUMENTS

NEGOTIABLE INSTRUMENTS

SECTION 62. NEGOTIABILITY

1. Meaning of negotiability. Certain classes of chose in action, called negotiable instruments, can be transferred (or negotiated) without the formalities necessary in assignments of choses in action under *s.* 136, the *Law of Property Act*, or the rules of Equity.

A *negotiable instrument* is a document evidencing an obligation, which:

(i) is transferable by mere delivery (or by delivery plus indorsement), (ii) such delivery operating to transfer all legal rights to the obligation evidenced, (iii) free of any defects in the transferor's title.

(A negotiable instrument *payable to bearer*, such as a bank note, is transferable by delivery alone. One *payable to the order* of a specified person, such as most cheques, is transferred by delivery of the instrument indorsed (signed) on the back by the payee or other transferor.)

2. Characteristics of negotiable instruments.

(a) *Title passes by delivery* (or by delivery + indorsement); whereas a legal assignment of an ordinary chose in action must be in writing under *s.* 136, *L.P.A.*, and any assignment not in writing is merely equitable: *see s.* **28.**

(b) *No notice is necessary to the debtor* or other obligee; whereas ordinary assignments must be notified under *s.* 136, *L.P.A.* or the Rule in *Dearle* v. *Hall*: *see s.* **28.**

(c) *The holder can sue in his own name*; whereas an equitable assignee of an ordinary chose in action cannot.

(d) *A bona fide transferee for value takes free of any defects in the transferor's title*; whereas an assignee of an ordinary chose gets no better title than his assignor had.

(e) *A transferee in due course (see s.* **65** *below)* takes *free of any defences* which could have been raised by the debtor against the transferor; whereas any defence available against an assignor of an ordinary chose in action can be raised against the assignee.

179

3. Examples of negotiable instruments. A chose in action may become negotiable either (*a*) by statute, or (*b*) by mercantile custom judicially recognised.

Instruments negotiable by statute include Bills of Exchange and Promissory Notes. *Instruments negotiable by custom* include bank notes, share warrants, bearer debentures, and exchequer bills.

> NOTE: The following are *not negotiable instruments*, though they are freely transferable: bills of lading, Post Office orders, share certificates, IOUs and receipts.

> EXAMPLE: A postal order and a £1 note are stolen from X. The thief sells both to Z. (i) The bank note is a negotiable instrument payable to bearer and Z becomes the legal owner of it: X cannot recover it from Z and can only sue the thief. (ii) The postal order is transferable, but not negotiable; therefore the seller of it cannot give a better title than he has himself. The thief has no title, therefore Z can get no title; X can recover the postal order or its value from Z (who can only sue the thief for damages).

4. Who can sue on a negotiable instrument? If a negotiable instrument is dishonoured (*i.e.* not paid when due), a holder for value can sue any person who signed the bill before it came into his possession.

The persons who may be liable are: (*a*) the drawer, *i.e.* the person who first issued the instrument, (*b*) the acceptor, *i.e.* the person (if any) who has accepted liability on the instrument, and (*c*) any indorser, *i.e.* any person who has transferred the instrument to another and indorsed it to effect the transfer (he will also have a right of action against accommodation parties, *i.e.* persons who have signed an instrument merely to lend the credit of their names to the instrument).

EXCEPTIONS: *A signatory may avoid liability* in the following cases:

(i) Where he signed under a *fundamental mistake* as to the nature of the document: *see s.* **15**.
(ii) Where his signature was *forged* (since then he has not signed it himself), *unless he is estopped* from denying the genuineness of the signature, *e.g.* where he facilitated the forgery.
(iii) Where he signed *sans recours* ("without recourse"), indicating that he accepted no liability on the instrument.
(iv) Where for some reason the law will not allow him to be sued, *e.g.* infants, bankrupts, enemy aliens, etc.

SECTION 63. BILLS OF EXCHANGE

1. Bills of Exchange Act, 1882. This act codified the law relating cheques and other bills of exchange, the most important kinds of negotiable instruments.

(Most of the rules laid down by the act as applying to bills of exchange generally apply also to cheques, which are bills of exchange drawn on a banker. But since cheques are bills payable on demand, the rules relating to presentation for acceptance do not apply to them.)

2. Bills of exchange defined. A bill of exchange is *"An unconditional order in writing, addressed by one person to another, signed by the person giving it, requiring the person to whom it is addressed to pay on demand, or at a fixed or determinable future time, a sum certain in money to or to the order of a specified person or to bearer"*: *Bills of Exchange Act*, 1882, *s*. 3 (1).

The person issuing the order is called the *drawer*, and the person to whom it is addressed is the *drawee*. If the bill is made payable to a named person, or to his order, it is an *Order Bill* and he is the *payee*. Otherwise a bill may be payable to *bearer*, and such a *bearer bill is transferable by mere delivery* (without any indorsement). An Order Bill, however, requires to be indorsed by the payee to effect transfer.

(The definition of bills of exchange should be memorised, and the comments on the definition (below) studied carefully.)

3. "Unconditional order." It must be a positive order to pay, not a mere request or authorisation. The usual wording is "Pay X . . .", though "Please pay X . . ." is also regarded as unconditional.

An order is not unconditional if:

(a) It gives the drawee a *discretion* whether to pay or not, *e.g.* "Pay X, if satisfied with goods consigned."
(b) It orders payment from a *particular fund*, *e.g.* "Pay X out of my current account." (But where an unconditional order to pay is merely coupled with mention of a particular fund, for the guidance of the drawee, this is sufficiently unconditional.)
(c) It requires the drawee to do *something more than to pay* money, *e.g.* "Pay X and notify me in writing."

4. Parties to a bill. The three necessary parties are the drawer, the drawee, and the payee (or bearer). One person

G

may fulfil two different capacities, *e.g.* where he draws a bill
payable to himself, or payable to the drawee (such as a cheque
on X Bank and payable to the bank in payment of a debt).
In such cases the bill is fully valid and can be negotiated in the
normal way.

But where the drawer and drawee are the same legal person
(*e.g.* where a branch of a company draws a bill on its head
office), the order is not strictly a bill of exchange, but a promissory note in favour of the payee: *B.E.A.*, *s.* 5 (2).

A bill is also treated as a promissory note if the payee is a
fictitious person or lacks contractual capacity: *B.E.A.*, *s.* 5 (2).

5. Addressed to drawee. He must be *identified* with reasonable certainty (depending on the circumstances).

A bill can be addressed to *joint drawees* (*e.g.* to X, Y, and Z),
but not to alternate drawees (*e.g.* X, Y, or Z).

6. Dating a bill. If a bill is *undated* the holder may insert
what he believes to be the correct date of issue (which may be
necessary for calculating time for payment).

If an *incorrect date* is inserted the bill is nevertheless enforceable by a holder in due course as though the date were correct:
B.E.A., *s.* 12.

A bill should bear the correct weekday date, but is not
invalid merely because it is post-dated, ante-dated, or Sunday
dated.

Any date appearing on a bill is *presumed to be the correct one*
unless the contrary is proved: *B.E.A.*, *s.* 13.

(NOTE: By B.E.A., *s.* 45, the drawer and indorsers are discharged from liability if the bill is not presented for payment on
the due date. B.E.A., *s.* 12 (above) therefore protects a holder in
due course against *s.* 45, where he has in good faith relied on an
incorrect date.)

7. Consideration and capacity.

(a) *Consideration.* Bills of exchange require to be supported
by consideration like other simple contracts, *but note*:

  (i) *Consideration is presumed, in favour of a holder.* Thus the
      normal burden of proof is reversed; in other contracts
      the person seeking to enforce the contract must prove
      that he has given consideration, in bills of exchange it is
      for the defendant to show that no consideration has been
      given.

    (ii) *Past consideration suffices, i.e.* any antecedent debt or other obligation: *B.E.A., s.* **27.**

  (b) *Capacity to contract* by bill of exchange is generally co-extensive with ordinary contractual capacity: *see s.* **13.** Thus an infant incurs no liability by signing a bill, but adult signatories to the same bill would be fully liable.

8. Sum payable. A bill must order the payment of a "sum certain in money," *i.e.* not in goods or services, etc. (Note also that the words used are "sum certain," not "a certain sum" which could mean an unspecified sum.)

  (a) *A sum may be certain within the meaning of the Act even though it is to be paid:*
    (i) *with interest* (usually calculated from the date of the bill),
    (ii) *by instalments,* or
    (iii) according to some indicated *rate of exchange, e.g.* where a bill drawn in pounds in Britain is payable in dollars in the U.S.A.: *B.E.A., s.* 9 (1).
  (b) *Words and figures.* Where the sum payable is stated in both *words and figures* (though this is not legally necessary) which do not agree, the sum denoted by the words is the amount payable: *B.E.A., s.* 9 (2).

9. Order and bearer bills. A bill may be drawn payable to bearer, or to the order of the drawer, payee, or (sometimes) drawee: *B.E.A., s.* 3 (1).

  (a) *Order bills* are those payable to a named payee or some person designated by him.

A bill is an order bill if:
    (i) the bill itself so states, or
    (ii) it is payable to a specified person without further words prohibiting transfer, *e.g.* "Pay X" or "Pay X or order." (But a bill payable to "X only" is not an order bill and in fact is not really a negotiable instrument at all, but an ordinary chose in action. Such a bill is enforceable by X, but if X sells it to Y, Y cannot enforce it against the drawer or drawee except through the agency of X.)

  (b) *Bearer bills* are those transferable by mere delivery.

A bill is a bearer bill if:
    (i) the bill itself so states,

     (ii) the last or only indorsement is in blank (see Blank indorsements, *s.* **64** below), or

     (iii) the bill is payable to a fictitious or non-existent person: *B.E.A.*, *s.* 7 (3) and 8.

    (*A non-existent person* is one of whose existence the drawer is unaware, or who does not exist at all. *A fictitious person* is one of whose existence the drawer is aware, but who was not intended by the drawer to receive payment: ✱ *Bank of England* v. *Vagliano Bros.* (1891).)

10. Inland and foreign bills.

(a) *An Inland bill* is one which is or purports to be (i) both drawn and payable within the British Isles, or (ii) drawn within the British Isles upon some person resident therein: *B.E.A.*, *s.* 4 (1).

(b) *Foreign Bills* are all other bills. But unless the contrary appears on the face of the bill the holder may treat it as an inland bill.

(This distinction is only important regarding (i) procedure on dishonour: *see s.* **66** *below*, and (ii) stamp duty.)

11. Bills in a set. A set of bills means a bill executed in *duplicate*, triplicate, etc. The payment of one part of a bill in set discharges the other parts also: *B.E.A.*, *s.* 71.

But if the drawee *mistakenly accepts two or more parts* of the same bill he will be liable on each part accepted as if it were a separate bill. Similarly a holder who indorses several parts is liable on each.

12. Inchoate instruments. Where a person *signs a blank piece of paper and* (a) *delivers* it to another, (b) *intending* it to be converted into a bill, it operates as authority to fill it up as a complete bill for any amount, using the signature already upon it as that of drawer, acceptor, or indorser: *B.E.A.*, *s.* 20 (1).

    Such a bill can only be enforced against the original signer if it is:

     (i) filled up within a *reasonable time of delivery*, and

     (ii) completed strictly *within the limits of the authority* given: *s.* 20 (2).

But after completion the bill is fully enforceable in the usual way. Thus where S signs an inchoate instrument and delivers it to X with authority to complete it for not more than £100, if X fills it up for £1000 he cannot force S to accept liability for that amount. But if X sells (negotiates) the bill to H, who takes it in good faith and without notice of the £100 limit, H as a holder in due course could enforce the bill for the full £1000 against S. (As to the meaning of "holder in due course," *see s.* **65**, **10**.)

13. Material alterations: s. 64.

(a) *What alterations are material:* amount, date, payee's name, terms of acceptance, place for payment, crossings on a cheque, altering order to bearer. (Alteration of the place where drawn is material if it changes an inland bill into a foreign bill, or *vice versa*.)

(b) *Effect. An unauthorised alteration discharges* from liability all persons who became party to the bill before the alteration, unless they expressly or implied assent to the alteration: ✱ *B.E.A., s.* 64.

(c) *Apparent and non-apparent alterations.* The effect of *s.* 64 differs slightly where the alteration is not apparent.

   (i) *Alteration not apparent:* a holder in due course can enforce as if it had not been altered, *i.e.* with the alteration deleted: *s.* 64.

   (ii) *Alteration apparent:* all parties prior to the alteration are discharged from liability (even against a subsequent holder in due course). But the bill will be valid and enforceable as between persons who became parties subsequent to the alteration.

EXAMPLE: S draws a cheque for £100 in favour of X, who fraudulently alters the amount to £1000 and sells (negotiates) it to Y who negotiates it to Z. Here: Z can enforce it against Y and X, even if the alteration is apparent; but he has no remedy against S unless he is a holder in due course and the alteration was not apparent (when he can make S liable for the unaltered amount).

(d) *Cheques:* The provisions of *s.* 64 apply to cheques, but note if a cheque is altered and the drawer later authorised the alteration (usually by initialling it) the effect is (i) the drawer is bound by the cheque as altered, (ii) other parties are protected by *s.* 64 unless they too have assented to the alteration.

14. Overdue bills. A bill is deemed to be overdue in the following circumstances:

- (*a*) Bills payable on demand are overdue when they have been in *circulation for an unreasonable time.*
- (*b*) Other bills are overdue when the *date fixed for payment has passed* without the bill being presented: *B.E.A.*, *s.* 36.

Effect of a bill being overdue is (i) that it can still be negotiated, but (ii) a transferee can get no better title to it than his transferor had, *i.e.* he cannot be a holder in due course.

(A holder in due course is one who takes a bill in good faith and for value *before* it is overdue, and he gets a perfect legal title to the bill irrespective of any defects in his transferor's title.)

15. Lost bills. If a bill is lost before it is overdue, the holder can compel the drawer to issue a *replacement* (though he cannot compel any other parties to sign the copy): *s.* 69.

Where this happens the drawer can demand *security* from the holder, to guard against the possibility of having to pay twice over, *i.e.* on the original bill and on the replacement.

16. Bills as conditional payment. A creditor who receives a cheque or other bill in settlement of his debt is not regarded as finally paid, since he has not received cash but merely a contractual right to obtain cash under the terms of the bill.

Payment by bill of exchange therefore is conditional, *i.e.* subject to a condition that if the bill is dishonoured the creditor shall have a right of action for the debt against the debtor: *see s.* 22.

17. Stamp duty. All bills of exchange must now be stamped 2*d.*: *Finance Act*, 1961, *s.* 3.

SECTION 64. SIGNATURE, DELIVERY, AND INDORSEMENT

1. Meaning of negotiation. A bill is negotiated when it is transferred *in such a way as to constitute the transferee the holder* of the bill, *i.e.* by delivery of a bearer bill, or by delivery plus indorsement of an order bill: *B.E.A.*, *s.* 31.

Negotiation may be prohibited by clear words written on the face of the bill, *e.g.* by marking the bill "Not negotiable."

NOTE: The addition of the words "*Not negotiable*" has differing effects in cheques and other bills.

  (i) *A cheque* crossed "not negotiable" remains transferable, but the transferee gets no better title than his transferor possessed, *i.e.* the instrument descends to the status of an ordinary assignable chose in action: *see s.* **67** *below.*
 (ii) *Any other bill* marked not negotiable ceases to be transferable altogether: *Hibernian Bank* v. *Gysin & Hanson* (1938).
(iii) A cheque or other bill marked "*Not transferable*" ceases to be transferable altogether (and therefore is not really a bill of exchange).

2. No liability without signature. Liability on a bill is incurred only by a person who has signed it, either as drawer, acceptor or indorser: *s.* 23.

  (a) *Signature in an assumed name,* or on behalf of a firm confers full liability: *s.* 23.
  (b) *Agent's signature.* Any agent signing a bill incurs full personal liability unless he makes it clear that he signs merely on behalf of someone else, *e.g.* by signing "*per pro*" or "*for and on behalf of*" his principal: *s.* 26. Thus a company director who signs a cheque merely as "director" or "manager" will be personally liable on the cheque: he should sign "J. Jones, director, *per pro* X Co. Ltd."
  (c) *Transferor by delivery.* A person who transfers a bill by delivery without indorsement (*i.e.* a bearer bill), is not liable upon it (except to his immediate transferee): *s.* 58.
  (d) *Indorsement by a stranger.* A person who is not a party to a bill but who signs it for any reason, is *fully liable* on the bill by reason of his signature, to a holder in due course: *s.* 56.

3. Signature sans recours. The drawer or any indorser can negative or limit his liability by clear words accompanying his signature on the bill: *s.* 16.

  (a) Signature *sans recours* ("without recourse") negatives all liability of the signer on the bill.
  (b) Signature *sans frais* ("without expenses") limits the signer's liability to the actual value of the bill, *i.e.* excludes liability for any expenses arising through dishonour and subsequent action for enforcement.

4. Forged signatures: s. 24. "Where a signature on a bill is *forged or placed thereon without the authority* of the person whose signature it purports to be, the forged or unauthorised signature is *wholly inoperative*" and no rights can be acquired by reason of such signature (unless the party against whom enforcement is sought is for some reason estopped from denying the genuineness of the signature).

NOTE:

(a) *Forged or unauthorised.* A forged signature is one which is *false or altered, e.g.* where X signs S's name to a cheque, or alters a signature to that of another person.

    An unauthorised signature is where X signs his own name, but without authority to do so, *e.g.* where an agent without authority to do so signs a cheque on behalf of his principal.

(b) *Ratification of unauthorised signatures.* An unauthorised signature can be ratified by the person by whose authority it purports to be made, thus validating it.

    (*A forgery cannot be ratified* in any circumstances since falsely making or altering any document is a criminal offence, and as such can never be validated: *Forgery Act*, 1916.)

(c) *Estoppel.* If a person knows that his signature to a bill has been forged, but leads others to believe that the signature is genuine he will be estopped from denying the genuineness of the signature and will be fully liable on the bill, *e.g.* where S habitually lets his wife forge his signature to cheques and obtain cash thereon, he may be estopped from denying the genuineness of such signature if a dispute later arises.

5. Effect of forged signatures.

(a) *Forgery of drawer's signature:* the bill is void since it fails to satisfy the definition in *B.E.A., s.* 3 (1) of an order "addressed by one person to another, *signed by the person giving it.*"

    (But the bill will remain *valid as between subsequent parties* to it, *e.g.* X draws a cheque in favour of himself on S's bank and forges S's signature as drawer. He then negotiates the cheque for value to Y. Here S incurs no liability on the bill (unless estoppel applies), but Y has full rights of action against X.)

(b) *Forgery of the acceptor's signature:* the acceptor incurs no liability, but a holder has full rights against other persons whose signatures are genuine, *i.e.* the drawer and indorsers.

(c) *Forgery of indorsement:* If the bill is an *order bill* indorsement is vitally necessary to effect legal transfer; therefore any forgery of such indorsement nullifies transfer. Thus the transferee gets no title to the bill, and has no claims against persons who became parties to it before the forgery. (But by *s.* 55 the bill will be valid and enforceable as between parties subsequent to the forgery.)

EXAMPLE: S draws a cheque in favour of A, who negotiates it to B. X steals it from B and negotiates it (by forging B's indorsement) to Y who negotiates it to Z. Z can enforce the bill against Y (and X), and Y can claim compensation from X. But neither Y nor Z have any claims against S, A, or B. (But B could compel S to issue another cheque, on giving adequate security: *see* **63**, 15 *above*.)

NOTE: In cases (a) and (c) above no person who takes the bill subsequent to the forgery can be a holder in due course (though by *ss.* 54, 55 he may have the legal rights of such a holder against persons who became parties subsequent to the forgery).

6. Delivery of bills. No person is liable upon a bill unless he has (i) *signed it*, and (ii) *delivered it*. An order bill must have the signature of the transferor on it in order to effect a valid transfer; but a bearer bill is transferable by delivery without indorsement.

NOTE:

(a) *Importance of delivery.* No person is liable on a bill, even if he has signed it, if he can prove positively that he did not deliver it, either actually or constructively. *Delivery means* deliberately and unconditionally transferring possession to another: *B.E.A.*, *s.* 21, (1). Thus if a bill is stolen from X, he has not delivered it and he (and prior parties) incur no liability except under (b) below.

(b) *Delivery presumed.* (i) Delivery is *conclusively presumed* in favour of a holder in due course, who can thus enforce a bill even against a person who can show that he did not deliver it: *s.* 21 (2) (ii) Delivery is also *rebuttably presumed* in favour of any holder (though here it can be disproved so as to avoid liability): *s.* 21 (3).

(c) *When delivery is rebuttably presumed.* Delivery is not presumed conclusively where (i) the bill was not complete or was irregular when it left the possession of the party to be charged, *e.g.* an inchoate instrument, or (ii) where the person seeking to enforce it is not a holder in due course.

(d) *Conditional delivery.* Where a bill is delivered subject to the fulfilment of some condition, delivery is incomplete until the condition is satisfied, and the bill is not enforceable between the parties to the conditional delivery. (But such bill is fully enforceable by a holder in due course: see (b) above.)

(e) *When deliverer liable.* Although a person who delivers a bill without signing it is not generally liable on the bill, he impliedly warrants (i) that he will indemnify his immediate transferee (but no one else) (ii) that the bill is genuine, and (iii) that he is entitled to transfer it. (This warranty does not apply if the transferee has not given value for the bill.)

7. Valid indorsements. An order bill requires the indorsement (signature) of the transferor in order for the transfer to be effective:

Requirements of valid indorsements:

(a) *It must be written* (on the back of the bill). The signature of the indorser is sufficient, without further words indicating transfer: *s.* 32 (1).

Indorsement may be in ink, print, pencil, etc. (but banks discourage indorsements in pencil, since they are easily obliterated; and indorsement by rubber stamp on a cheque will not usually be accepted by a bank).

(b) *Partial indorsement is ineffective.* The indorsement must relate to the full value of the bill: *s.* 32 (2).

(c) Where there are *several payees*, all should indorse (unless one has authority to indorse on behalf of the others, *e.g.* in a partnership): *s.* 32 (3).

(d) *Manner of indorsement should correspond exactly* with the drawing, *e.g.* if the payee's name is misspelt he should indorse in the misspelt version (adding the correct spelling if he wishes); *s.* 32 (4).

(e) *Allonge.* Where there is *insufficient space* on the bill for further indorsements, an additional piece of paper (called an allonge) may be glued to the bill to receive further indorsements.

(f) *Indorsement by agent.* An agent is personally liable as indorser unless he makes it clear that he indorses only on behalf of another, *e.g.* by indorsing "per pro" his principal: *see s.* **32,** 4.

(g) *Blank and Special indorsements.* If the indorser merely signs his own name (without adding that of the transferee), the indorsement is said to be *in blank* and the bill becomes payable to bearer (so that it can be further negotiated by mere delivery).

If the indorser adds the name of the transferee the bill is *specially indorsed,* and is payable to order, *i.e.* if the transferor wishes to negotiate it further he must himself indorse the bill.

(Thus by means of its indorsements, an order bill may be converted into a bearer bill at any time, and vice versa.)

8. Restrictive and conditional indorsements.

(a) *A restrictive indorsement* is one which prohibits further transfer or *limits transferability, e.g.* "Pay X only, signed J. Smith," or an indorsement indicating that the indorsee is to receive payment only as agent for the indorser: *s.* 35 (1).

By this means an indorser can *deprive the bill of its negotiability.* This will not affect the rights of the transferee as against the indorser, but will prevent him passing a full title to any further transferee: *s.* 35 (2).

(b) *Conditional indorsement* is one which makes payment or transfer subject to some condition, *e.g.* "Pay X, after his marriage to Z."

Such a condition can be ignored by the payer: *s.* 33.

(c) *Indorsement sans recours.* If the indorser seeks to restrict his liability to the transferee by indorsing *sans recours,* or *sans frais (see* 3 *above),* the transferee can refuse to accept the bill with this indorsement. If he does take the bill so indorsed, he is bound by the restriction.

(d) *Falculative indorsement* is one in which the indorser waives some of his legal rights in favour of the transferee, *e.g.* indorsement with "notice of dishonour waived": *s.* 16 (2). In such a case the transferee and subsequent transferees can enforce the bill against the indorser without giving notice of dishonour, etc.

SECTION 65. LIABILITY OF PARTIES

1. Parties to a bill. A party means a person who is liable on the bill, *i.e.* the drawer, acceptor, and indorsers.

However, the payee (before he indorses the bill) has rights under it, and can also be described as a party.

2. Order of liability.

(a) *Before acceptance* the drawer is the principal debtor and primarily liable.

(b) *After acceptance,* the drawee takes over primary liability (and the drawer and indorsers are merely sureties for him).

(c) *After indorsement,* the indorser becomes liable as a surety for the value of the bill.

The holder can thus enforce the bill against the drawer, the acceptor (primarily) and any indorsers. He can sue any one or he can sue any combination of them, and each is liable for the full value of the bill.

(*As between themselves* the parties have *no right of contribution*: contrast guarantors, *see s.* **75**. But any party who has been made to pay the full amount on the bill has a right of action for that amount against his immediate transferor.)

3. The drawer: s. 55.

(a) *Liability.* He engages that (i) on due presentment it will be *paid* according to its tenor, and (ii) *if dishonoured*, he will compensate the holder or any indorser who has suffered loss thereby (provided necessary proceedings on dishonour are taken).

(b) *Estoppel.* He is precluded from denying to a holder in due course the existence and capacity of the *payee*.

4. The drawee/acceptor. He is the person to whom the order is addressed. He is under no liability on the bill unless and until he accepts it, after which he assumes primary liability (and is called the acceptor).

Where a bill is *not payable on demand* it must be presented to the drawee for him to signify his acceptance of liability (or to reject it), and later presented to him again for payment. A bill *payable on demand*, such as a cheque, is merely presented for payment without any prior presentation for acceptance.

(a) *Acceptor's liability.* He engages that he will *pay* the bill on due presentment for payment according to its tenor.

(b) *Estoppel.* He is precluded from denying (i) the existence, capacity and signature of the drawer, (ii) the existence and capacity of the payee of an order bill (though he may deny the validity or genuineness of the payee's indorsement): *s.* 54.

5. Indorsers. They are people (including the payee) who indorse an order bill in order to transfer it.

(a) *Liability.* They engage (i) that on due presentment the bill will be accepted and paid according to its tenor, and (ii) that if it is dishonoured they will compensate the holder (or any indorser who is compelled to pay it) providing necessary proceedings for dishonour are taken: *s.* **66**.

(b) *Estoppel.* An indorser is precluded from denying (i) to a holder in due course—the genuineness of the drawer's signature and of all indorsements prior to his own, (ii) to a later indorser—the validity of the bill or his own title when he indorsed it.

(Remember that any person signing a bill otherwise than as drawer or acceptor incurs the full liability of an indorser.)

6. Accommodation party. This means a person who has signed a bill as drawer, acceptor or indorser *without receiving value* therefor.

An accommodation party is *liable* on the bill to any holder for value, but not to the person whom he has accommodated, *i.e.* the person to whom he lent the credit of his name.

An accommodation bill is one of which the acceptor is an accommodation party: *s.* 59 (3), *i.e.* a person who accepts for the honour of the drawer of some other party. (When a bill is not accepted by the original drawee, some other person may step in to accept the bill to save the drawer or any indorser from being sued for dishonour. This is called acceptance for honour.)

7. Referee in case of need. The drawer or any indorser who fears that a bill may not be accepted by the drawee, may designate some other person in addition to the drawee as "referee in case of need," to whom the holder may apply for payment (if he wishes) in the event of dishonour by the drawee: *s.* 15.

If the referee accepts liability, the bill becomes an accommodation bill and he is said to be accepting for honour of the drawer or any indorser on whose behalf he intervenes: *ss.* 65–68.

8. Fictitious and non-existing payees: s. 7. Where the payee of a bill is a fictitious or non-existing person, the bill may be treated as payable to bearer (and can be negotiated without the indorsement of such payee): *s.* 7 (3).

(a) *Fictitious payee* means someone whom *the drawer did not intend* to receive payment, though he may be an existing person and may be named by the drawer as payee.

EXAMPLES: (i) V's clerk G obtained V's acceptance of bills G had forged, and apparently drawn by a customer of V in favour of X, a person known to V. G then forged X's indorsement to the bills and obtained their value. HELD: The clerk was the real drawer of the bills, and he knew of X's existence but did not intend him to obtain payment, therefore X was a fictitious payee and the bills were payable to bearer: * *Bank of England* v. *Vagliano Bros.* (1908).

(ii) A clerk induced his employer to draw cheques payable to X, to whom the employer owed money. The employer intended X to be the payee, but the amounts of the cheques were forged by the clerk, who later forged X's indorsements and obtained payment. HELD: The cheques were not payable to a fictitious payee since the drawer intended X to receive payment, though not of the amounts stated. Thus the cheques were order bills, needing a valid indorsement by X to effect transfer, therefore the forged indorsements by the clerk were ineffective and the transferee obtained no title: *Vinden* v. *Hughes* (1905).

(b) *Non-existing payee* means someone (living or not) *of whose existence the drawer is unaware*, even though he may have intended him to receive payment.

EXAMPLE: A clerk induced his employer to draw cheques in favour of X (an actual person), by pretending that the money was owing to X. The clerk then forged X's indorsements and obtained the value of the cheques. HELD: X was a non-existing payee, and these cheques were therefore bearer bills. Consequently transfer would have been effective without indorsement at all: *Clutton* v. *Attenborough* (1897).

9. Position of holder.

(a) *Meaning of holder.* He is *the payee or indorsee* of a bill, who is in possession of it, or *the bearer* of a bearer bill: *s.* 2.

Thus a person who takes an order bill by means of a forged indorsement is not a holder, since he is neither the indorsee of it, nor the bearer of a bearer bill.

(b) *Position of holder.* He can *enforce* the bill (i) against any person who has signed it, and (ii) against the transferor from whom he obtained it, whether that person signed it or not.

To have full rights of enforcement he should (i) have given value himself (in which case he is probably a holder in due course: *see below*), or (ii) have obtained it from a person who has given value for it (in which case he is a holder for value: *see* 11 *below*).

But in any case the law presumes in favour of any holder that his possession is supported by valuable consideration, and in any action brought by the holder it will be for the defendant to disprove this presumption (not for the holder to prove the existence of consideration): *see s.* **63,** 7 *above.*

10. Holder in due course: s. 29.

(a) *Meaning.* He is a holder who has taken a bill (i) complete and regular on the face of it (ii) before it was overdue and without notice that it had been dishonoured (if such was the case), (iii) in good faith and for value and (iv) without notice of any defect in the transferor's title: *s.* 29 (1).

NOTE: (i) That the *payee* cannot be a holder in due course, since he did not take the bill by the process of negotiation, *i.e.* he was one of the original parties to the issue of the bill: *R.E. Jones Ltd.* v. *Waring & Gillow, Ltd.* (1926).

(ii) A person who derives his title through a *forged indorsement* cannot be a holder in due course, since a holder is a person who derives his title through a valid indorsement (*s.* 2) and a forgery is an invalid and inoperative indorsement (*s.* 24).

(b) *Rights.* A holder in due course can (i) sue on the bill in his own name, and (ii) defeat any defences arising from defects of title or arising from the relations of the parties before he took the bill.

Thus the only defences that can be raised against his claims are (i) that he does not satisfy the definition given in *s.* 29 (1), *e.g.* that the bill was overdue when he took it, or had some patent defect (such as disagreement of words and figures of the amount), (ii) that a forged indorsement vitiates his title, (iii) that issue, acceptance or negotiation of the bill were produced by fraud, coercion or illegality (in which case the holder in due course can still enforce the bill but only if he can prove positively that subsequent to the alleged fraud, coercion or illegality, value has in good faith been given for the bill, *i.e.* the burden of proof shifts to the holder): *s.* 30 (2).

(c) *Presumption in favour of holder.* Every holder of a bill is presumed to be a holder in due course until the contrary is proved.

(d) *Good faith.* Negligence of the holder (*e.g.* failure to make reasonable enquiries) does not preclude him from being a holder in due course, *i.e.* does not necessarily amount to bad faith.

11. Holder for value.

(a) *Meaning.* He is a holder of a bill for which *value has at some time* been given; he need not have given value himself.

(b) *Rights.* He can enforce the bill against all persons who became parties prior to the giving of such value; *s.* **27.** (Remember also the presumption in favour of all holders that value has been given for the bill: *s.* **63, 7.**)

He can *sue* on the bill in his own name, but he obtains *no better title than his transferor possessed.* Thus if a holder in due course gives the bill as a present to V, V is a holder for value (since value has been given by the holder in due course) and has as good a title as his transferor, *i.e.* in this case, a perfect title.

EXAMPLE: S draws a cheque in favour of A, who indorses it for value to B, who gives it gratuitously to C who gives it gratuitously to D. Presuming all indorsements are valid, D is a holder for value (even though he did not himself give value) and can enforce the cheque against all persons who became parties prior to value being given, *i.e.* against S and A, but not against B or C.

SECTION 66. ACCEPTANCE, PAYMENT, AND DISHONOUR

1. Acceptance of bills of exchange. Bills not payable on demand must be accepted by the drawee as a pre-requisite to payment. (Bills payable on demand, including cheques, by-pass this intervening stage and proceed straight to payment.)

(a) *Drawee's liability.* The drawee is under no liability to holders of the bill until he accepts liability, by signing across the face of the bill. (Though he may be liable to damages for breach of contract to the drawer if he improperly refuses to accept a bill which he was contractually bound to accept.)

Acceptance is *signified by* the drawee signing across the face of the bill, with or without addition of the date or such words as "accepted": *s.* **17.**

(b) *When made.* Acceptance may be made at any time, even before the drawer's signature of the bill (though usually after). A bill may also be accepted when overdue or when previously dishonoured: *s.* **18.**

If a bill payable after sight is dishonoured by non-acceptance but the drawee later changes his mind and accepts it, the holder is entitled to have the acceptance back-dated to the date when it was first presented for acceptance: *s.* 18 (3). This may be important, *e.g.* where a bill is payable 3 months after sight by the drawee.

(c) *Kinds of acceptance.* Acceptance may be either *general* (unqualified acceptance of the bill as drawn) or *qualified.* The holder is entitled to general acceptance, and may treat the bill as dishonoured if only a qualified acceptance is offered: *s.* 44 (1). If he takes a qualified acceptance he loses his right of recourse against prior parties to the bill (except such of them as authorised him to do so): *s.* 44 (2).

(d) *Kinds of qualified acceptance.*

  (i) *Conditional, e.g.* "Accepted subject to deduction for expenses."
  (ii) *Partial, e.g.* for part only of the sum specified.
  (iii) *Local, i.e.* payable only at a particular place. (Merely naming a place for payment is general acceptance, unless it is to be made only at the place named.)
  (iv) *Qualified as to time, e.g.* "accepted payable in 6 months" where the bill specified 3 months.
  (v) *Acceptance by some only* of several joint drawees.

2. Presentment for acceptance. A bill payable after sight must be presented for acceptance within a reasonable time, and if not so presented the drawer and all indorsers prior to presentation are discharged from liability: *s.* 40 (1).

Presentment is only necessary where:

  (i) The bill is *payable after sight* or after demand (since presentation will enable calculation of the period after which the bill shall be payable).
  (ii) There is an *express stipulation* for presentment.
  (iii) The bill is payable *elsewhere than at the residence* or place of business of the drawee, *e.g.* at a bank. (But the drawee for his own convenience may nominate his bank or some other place as the place for payment, in which case the bill is said to be *domiciled.* Domiciling a bill is not qualified acceptance, unless it is done in such a way as to prohibit the holder from seeking payment anywhere else.)

3. Presentment for acceptance is excused, and the bill may be *treated as dishonoured* where:

(*a*) The drawee is dead, bankrupt, lacks capacity or is a fictitious person.

(b) Presentment is impossible, *e.g.* because the drawee cannot be found.

(c) Acceptance is refused: *s.* 42 (2).

4. Presentment for payment. A bill not payable on demand must be presented for payment on the due date (as fixed by the bill, *e.g.* three months after acceptance, or "after sight"), subject to any allowance for Days of Grace: see below.

(a) *Days of Grace:* Three days are added to the time for payment fixed by the bill (unless the bill expressly provides otherwise) and payment falls due on the last day of grace: *s.* 14 (1). Where the bill is payable by instalments the days of grace are available for each instalment.

    If the last day of grace falls on: (i) a Sunday, Christmas Day, or Good Friday, the bill is payable on the preceding business day, (ii) a Bank Holiday (other than Christmas Day or Good Friday), or a Sunday immediately preceded by a Bank Holiday, the bill is payable on the next ensuing business day.

(b) *Presentment must be at a reasonable hour* on a business day, and at the proper place: *s.* 45 (3).

(c) *Delay in presentment is excused* if due to circumstances beyond the holder's control: *s.* 46 (1).

(d) *A bill not presented within due time* is not invalidated, but it cannot be enforced against persons who drew or indorsed it unless such person's signature was added within a reasonable time. (Compare the position of the drawer of a *cheque*, who is discharged by delay only to the extent he has suffered damage: *s.* 74 and *see s.* **67,** 2.)

(e) *Presentment for payment may be excused* where: (i) after reasonable diligence it cannot be effected, *e.g.* because the acceptor cannot be found; (ii) the drawee is a fictitious person; or (iii) presentment has been waived: *s.* 45 (2).

(f) *A bill is dishonoured by non-payment when* (i) it is properly presented but payment is refused or cannot be obtained, or (ii) presentment is excused: *s.* 47 (1). An offer of partial payment can be treated as dishonour, or it can be accepted and the bill treated as dishonoured for the balance.

5. Procedure on dishonour. The holder of a dishonoured bill must notify the fact of dishonour to all prior parties against whom he reserves a right of action; persons not so notified are discharged.

Similarly any indorser must reserve his rights of action by notifying parties prior to himself.

(a) *Inland Bills:* Notice of dishonour can be in *any form,* oral or written, providing it clearly identifies the bill: *s.* 49 (5). Return of a dishonoured bill is sufficient notice to the drawer: *s.* 49 (6). Notice must be given within a reasonable time of dishonour: *s.* 49 (12).

(b) *Foreign Bills: Noting and Protesting.* Formal notice of dishonour is required in the case of foreign bills (and is optional in the case of inland bills).

Formal notice is achieved by getting the bill re-presented by a *notary public* (or, if none can be found, by a householder in the presence of witnesses), who *notes* on the bill the answer obtained, if any.

The notary or householder then issues a formal certificate of dishonour (called the *Protest*), setting out the circumstances of dishonour. The Protest and a copy of the noted bill are then sent by the holder to the person or persons he intends to make liable.

6. Notice of dishonour is dispensed with:

(a) When after exercise of reasonable diligence it *cannot be given, e.g.* where the address cannot be found.

(b) *When waived,* expressly or by implication, by the person entitled to notice.

(c) *As regards the drawer:* (i) where drawer and drawee are the same person, (ii) where the drawee is a fictitious person or lacks capacity, (iii) where the drawer is the person to whom presentment for payment was made, (iv) where the drawee was under no obligation to the drawer to accept the bill, or (v) where the drawer has countermanded payment.

(d) *As regards the indorser:* (i) where the drawee is a fictitious person or has no capacity, and the indorser was aware of this when he indorsed, (ii) where the indorser is the person to whom the presentment was made, or (iii) where the bill was accepted or made only for the indorser's accommodation.

7. Discharge of bills occurs:

(a) *By payment in due course, i.e.* to a bona fide holder without the payer having notice of any defect in the holder's title: *s.* 59.

Note that by *s.* 60 where a banker, in reliance on a forged indorsement, pays a bill drawn on him (i) in good faith and (ii) in the ordinary course of business, the bill is effectively discharged and the bank incurs no liability. (*The Cheques Act,* 1957, *s.* 1, reduces the importance of this rule by providing that indorsements are no longer necessary in most cases: *see s.* **67.**)

(b) *By an acceptor becoming the holder of all rights* on the bill at or after its maturity: *s.* 61.

(c) *By renunciation by the holder* of all rights against the acceptor: *s.* 62. (Renunciation must be in writing, or the bill must be delivered up to the acceptor.)

(d) *By intentional cancellation* by the holder or his agent: *s.* 63. (Unintentional cancellation is ineffective.)

(e) *By material alteration of the bill or its acceptance,* without the consent of all parties liable upon it, *e.g.* by alteration of date, amount, etc.: *s.* 64.

SECTION 67. CHEQUES

1. Definition. A cheque is a bill of exchange drawn on a banker and payable on demand: *B.E.A., s.* 73.

It is not necessary that the words "on demand" should appear on a cheque, since all bills are treated as payable on demand where no time is specified for payment: *s.* 10.

2. Stale and overdue cheques.

(a) *A stale cheque* is one which has been in circulation for a considerable period of time. Banks generally refuse to honour a cheque more than six months old.

(b) *An overdue cheque* is one which has been in circulation for an unreasonable time: *s.* 36. (A person who takes an overdue cheque cannot be a holder in due course.)

NOTE:

(i) *What is a reasonable time?* This depends on all the circumstances of each case. Thus where a cheque is intended by the drawer to be presented within two or three days, failure to present within that time might amount to unreasonable delay: *Wheeler* v. *Young* (1897). By contrast, if a cheque was issued overseas for payment in Britain time would have to be allowed for its transmission to Britain in computing what is a reasonable time.

(ii) *Discharge of drawer.* If not presented within a reasonable time the drawer is discharged to the extent of any damage he suffers from the delay. In the absence of such damage he remains fully liable for 6 years, after which his liability is statute-barred: *Limitation Act,* 1939.

(iii) *Summary on delay in presentation.* (a) *Bills other than cheques*—drawer and indorsers completely discharged: *B.E.A., s.* 45; (b) *Delay re cheques:* (i) indorsers discharged under *s.* 45; (ii) drawer discharged only to extent of damage suffered: *s.* 74.

(iv) *Damage suffered by drawer.* Example: A drew a cheque for £100 in favour of B, who failed to present it for some time. When drawn, A's account had funds to meet the cheque, but during the intervening time the bank went into liquidation. HELD: B could claim for the money as a creditor of the *bank*, but A was under no liability and B had no claim against him: *Wheeler* v. *Young* (1897).

3. Undated and post-dated cheques.

(a) *Undated cheques.* A banker is not bound to honour such a cheque, but it must be remembered that any holder is entitled to fill in the correct date: *s.* 20 (1). Any date appearing on a bill is presumed to be the correct date.

(b) *Post-dated cheques.* These are not really cheques, since they are not payable on demand. However, a banker is entitled to pay a post-dated cheque when it falls due. If he pays it before its date he cannot debit the customer's account, and must bear the loss if the customer stops the cheque before its due date.

(Post-dated cheques are frequently used today instead of bills of exchange payable at some time after sight, *e.g.* where a purchaser of goods issues a post-dated cheque for goods to be delivered later, thus being entitled to stop the cheque if the goods are not delivered when agreed.)

4. Stamping. A cheque must be stamped (2*d.*). The stamp can now be impressed, printed or merely adhesive (though an adhesive stamp must be cancelled by the person issuing the cheque): *Finance Act,* 1961.

5. Payment by cheque.

(a) *Conditional payment.* Payment by any bill is conditional only. A creditor is entitled therefore to refuse payment by cheque, and in any case payment is not effective until the cheque is honoured. (But a creditor who takes a cheque in payment may be estopped from action against the debtor if the cheque is dishonoured because he negligently failed to demand payment himself. Though the cheque will remain enforceable by other parties against the drawer for six years: *Limitation Act*, 1939.)

(b) *Cheques through the post.* If a cheque is sent through the post and is lost, the loss falls on the sender, unless the creditor requested this method of payment: *see s*. **22**. Such a request will not be implied; it must be express: *Pennington* v. *Crossley & Sons* (1897).

(c) *Cheques as evidence of payment.* An unindorsed cheque which appears to have been paid by the banker on whom it was drawn is prima facie evidence of receipt by the payee of the sum stated on the cheque, even without the payee's indorsement: *Cheques Act*, 1957, *s*. **3**.

6. Crossings on cheques. The object of crossing a cheque is *to convey instructions* that it is not to be paid otherwise than through a bank, or to make some other stipulation as to the manner of payment: *s*. **76**.

A crossing is a *material part* of a cheque and any unauthorised alteration of a crossing is unlawful (*s*. **78**) and discharges the cheque: *s*. **64**.

The drawer or any holder may cross a cheque, or add to an existing crossing, *e.g.* where the holder of a cheque crossed generally adds the words "Not negotiable."

Crossings are usually intended as instructions to the paying banker, but a crossing "account payee" is an instruction to the collecting banker.

7. Types of crossing.

(a) *General crossing:* indicated by drawing two transverse lines across the face of the cheque, thus / /, with or without the addition of the words "& Co." between the lines (or such other words as "not negotiable": see below).

    The effect of such a crossing is to make the cheque payable only to a collecting banker, *i.e.* it precludes the paying banker from paying cash for the cheque across the counter.

(b) *Special crossing:* indicating the name of a particular banker, with or without the addition of two transverse lines. *The effect* is that the paying banker must pay the cheque only to the collecting banker named on the crossing, and to no other.

(c) *Not negotiable:* this general crossing deprives the cheque of its negotiability, and it becomes an ordinary transferable chose in action, *i.e.* it can be assigned, but the assignee obtains no better title than was possessed by his assignor: *s*. **81**.

Thus where a clerk took a blank cheque from his employer, which was already crossed "not negotiable," and fraudulently made it payable to P, it was HELD that the employer could recover the value from P (who had obtained cash), since the clerk had no title to the cheque and P could get no better title than the clerk had: * *Wilson & Meeson* v. *Pickering* (1946).

(d) *Account payee (or Account payee only):* this is not a statutory crossing but is recognised and obeyed by banker's custom. A collecting bank which collects for some person other than the payee named may therefore be liable for negligence. (A paying banker is not generally affected by this crossing.)

8. Alterations on a cheque. Any material alteration of a cheque or other bill discharges from liability any party to the bill who did not assent to the alteration. On a cheque, alterations of date, amount, name of payee, or of any crossing would be material.

Bankers therefore should not pay a cheque unless any alteration is initialled by the drawer, and where the words "or order" have been altered to "bearer" the normal practice is to insist on the drawer's full signature by way of assent.

(Note the distinction between apparent and non-apparent alterations: *see s.* **63**, 13, *above*.)

9. Indorsements. The general rules about indorsements apply to cheques.

Note that the * *Cheques Act*, 1957, *s.* 1 dispenses with the need for an indorsement where the apparent payee or indorsee of a cheque is paying it into his own account. But the *Committee of the London Clearing Banks* has listed the following instruments as still requiring indorsement:

(a) Cheques with receipt forms attached.
(b) Bills other than cheques.
(c) Promissory notes.
(d) Drafts drawn on H.M. Paymaster, etc.
(e) Cheques cashed over the counter.

10. Duty of bankers as to crossed cheques. The banker is liable to the true owner for any loss occasioned where:

(a) He pays a cheque which is *crossed specially to more than one banker* (unless the additional special crossing merely indicates that one of the bankers named is to collect merely as agent for the other).

(*b*) He pays a cheque *crossed generally otherwise than to a bank, i.e.* treats it as an open cheque.

(*c*) He pays a cheque *crossed specially otherwise than to the banker named* in the crossing or his agent: *s.* 79.

11. Protection of paying banker. The drawee bank is statutorily protected against liability if it pays in the following circumstances:

(a) *Cheques with forged indorsements:* provided they are paid (i) in good faith and (ii) in the ordinary course of business: ✳ *B.E.A., s.* 60.

(b) *Crossed cheques:* provided the bank pays a cheque drawn upon it, (i) in accordance with the crossing, (ii) in good faith, and (iii) without negligence: ✳ *B.E.A., s.* 80.

(c) *Cheques not indorsed or irregularly indorsed:* provided the cheque is drawn on the bank and is paid (i) in good faith, (ii) in the ordinary course of business: ✳ *Cheques Act,* 1957, *s.* 1.

12. Protection of collecting banker. A collecting banker, that is one who presents a cheque to the drawee bank on behalf of a customer, is protected from liability where he receives payment for a *customer* who has no title or defective title, provided he does so (i) in good faith and (ii) without negligence (whether or not the cheque is crossed): ✳ *Cheques Act,* 1957, *s.* 4.

NOTE:

(*a*) *The section applies only to customers.* A person becomes a customer as soon as he opens an account, *i.e.* where the bank obliges someone, not having an account, by cashing his cheques from time to time, this does not make such person a customer: *Commissioners of Taxation* v. *English, Scottish & Australian Bank Ltd.* (1920).

(*b*) The following have been held to amount to *negligence* by a collecting bank:

(i) *Opening an account* for someone without making *adequate enquiries* about him: *Hampstead Guardians* v. *Barclays Bank* (1923).

(ii) Collecting payment for a customer of a cheque made out to the *customer's employer* without making enquiries: *Underwood Ltd.* v. *Martins Bank* (1924).

(iii) Paying into a customer's private account a cheque payable to him in an *official capacity*: *Ross* v. *London County Bank* (1919).

(iv) Receiving payment for a customer of cheques clearly indicating they are payable to him only as *agent* for someone else: *Bute (Marquess)* v. *Barclays Bank* (1955).

(v) Where a bank uses a computer to identify the branch on which a cheque is drawn and a customer with accounts at two branches alters a cheque from branch A to draw it on branch B and the computer fails to recognise the change, if the customer then stops the cheque by notice to branch B and the computer directs the cheque to branch A which pays the cheque, the bank may be liable for negligence: *Burnett* v. *Westminster Bank, Ltd.* (1966).

(c) Where a collecting banker is negligent he may be sued for damages for the *tort of conversion* by the true owner of the cheque.

NOTE: There is no corresponding duty of care imposed on the drawer or acceptor of any bill: *Scholfield* v. *Londesborough* (1896).

13. Termination of banker's authority: s. 75. A banker's authority to pay a cheque drawn by his customer is terminated by:

(a) *Countermand of payment,* written or oral, though if oral countermand is made, it is the practice to insist on written confirmation and merely to postpone payment pending receipt of confirmation.

(b) *Notice of the customer's death.* Observe that it is not the death which terminates the authority, but notice of the death.

(c) *Notice of the lunacy* of the customer.

(d) *Notice of the presentation of a bankruptcy petition* against the customer.

Note that if the bank receives notice of an *act of bankruptcy* committed by the customer, if can still pay out to the customer himself but should not pay out cheques drawn by him in favour of third parties (otherwise it may be liable to make good such payments to the trustee in bankruptcy): *Re Keever* (1966).

(e) *The making of a receiving order* in bankruptcy against the customer.

(f) *The service of a garnishee order* attaching the balance of the customer's account, *i.e.* a court order addressed to a debtor commanding him not to pay the stated debt to his creditor but to hold the money pending further orders from the court (which may eventually direct that the money shall be paid to some other person).

(g) *Notice of a breach of trust, i.e.* when a customer is about to use trust funds for his own purposes.

(h) *Notice of a defect in the presenter's title.*

(i) *Insufficient credit* in the customer's account, or where payment would increase the customer's indebtness beyond some agreed limit.

The bank is entitled to refuse to pay a cheque if it exceeds the customer's entitlement by as little as a half-penny, and it cannot pay part of a cheque. If it wrongly refuses to honour a cheque properly drawn it is liable to the customer for damages for breach of contract, but is not liable to the holder. A bank may also be liable for damages for libel if it makes a defamatory comment unjustifiably on a cheque, *e.g.* where it wrongly marks a cheque "No funds."

SECTION 68. PROMISSORY NOTES AND MISCELLANEOUS INSTRUMENTS

1. Promissory note: s. 83. This is an unconditional promise in writing by one person to another, signed by the maker, and engaging to pay on demand or at a fixed or determinable future time a sum certain in money to or to the order of a specified person or to bearer.

A promissory note is *inchoate* and incomplete until delivery to the payee or bearer: *s.* 83.

2. Differences from bills of exchange.

(a) *Acceptance* of a note is never necessary, since there is no drawee.

(b) A promissory note (unlike a bill) cannot be drawn *in a set.*

(c) The maker is the *person liable* to pay. (In a bill, the drawer is only liable until the drawee accepts.)

(d) A promissory note must contain an *unconditional promise* to pay. (The acceptor of a bill may make a conditional promise to pay.)

(e) A promissory note is a *promise to pay*: a bill is an order to pay.

(f) *A bill may be treated as a promissory* note where (i) drawer and drawee are the same person; (ii) the drawee is fictitious or lacks capacity; *s.* 5 (2).

3. Bank notes. These are promissory notes payable to bearer. When presenting a note for payment it is not necessary for the bearer to reveal how he came by the note, but if the circumstances arouse suspicion the bank would be entitled to refuse payment until satisfied of good faith; if, however, the bearer sued the bank for its refusal, the burden of proving bad faith would rest on the bank.

4. Joint, and joint and several notes. Where a note is issued by two or more persons, their liability may be joint or joint and several, depending on the circumstances.

(a) *On a joint note*, each maker is fully liable for the whole amount, but a person suing to enforce the note has only *one cause of action* and can sue all, or one or any combination, but cannot later bring a second action against parties not sued in the first: see also *s.* **35,** 4.

If the maker of a joint note dies, his estate ceases to be liable on the note.

(b) *On a joint and several note*, each maker is fully liable but a holder has *several rights of action, e.g.* he may sue all, or any one, or bring successive actions against the makers. And the death of a maker does not relieve his estate from liability on the note.

NOTE: Where a note runs "I promise to pay" and is signed by two or more makers, it is deemed to be a joint and several note: *s.* 85.

5. Miscellaneous banking instruments.

(a) *Bankers' Drafts.* These are drafts to order payable on demand, drawn by an office of a bank upon itself or upon some other office of the same bank: *Bills of Exchange Act* (1882) *Amendment Act*, 1932.

Drafts may be crossed, and the crossing has the same effect as the crossing on a cheque. *The Cheques Act*, 1957, extends the protections given bankers by the *B.E.A.* to cover bankers drafts.

(b) *Conditional orders.* These are documents ordering payment of money subject to the fulfilment of some stated condition. They may be crossed like cheques, and the *Cheques Act*, 1957 extends the provisions of the *B.E.A.* protecting bankers to conditional orders: *see s.* **67.**

Note that a document apparently a cheque may in fact be a conditional order, *e.g.* a cheque stating on it that payment is not to be made *unless* an attached receipt form is signed. But the mere fact that a cheque contains a receipt form does not make it a conditional order, unless payment is made conditional on the signing of the receipt.

(c) *Dividend and Interest warrants.* These are drafts issued by a company and ordering its bank to pay the stated sum to a named person. They can be crossed like cheques, and are covered by the protections given by the *Cheques Act*, 1957.

(d) *Deposit receipts.* These are acknowledgments by a banker that he holds funds to a certain amount for the depositor. They are not negotiable instruments.

6. Quasi-negotiable instruments. The following documents have some of the qualities of negotiability, but not all, and are therefore not negotiable instruments:

(a) *Bills of Lading:* receipts for goods shipped, signed by the carrier or his agent. A bill of lading is a *document of title* to the goods specified therein, and possession of the bill entitles the holder to delivery of the goods. But it is not a negotiable instrument, so that a transferee gets no better title than was possessed by his transferor.

(b) *Dock warrants:* documents issued by a dock or warehouse company acknowledging that it holds certain goods on behalf of the person named, or his indorsee. They are *documents of title* assignable by delivery plus indorsement, but they are not negotiable instruments and the indorsee gets no better title than his transferor.

(c) *American share certificates* usually have a transfer form printed on the back, and the owner can sign this form leaving the name of the transferee blank. This then operates as a power of attorney to a subsequent transferee to fill in his own name or the name of another, the person named being entitled to apply to the company for registration as a shareholder. Such transferee gets no better title than his transferor.

(d) *IOU*'s. These are merely written admission of the existence of a debt (with an implied promise to pay at some future date). They are not negotiable but *can be assigned* under *s.* 136, *L.P.A.*, 1925.

Note that if the document contained an express promise to pay, it would be a promissory note.

NEGOTIABLE INSTRUMENTS

1. How would you define a negotiable instrument? What are the characteristics of such an instrument, and how does it differ from other choses in action? (62. 1, 2, 3.)

2. What persons are liable on a negotiable instrument and to whom? (62. 4.)

3. Define a bill of exchange. Explain what is meant by saying that a bill must be unconditional. What is a conditional order and what is its effect? (63. 2, 3; 68. 5.)

4. What is meant by saying that there must be three parties to a bill of exchange? What is the effect where the drawer and drawee are one and the same person? (63. 4; 68. 2.)

5. X is the holder of an undated cheque, and when he presents it to his bank the bank refuses to take it. Explain why the bank refused it and what X can do to remedy the situation. (63. 6; 67. 3.)

6. "A cheque is an exception to the rule that past consideration is no consideration." Discuss. (12. 4 (F); 63. 7.)

7. What is meant by saying that a bill must order the payment of a "sum certain" and not a "certain sum" of money? (63. 8.)

8. Distinguish between order and bearer bills, and explain how each can be negotiated. Distinguish also between non-existing and fictitious payees. (63. 9; 62. 1; 65. 8.)

9. Explain briefly the meaning of: (a) Inland and foreign bills; (b) Bills in a set; (c) Inchoate instruments. (63. 10–12.)

10. What is, and what is the effect of, a material alteration of a bill? Why is it important to distinguish between apparent and non-apparent alterations? (63. 13; 67. 8.)

11. What is meant by an overdue bill? How does an overdue cheque differ from a stale cheque? (63. 14; 67. 2.)

12. X owes Y £100 and draws a cheque for that amount in favour of Y. The cheque is lost or stolen before Y is able to present it to his bank. Y now maintains that he has not been paid. What is the legal position? (63. 15, 16; 67. 5.)

13. What is meant by the negotiation of a bill? Explain the effect of marking a bill or a cheque "not negotiable." (64. 1.)

14. X negotiates a bearer bill to Y for value and later, when the bill is dishonoured, X maintains that he is under no liability (a) to Y, or (b) to any person to whom Y has negotiated the bill.

What is the legal position? (**64. 2.**) Would it make any difference to Y's position if he had not given value? (**63. 7.**)

15. Explain the effect of the following signatures on a bill of exchange: (*a*) signature of a stranger; (*b*) agent's signature; (*c*) signature *sans recours*; (*d*) signature *sans frais*. (**64. 2, 3.**)

16. "A forged or unauthorised signature is wholly inoperative on a bill of exchange." Discuss this statement, distinguishing between forged and unauthorised signatures and explaining how estoppel may operate to prevent a person whose signature has been forged from denying that he signed the bill. (**64. 4.**)

17. Distinguish carefully between the effect of forgery of the signature on a bill of: (*a*) the drawer; (*b*) the drawee; (*c*) an indorser. (**64. 5.**)

18. What is meant by the delivery of a bill? What is conditional delivery and what is its effect? (**64. 6.**)

19. "Delivery is presumed in favour of any holder of a bill of exchange." Explain this statement, and state the cases where delivery is not presumed conclusively. (**64. 6.**)

20. "An order bill is transferable by delivery plus indorsement." Explain this statement, and explain also what is meant by a valid indorsement. (**63. 9; 64. 7.**)

21. Explain the following terms: (*a*) Blank and special indorsements; (*b*) Restrictive indorsements; (*c*) Conditional indorsement; (*d*) Indorsement *sans recours*. (**64. 7, 8.**)

22. In what order are the parties to a bill liable upon it? Explain carefully the liability of: (*a*) the drawer; (*b*) the drawee; (*c*) an indorser. (**65. 2–5.**)

23. Explain the significance of the following terms: (*a*) Referee in case of need; (*b*) Accommodation party; (*c*) Accommodation bill; (*d*) Fictitious payee; (*e*) Non-existing payee. (**65. 6–8.**)

24. Distinguish carefully between the following terms in relation to bills of exchange: (*a*) holder, (*b*) holder for value, (*c*) holder in due course. (**65. 9, 10, 11.**)

25. What are the rights of a holder in due course and of a holder for value? (**65. 10, 11.**)

26. What is meant by saying that neither a payee of a cheque nor the paying banker can be a holder in due course? (**65. 10; 67. 1.**)

27. When does a bill of exchange require acceptance by the drawee in order to render it payable? (**66. 1, 2.**) What is, and what is the effect of, qualified acceptance? (**66. 1.**)

28. When is presentment for acceptance (*a*) necessary, (*b*) unnecessary? (**66. 2, 3.**)

29. Explain the following: (*a*) Days of Grace, (*b*) Noting and protesting, (*c*) Presentment for payment. (**66. 4, 5.**)

30. When is presentment for payment excused? (**66. 4.**)

31. When is a bill dishonoured (*a*) by non-acceptance, and (*b*) by non-payment? (**66.** 1, 4.)

32. When is notice of dishonour necessary and when is it unnecessary? What form should such notice take (*a*) in the case of Inland Bills, and (*b*) in the case of Foreign Bills? (**66.** 5, 6.)

33. What is a promissory note and how does it differ from a bill of exchange? (**68.** 1, 2.) What is the distinction between (*a*) joint notes and (*b*) joint and several notes? (**68.** 4.)

34. Define the following, and explain how far they are subject to the provisions of the Cheques Act, 1957: (*a*) Bankers' draft, (*b*) Conditional order, (*c*) Dividend warrant, (*d*) Deposit receipt. (**68.** 5.)

35. Some instruments are negotiable by statute, and others are negotiable by custom; others again have some of the characteristics of negotiable instruments, but not all." Explain this statement. (**62.** 3; **68.** 6.)

36. Define a cheque. How does a cheque differ from an ordinary bill of exchange? (**67.** 1; **63.** 2.)

37. An overdue cheque is one which has been in circulation for an unreasonable time. What is meant by "unreasonable time" in this context? (**67.** 2.)

38. The effect of delay in presenting a cheque differs from the effect of delay in presenting other bills. How? (**67.** 2.)

39. "A banker is not bound to honour an undated or post-dated cheque." Do you agree? (**67.** 3.)

40. On 1st June X sent to his insurance company a cheque to cover the insurance on his car. The cheque arrived on the 2nd June. On the 2nd June X was charged by the police with driving an uninsured vehicle, since his insurance expired in May. Explain why the prosecution would succeed. (**67.** 5; **22.** 5.)

41. What is the object of crossing a cheque, and what types of crossing are legally recognised? (**67.** 6, 7.)

42. When does a banker's authority to pay a cheque drawn upon him cease? (**67.** 13.)

43. State and explain briefly the protections given to paying bankers by statute. (**67.** 10, 11.)

44. A collecting banker who collects a cheque for the wrong person may be liable in tort to the true owner. What form does this liability take, and when does it arise? (**67.** 12.)

SPECIMEN QUESTIONS

1. Explain what is meant by accepting a bill of exchange, and state in what circumstances it is necessary that a bill of exchange be presented for acceptance.

What is the legal position of the parties where a bill of exchange drawn on B in favour of C is presented by C as a result of a fraudulent statement made by F? *C.I.S., Final, June* 1962. (**66. 1, 2.**)

2. (*a*) Explain the legal effect of crossing a cheque *a/c payee* only.

(*b*) How does the effect of such crossing differ from that of a crossing *not negotiable*?

(*c*) What is notice of dishonour, and when may it be dispensed with? *I.C.W.A., Final, June* 1961. (**67. 7; 66. 5.**)

3. E, an employee of F, forged D's signature to a bill of exchange drawn in favour of C, who was F's customer. The forged bill was accepted by F, the drawee. E forged C's indorsement and when the bill matured presented it to F's bank for payment. The bank paid.

Advise the bank as to its legal position. *C.I.S., Final, December* 1961. (**64. 4, 5.**)

4. How may the duty and authority of a banker to pay a cheque drawn on him by a customer be revoked? *A.C.C.A., Intermediate, June* 1961. (**67. 13.**)

5. Explain the liability of a banker who pays (*a*) a bill of exchange, and (*b*) a cheque, to a person claiming under a forged indorsement. Under what conditions, if any, is the banker protected? *Inst. of Bankers, Part II,* 1962. (**64. 5.**)

6. (*a*) What is meant by the acceptance of a bill of exchange?

(*b*) State and explain the different kinds of qualified acceptance which are set out in the Bills of Exchange Act, 1882.

(*c*) If the holder of a bill decides to take a qualified acceptance, what is the legal position of the drawer and the indorsers? *Inst. of Bankers, Part II,* 1963. (**66. 1.**)

7. Distinguish between a general acceptance and a qualified acceptance of a bill of exchange. What are the rights of the holder of a bill of exchange who is offered a qualified acceptance? If the holder takes a qualified acceptance, what are the positions of the drawer and the indorsers of the bill, respectively? *C.I.S., Final, June* 1961. (**66. 1.**)

8. What does the expression "fictitious" mean in regard to the payee of a bill of exchange and what are the consequences of making a bill payable to such a person? *A.C.C.A., Intermediate, Dec.* 1963. (**65. 8.**)

9. What is a material alteration of a bill of exchange and what is its effect upon the several parties to the bill? What is the position if the alteration is not apparent and the bill is in the hands of a holder in due course? *A.C.C.A., Intermediate, June* 1964. (**63. 13.**)

10. (*a*) Explain the legal nature of the relationship between banker and customer.

(*b*) In what ways may the authority of a banker to pay cheques drawn by a customer be revoked? *C.A., Final, June* 1963. (**33.** 4; **67.** 13.)

11. Williams sells goods to Thomas at the price of £100 and Thomas gives Williams a cheque for the amount, payable to Williams or order. What are Williams rights and liabilities in each of the following situations:

(a) Williams loses the cheque and asks Thomas for another, but Thomas declines to give one.

(b) Williams endorses the cheque to Rees to satisfy a debt of £85 which he owes to Rees. The cheque is subsequently dishonoured and Thomas cannot be traced. Rees claims the sum of £100 from Williams. *C.A., Final, Nov.* 1962. (**63.** 15, 16.)

12. A buys goods from B and asks B to accept C's cheque for part of the money and the balance in cash. He explains that he has no banking account of his own and that C's cheque is crossed. B agrees to this and the goods are given to A and he hands B the cheque and cash as arranged. The cheque is payable to "A or order," but B omits to obtain A's endorsement. He subsequently discovers his mistake.

(a) Is B entitled to ask for A's endorsement?

(b) Will B's rights against C be affected if he finds A obtained the cheque by fraud? *C.A., Final, May* 1962. (**64.** 7; **67.** 5; **65.** 9, 10.)

13. (a) Allen sells a typewriter to Baker, an infant, who pays for it by his cheque. Allen endorses the cheque to Cook who takes it in good faith and for value. The cheque is dishonoured on presentation. Can Cook enforce payment of the cheque against A or B?

(b) Davis, by mistake, draws a cheque payable to Evans, who does not exist. The cheque is negotiated by Franks by a forged endorsement to Green, who takes it in good faith and for value. Can Green enforce payment of the cheque? *C.A., Final, May* 1964. (**62.** 7; **64.** 5; **65.** 8.)

14. (a) Explain the rights and duties of a paying banker and a collecting banker in relation to cheques.

(b) How is a banker's authority to pay a cheque drawn on him by his customer terminated? *A.C.C.A., December* 1967. (**67.** 10–13.)

H

PART FIVE

SECURITIES

SECURITIES

SECTION 69. SECURITIES GENERALLY

1. Meaning of "security." A security is some right or interest in property given to a creditor so that, in the event of the debtor failing to pay his debt as and when due, the creditor may reimburse himself for the debt out of the property charged.

Both real and personal property may be charged with repayment of a debt in this way. (Real property means freehold land, and personal property includes leasehold land and all movable property, such as chattels and choses in action.)

2. Forms of security.

(a) *Mortgages.* A mortgage is an assurance to the creditor of the legal or equitable interest in property as security for the discharge of a debt, subject to a proviso that on repayment of the debt the property shall revert to the borrower.

The characteristic of a mortgage is that possession of the property remains vested in the mortgagor (the borrower), while the mortgagee (the lender) obtains some or all of the rights of ownership, or the right to obtain ownership if the debtor defaults.

Land is the form of property most usually mortgaged, but chattels can be mortgaged by *Conditional Bill of Sale* (*see s. 2 below*), and choses in action (such as insurance policies) can be mortgaged by assignment subject to a condition that on repayment the chose shall revert to the borrower.

(b) *Pledges or Pawns.* A pledge is a deposit of chattels with a lender as security for a debt. If the pledgee is a professional lender upon this type of security (a pawnbroker) the pledge is called a pawn.

A pledge *differs from a mortgage* in that the lender obtains possession of the chattel, while the borrower retains ownership.

(c) *Liens.* A lien is a right to retain property until a debt is paid (a possessory lien) or to seek a court order for sale of the property (equitable lien).

A lien *differs from mortgages and pledges* in that it arises by implication of law from certain situations, while mortgages and pledges are the result of express agreement between a borrower and a lender.

3. Legal and equitable interests. In English property law a distinction is drawn between legal interests in property (which are enforceable in any court and against any person), and equitable interests (which are personal rights against a particular individual and are not enforceable against other persons, save in certain exceptional circumstances: *see below*). Both legal and equitable interests in property can be used as security for loans, but the limited enforceability of equitable interests makes them less acceptable securities.

Differences between legal and equitable interests:

(a) *Creation.* A legal interest is one created in the correct *form* for the particular type of property, *e.g.* a deed of conveyance to create a legal interest or estate in land. An equitable interest is either (i) the result of an informal creation, *e.g.* a conveyance of land not under seal, or (ii) the result of a transfer of an existing equitable interest, since these cannot be converted into legal interests (even by conveyance under seal).

(b) *Enforceability.* If a person has a legal interest in property his claims are enforceable against all comers, and are indefeasible. But the holder of an equitable interest in property can (i) enforce his interest only against the person through whom he derives it, *i.e.* the owner of the parallel legal interest in the property, and (ii) can have his interest in the property destroyed if the legal owner sells the property to a purchaser for value without notice of the equitable interest attaching to the property.

(c) *Parallel interests.* In any one piece of property there may be parallel legal and equitable interests, vested in different persons. Thus, in a trust, the legal owner of property is compelled to hold the property as trustee for the benefit of the beneficiary, that is the owner of the equitable interest. (And the beneficiary's claims are enforceable only against the trustee, and can be extinguished if the trustee sells the property to a purchaser who buys without knowing of the beneficiary's interest.)

4. Legal and equitable mortgages. Just as there can be parallel legal and equitable ownership of land, mortgages can also be either legal or equitable. And where there are several mortgages of a piece of land some may be legal and others equitable.

Where the mortgagee obtains a legal interest in the property charged his mortgage is a legal mortgage; if he obtains merely an equitable interest, his mortgage is equitable (and is a weaker security).

SECTION 70. SUMMARY OF PROPERTY LAW

1. Understanding of property law. Students who are required to study the subject of securities need at least a background knowledge of the law of property. This section is intended to provide a superficial outline to facilitate understanding of the law relating to securities, but students who have no prior knowledge of the subject would be well advised to make a more detailed study of property law.

2. Ownership and possession. The owner of property is the person who has the maximum legal rights over the property (including the right to actual possession). He may however part with possession, without surrendering ownership, *e.g.* where the owner lends property to another.

Ownership is a legal concept; possession is a state of fact, and involves actual control over the property. When the owner of land leases it to a tenant, the tenant acquires legal possession and can assert his right of control against anyone (even against the owner, if the owner in breach of the lease attempts to regain possession).

3. Transfer of ownership.

(a) *Personal property.*

(i) *Chattels* can be transferred by mere delivery, with intention to pass ownership (and not merely possession).

(ii) *Choses in action* require to be assigned either in accordance with the method laid down by *s.* 136 *L.P.A.* or Equity (*see s.* **28**) or in accordance with some particular method laid down for particular choses, *e.g.* share transfers.

(b) *Real property*. Freehold land (and also leasehold) should be transferred *by deed* if legal ownership is intended to pass. Any attempted conveyance which is not by deed operates to transfer only an equitable interest in the property.

A deed is not necessary in the following cases:

(i) Leases for a term not exceeding three years.

(ii) Assents by personal representatives. A deceased person's land vests in his personal representatives and they can transfer it to the beneficiaries under the deceased's will (or upon his intestacy) by a mere written assent.

(iii) Disclaimers by a trustee in bankruptcy need only be in writing.

(iv) On redemption of a mortgage of land, the land revests in the mortgagor as soon as the mortgagee signs a receipt for the mortgage moneys.

4. Estates in land. An estate in land is a right to possession of the land (as distinct from a right over the land not amounting to possession, *e.g.* a right of way).

The only *legal estates* that can exist in land are:

(a) *Freehold* (technically called the *fee simple absolute in possession*). This is the maximum estate possible, and its characteristic is that it may endure forever, *i.e.* is not for a limited period like a lease.

Theoretically the freeholder is the owner of everything *on, above, or below* his land. But in practice his rights are restricted by the law; thus he must allow aeroplanes to pass over: *Civil Aviation Act*, 1949, and he must not alter the use of his land without consent: *Town and Country Planning Act*, 1947, and most minerals under his land belong to the state: *Coal Nationalisation Act*, 1947.

(b) *Leasehold* (technically called a *term of years absolute*). This is an estate granted by a freeholder to a tenant for a limited period.

During continuance of the lease the tenant is entitled to exclusive possession of the land, and if he holds under a long lease (99 years or more) he can be regarded as virtually the owner for most practical purposes, *e.g.* he can sell or mortgage his lease.

5. Legal interests in land. These are rights over the land of another *not amounting to possession*.

Like legal estates they can only be *created by deed.* Some
legal interests can be mortgaged, but they are not usually
considered desirable securities.

The principal legal interests are *easements* (rights of way,
light, support, etc.), *profits* (*e.g.* rights to hunt, shoot, or fish
on another's land), and *rentcharges* (the right of a person with
no possessory rights to receive a yearly sum out of the profits
of the land).

A certain type of mortgage, called a *charge by way of mortgage,*
is also a legal interest in land (providing it is created by deed).

6. Equitable interests in land. Every type of legal estate or
interest has its parallel in Equity, and there are some types of
estate or interest which cannot exist in modern law but which
are still recognised and enforced in equity.

Equitable interests take the following forms:

(a) *Informal creations of estates or interests in land, i.e.* where
the grantor *intends* to create a legal estate or interest but
fails to adopt the proper form of transfer, usually a deed.
(In such cases the grantee can often obtain an order of
specific performance against the grantor compelling him to
execute the necessary deed and so convert the grant into a
legal estate or interest.)

(b) *Deliberate grants of equitable interests, e.g.* where the grantor
conveys the legal estate to T with instructions that he shall
hold the property on trust for B, so that T acquires the legal
estate and B acquires an equitable interest in the property.
(Similarly if B sells his interest, he can give no better than
he has got himself, *i.e.* can only convey an equitable interest
to the purchaser.)

(c) *Estates and interests not recognised by law.* Any attempt to
create a legal estate other than freehold or leasehold, or
a legal interest other than the types recognised by the law
of Property Act (easements, profits, rentcharges, mortgage
charges, etc.), operates to create an equitable interest only.

Thus if the grantor attempts to *entail* the land granted
("To X and his heirs male"), the rights of the heirs will be
equitable only. Similarly *future interests,* such as remainders,
("To X for life, remainder to B") can exist only as equitable
interests.

7. Registration of title. In certain parts of England the
ownership of legal estates in land can be registered at the

central land registry, *e.g.* the home counties, and the towns of Hastings, Oldham, Oxford, Leicester, etc.: *Land Registration Act,* 1925. (The Act makes possible the extension of the system to other parts of the country, and this is proceeding gradually.)

(a) *Registrable estates.* Only legal estates can be registered, and the following leases cannot be registered: (i) leases with 21 years or less remaining unexpired, (ii) non-assignable leases, (iii) mortgage leases: (*see below.*)

The purpose of registration is (i) to provide easily accessible evidence of ownership, and (ii) to facilitate conveyancing (by substituting a simple certificate or transfer for the old complicated conveyance).

(b) *Titles registrable.* The following forms of title can be registered:

    (i) *Absolute title.* This vests in the person named the full fee simple or leasehold estate, subject to any charges upon the land which are stated in the register. (*See* 8 *below.*)

   (ii) *Qualified title.* This has the same effect as absolute title, except that the land is held subject to some defect in title specified in the register.

 (iii) *Possessory.* Any person who has possession of land of which there appears to be no legal owner can register with a possessory title. This will then be the same as an absolute title, subject only to any claims against the land arising before registration, *e.g.* it can be defeated if the true owner of the land is found and proves his title.

 (iv) *A good leasehold title.* This vests the lease in the tenant, but recognises the possibility that the lessor may not have had power to grant the lease in the first place.

(c) *Effect of registration.* An *absolute title* is virtually a guarantee by the State of the authenticity of the title registered. After a piece of land has been registered, further transfers will be by cancellation of the existing entry and substitution of a new entry in the name of the transferee. The new owner is then given a Land Certificate which states his title, and all charges and encumbrances on the land (except the covenants in a lease: *see* 8 *below*) and is virtually his title deed.

8. Registration of charges. Registration of *title* is only available in a few areas, but *charges* or encumbrances on the land can be registered in whatever part of England or Wales they occur: *Land Charges Act,* 1925.

The following registers exist:

(a) *Register of Pending Actions, i.e.* proceedings pending in any court and affecting the land, such as a petition for the bankruptcy of the tenant.
(b) *Register of Annuities and Rent Charges* payable out of the profits of a piece of land.
(c) *Register of Writs and Orders* affecting land, *e.g.* a receiving order in bankruptcy.
(d) *Register of Deeds of Arrangement.*

NOTE: *Failure to register* the above may make them *void* against a purchaser of the land, since he may buy without notice of their existence.

(e) *Register of Land Charges.* For the purposes of registration, land charges fall into the following categories:
   (i) *Class A land charges:* statutory charges on land made pursuant to the *application of some person* and by virtue of a court order.
   (ii) *Class B land charges:* statutory charges arising *otherwise than pursuant to the application of any person, i.e.* imposed by the statute itself.

   (iii) *Class C land charges:*
      (a) *Puisne mortgages, i.e.* legal mortgages not protected by a deposit of title deeds: *see s.* **71** *below.*
      (b) *Limited owner's charges, i.e.* equitable charges on trust property in favour of the principal beneficiary or "tenant for life," and usually arising where he has spent some of his own money on improving the land and acquires a charge on the land for the money expended.
      (c) *General equitable charges, i.e.* those not secured by deposit of title deeds, and including mainly equitable mortgages and vendors' liens.
      (d) *Estate contracts, i.e.* options or contracts for the sale or lease of land. A purchaser who has paid for land but not yet had it conveyed to him can register his contract to prevent any subsequent purchaser buying the land.
   (iv) *Class D land charges, i.e.* (i) charges for death duties, (ii) restrictive covenants affecting freehold, (iii) equitable easements.
   (v) *Class E land charges:* annuities created before 1926.

   Failure to register in Class C (a), (b), or (c) renders the charge void against any purchaser for *value* of any conflicting interest in the land. Failure to register in Class C (d), and Class D renders the charge void as against a purchaser for *money* or money's worth of the legal estate only. *Value* includes marriage, which is recognised as valuable consideration for this purpose.

SECTION 71. MORTGAGES OF LAND

1. Legal mortgages before 1926. Mortgages of land were generally created by conveying to the mortgagee the entire estate or interest of the mortgagor, subject to a promise by the mortgagee to reconvey the property back to the mortgagor on repayment of the loan plus interest on a certain date (usually six months from the date of the mortgage).

After the date fixed for repayment (*the legal date for redemption*) the mortgagor lost his legal right to the land. From this time onwards he was regarded as having merely an equitable right to redeem, amounting to an equitable interest in the property. The mortgagor's possession of both (a) *a legal right to redeem* on the contracted date, and (b) *an equitable right to redeem* later, was called his *equity of redemption* and was an equitable interest in land which he could sell, leave by will, mortgage, etc.

2. Legal mortgages since 1925. The mortgage by conveyance was abolished by the *Law of Property Act, 1925*, which provided that legal mortgages can now take only the *following forms*:

(a) *Lease to the mortgagee for a long term of years*, subject to a proviso for *cesser on redemption*, *i.e.* a proviso that the lease shall cease automatically on repayment of the loan plus interest.

    (Mortgages of *freehold* are usually by lease for 3000 years, and mortgages of *leasehold* by lease for the maximum period possible, *e.g.* the period of the tenant/mortgagor's lease less ten days. Thus if A has a lease for 99 years, of which 67 years remain unexpired, he may create a mortgage in favour of B by granting him a mortgage lease for 66 years plus 355 days.)

(b) *Charge by deed expressed to be by way of legal mortgage*. The deed simply states that in consideration of the loan made by the mortgagee, the mortgagor charges his land with repayment of the debt. If he fails to repay, the mortgagee can exercise the same remedies as a mortgagee having a mortgage lease: see below.

NOTE: Any attempt to create a mortgage by the old method of conveying the freehold to the mortgagee operates as a grant of a mortgage lease of 3000 years, subject to cesser on redemption: *L.P.A.*, *s.* 85.

3. Equitable mortgages. If the mortgagee receives merely an equitable interest in the land his mortgage is said to be equitable. This may occur in the following ways:

(a) *Any mortgage of an equitable interest,* whether by deed or otherwise.

   If the mortgagor himself has merely an equitable interest in the property (*e.g.* as a beneficiary under a trust), he can only confer a like interest on the mortgagee.

   Such a mortgage may be *by lease or by charge* (as in legal mortgages), or by *mere deposit of title deeds* with the mortgagee (usually accompanied by a note explaining the purpose of the deposit). Such equitable mortgages must be *in writing* (whether by deed or not), signed by the mortgagor or his agent: *L.P.A.*, *s.* 53.

(b) *Any informal mortgage of a legal estate or interest.* Thus an attempt to create a legal mortgage otherwise than by deed, operates to create an equitable mortgage.

(c) *Any binding contract to grant a legal mortgage* operates immediately to give the mortgagee an equitable mortgage of the land. This will be automatically converted into a proper legal mortgage as soon as the mortgagor executes the necessary deed (and if he refuses to do so the mortgagee can obtain an order for specific performance against him, compelling execution of the appropriate mortgage deed): ✻ the Rule in *Walsh* v. *Lonsdale* (1882).

   For there to be a *binding contract* there must be: (i) written evidence of the contract, signed by the mortgagor or his agent, or (ii) a sufficient act of part performance by the mortgagee: *see s.* **11.**

4. Capacity to create mortgages. Generally any adult can create a mortgage, but note:

(a) *Infants'* mortgages are void. (But until the contrary is proved every party to a conveyance is presumed to be of full age: *L.P.A.*, *s.* 15.)

(b) Mortgages by statutory or registered *companies* are void if ultra vires.

(c) *Lunatics'* mortgages are void if the lunatic has been certified. (Otherwise they are generally voidable.)

(d) *Trustees* cannot mortgage trust property unless so authorised (i) by the trust instrument, of (ii) by statute, *e.g.* in a Trust for sale, where trustees have implied power to mortgage property: *L.P.A., s.* 28.

5. Remedies and rights of a legal mortgagee.

If the loan, or any interest is unpaid when due, or if the mortgagor breaks some covenant in the mortgage deed, the mortgagee has the following *concurrent remedies*:

(a) *To sue for debt* on the mortgagor's personal covenant to repay. This is the basic remedy and is open to all creditors whether secured by mortgage or not.

(b) *To take possession* of the land, whether the mortgage is by lease or by charge: *L.P.A., s.* 87.

But a mortgagee who takes possession must account to the mortgagor for any loss to the property occasioned by his default, and because of this liability the remedy of possession is rarely exercised: *White* v. *City of London Brewery* (1889).

(c) *To foreclose, i.e.* to obtain a court order extinguishing the mortgagor's rights in the property, and vesting the legal estate in the mortgagee.

Foreclosure is disfavoured by the courts, since it may confer excessive profits on the mortgagee. Consequently the court will first issue a *foreclosure order nisi*, ordering the mortgagor to pay his debt within six months. If he fails to obey this order, the court will then either (i) issue a foreclosure order absolute, vesting the property finally in the mortgagee, or (ii) order sale of the property.

(d) *To sell the land* under the power implied in all mortgages by deed (whether legal or equitable), unless otherwise agreed: *L.P.A., s.* 101, *see 6 below.*

(e) *To appoint a receiver*, under the power implied in all mortgages by deed (whether legal or equitable), unless a contrary intention is expressed: *L.P.A., s.* 101.

The receiver takes possession of the property and collects all rents and profits, applying them in payment of the due debt: *see 7 below.*

The above remedies are *concurrent, i.e.* the mortgagee could for instance appoint a receiver, apply to the court for foreclosure and at the same time sue the mortgagor for debt.

In addition to these remedies, the mortgagee has the following *subsidiary rights*:

(i) *To insure the property* against fire to two-thirds of its value or the estimated cost of replacement.

(ii) *If he is in possession,* he can (*a*) grant *leases,* and accept surrenders of leases, and (*b*) cut and sell *timber.*

Leases granted for occupational or agricultural purposes must not be for more than 50 years, and building leases must not exceed 999 years. The lease must take effect in possession within 12 months of being granted, and must be at the best rent obtainable.

The mortgagor can also grant leases during the continuance of the mortgage, but only with the consent of the mortgagee. Leases granted by either party will be binding on the other if consent was obtained.

6. Mortgagee's power of sale. The power may be given *expressly* by the mortgage deed (in which case its exercise will be governed by the terms of the deed), or may arise by *implication* of law (in all mortgages by deed, whether legal or equitable).

The implied power to sell *arises* as soon as the legal date for redemption has passed, but only becomes *exercisable* when:

(*a*) Some interest is two months in arrear; or
(*b*) There has been a breach of some covenant in the mortgage deed, other than the covenant to repay, *e.g.* the mortgagor may have failed to insure against fire when he has covenanted to do so; or
(*c*) The mortgagor fails to repay the loan after having been given three months' notice requiring him to do so: *L.P.A., s.* 103.

Once the mortgagee has exercised his power to sell and has signed a binding contract in favour of a purchaser, the mortgagor cannot prevent the sale by repaying the loan; but he can stop the sale at any time *before* the signing of such contract: *Waring* v. *London Assurance* (1935).

Normally the mortgagee can utilise his power of sale without the court's assistance, but in the following cases he must have *consent of the court* before selling:

(i) If he has obtained a foreclosure order nisi.
(ii) If the power of sale becomes exercisable because the mortgagor has become bankrupt.

The mortgagee must (i) exercise his power of sale in good faith, and (ii) obtain a proper price (not necessarily the best price obtainable). Proceeds of sale are applied (in order): (i) to discharge prior encumbrances if any (*e.g.* earlier mortgages having priority over the seller's), (ii) in paying costs of the sale, etc., (iii) in discharge of the mortgage, and (iv) the residue is held by the mortgagee on trust for the mortgagor, or other person entitled (*e.g.* a mortgagee having the next claim after that of the seller).

A purchaser from the mortgagee is not bound to enquire whether he is exercising his power of sale properly, but is bound to ascertain whether he has a power of sale, *e.g.* by discovering whether the mortgage is by deed, and whether *s.* 103 has been satisfied.

7. Appointment of a receiver. Where the mortgagee does not wish to sell the mortgaged property, or is unable to do so for some reason (*e.g.* because the property is leased to a tenant, so that its value to a purchaser would be diminished by the fact that it cannot be sold with vacant possession), he may appoint a receiver to take possession of the property and *collect all rents and profits* and apply them in payment of interest and/or capital outstanding.

A receiver may be appointed wherever the power of sale becomes exercisable under *s.* 103: *see* 6 *above.* The receiver must be appointed *in writing* by the mortgagee, and can be removed in the same way.

The receiver in possession is regarded in law as the *agent of the mortgagor*, who is therefore responsible for his defaults. If therefore the property sustains any loss by reason of the misconduct of the receiver, it is the mortgagor (and not the mortgagee) who must make good the loss.

NOTE:

(*a*) The receiver has all necessary *legal remedies* to compel debtors to pay money owing to the estate, *e.g.* he can distrain on the goods of a tenant and sell them to raise rent due to the mortgagor.

(*b*) The receiver is entitled to *payment* for his services at a rate not exceeding 5% of the gross amount raised by him. He is entitled to deduct this commission before handing any money to the mortgagee.

(*c*) Money received by him must be *applied* (in order) in paying (i) rents, rates, taxes, etc. (ii) annual sums owing under prior charges (iii) his own commission, insurance and repair costs (if repairs are authorised by the mortgagee) (iv) interest due on the mortgage under which he is appointed (v) capital moneys, if required by the mortgagee (vi) residue to the mortgagor.

(*d*) A person paying the receiver is not bound to ascertain if the power under which he was appointed has been properly exercised.

8. Remedies of equitable mortgagees. These are basically the same as those of a legal mortgagee, and again are concurrent.

(a) *To sue* for debt.

(b) *To sell*, if the mortgage is by deed (in which case power is implied as in 6 above). If the mortgage is not by deed, there is no implied power but an express power may be included.

(c) *To appoint a receiver* if the mortgage is by deed, and otherwise only if there is an express power.

(d) *To foreclose*, if the mortgage is by lease (if the mortgage is by equitable charge, there is no power of foreclosure).

(e) *To take possession only* if there is an express power given by the mortgage.

9. Consolidation and tacking.

(a) *Consolidation* is the mortgagee's power to insist that several mortgages must be redeemed simultaneously or not at all. Consolidation is only allowed where:

    (i) Power to consolidate is *expressly reserved* in both or all the mortgages to be consolidated: *L.P.A.*, *s.* 93;

    (ii) The legal date for redemption has expired;

    (iii) The same mortgagor created both or all the mortgages; and

    (iv) The same mortgagee has at some time acquired all the mortgages to be consolidated: *Pledge* v. *White* (1896).

(b) *Tacking of further advances.* If A borrows money from X on a first mortgage, and from Y on a second mortgage, X is entitled to payment in priority over Y. If X then makes a further loan to A on security of the same property, this will be a third mortgage and Y's second mortgage will have priority over it, unless X is entitled to tack the third mortgage on to the first so as to gain overall priority.

    Tacking is *only allowed where* (*L.P.A.*, *s.* 94):

    (i) Any intervening mortgagee agrees; or

    (ii) An obligation to make further advances was imposed on X in the first mortgage, *i.e.* where in effect loans are to be made by instalments pursuant to the first mortgage; or

(iii) No notice of the intervening mortgage was available to X when he made his further advance. (Registration of intervening mortgage as puisne mortgages in Class C of the Land Charges Register constitutes notice for this purpose: *see s*. 70 *above*.)

10. Attornment clause. Mortgages sometimes contain a clause by which the mortgagor attorns as tenant of the mortgagee, *i.e.* agrees to retain possession of the land only as a *tenant of the mortgagee*, at a nominal rent.

The advantage of such a clause is that it enables the mortgagee to evict the mortgagor for failure to pay (or for breach of any other covenant in the mortgage), and so obtain possession more speedily than is usually possible by proceedings under the power of possession given by the mortgage. Usually the mortgagor can be evicted without notice, or with such notice as the mortgage deed provides.

11. Priority of mortgages. The mortgagor may create several mortgages on the same property, and where this happens the value of the property (if sold) may not be sufficient to repay all the mortgagees in full. It then becomes important to ascertain which mortgagee is entitled to be paid first, which second, etc.

The rules governing priorities are laid down by *L.P.A.*, *s*. 97, and *L.C.A.*, *s*. 13, as follows:

(a) *Mortgages of the legal estate:*

(i) The mortgagee holding the *title deeds* ranks first, whether his mortgage is legal or equitable (provided he is not guilty of any fraud himself, and has not enabled the mortgagor to perpetrate any fraud, *e.g.* by parting with the deeds to enable the mortgagor to create another mortgage by concealing the first).

(ii) All legal *puisne mortgages* (legal mortgages not protected by deposit of deeds) and all equitable mortgages not protected by deposit of deeds, rank for priority from the date of *registration: L.P.A.*, *s*. 97. (If not so registered, they are void against a purchaser for value of the land: *L.C.A.*, *s*. 13 (2).)

(b) *Mortgages of equitable interests* rank for priority according to the rule in *Dearle* v. *Hall* (1823) as amended by *L.P.A.*, *ss*. 137 and 138.

Under this rule priorities rank from the *date of notice* (in writing) to the holder of the legal interest on which the mortgaged equitable interest depends.

Thus the *persons to be notified* are:

(i) The trustees, in the case of settled land.

(ii) The trustees, in a trust for sale.

(iii) The estate owner, in all other cases.

(The trustees or estate owner must produce the notice if requested by any person interested in the equitable interest: *L.P.A.*, *s.* 137 (8).)

12. Sub-mortgages. A mortgagee can use his mortgage as security in order to borrow money himself, *i.e.* he can sub-mortgage it.

Such a sub-mortgage, if by lease, must be for a term shorter than that granted to the mortgagee himself, *e.g.* the mortgage lease less ten days.

The remedies of a sub-mortgagee are basically the same as those of any mortgagee, *i.e.* he can take possession, sell, appoint a receiver, etc., where the original mortgagor is in default: *L.P.A.*, *s.* 103. In addition he has remedies against the sub-mortgagor, *i.e.* he can sell the original mortgage, and sue the sub-mortgagor for debt.

13. Redemption of mortgages. On repayment of the mortgage advance and acknowledgment of receipt by the mortgagee, the mortgage automatically terminates without the need for any reconveyance to the mortgagor: *L.P.A.*, *s.* 115. The receipt is usually under seal, but this is not necessary, though by *L.P.A.*, *s.* 69 a sealed receipt authorises a solicitor to collect payment on behalf of the mortgagee and then surrender the receipted mortgage.

14. The equity of redemption. Theoretically, when the agreed date for redemption has passed the mortgagor loses his legal right to redeem, but a further equitable right to redeem still remains. (The two rights of redemption together are called the Equity of Redemption: *see* 1 *above*.)

The equity of redemption is *extinguished by* (i) sale or foreclosure by the mortgagee, (ii) the mortgagor releasing it to the mortgagee, or (iii) by lapse of time under the *Limitation Act*, 1939, *i.e.* by lapse of twelve years from the date of the last unsatisfied demand for payment by the mortgagee, and where the mortgagee has been in possession for twelve years: *L.A.*, *s.* 12. (The Act does not apply to mortgages of personalty: *Weld* v. *Petre* (1929).)

(Note that the *Limitation Act* also applies in favour of the mortgagor, *i.e.* he cannot be sued for capital after 12 years from the date payment fell due, or for interest 6 years after any payment thereof fell due: *L.A.*, *s.* 18.)

15. Clogs on the equity of redemption. Any agreement which attempts to bar the mortgagor's right to redeem is void. Similarly provisions in a mortgage which would mean that after redemption the mortgagor would not get back his property free of the mortgagee's claims are also void.

Such stipulations in a mortgage are called *clogs on the equity of redemption*, since they attempt to defeat the mortgagor's equitable rights.

EXAMPLES:

(a) *A mortgage cannot be made irredeemable.* But it is legitimate for the mortgagee to insist that redemption shall be postponed for a reasonable period, *e.g.* that the mortgagor shall not redeem within 20 years: *Knightsbridge Estates Trust Ltd.* v. *Byrne* (1939).

(b) After redemption the mortgagor *must get back his property unfettered*, *i.e.* free of all claims by the mortgagee. Thus where a mortgagor of an inn covenanted to buy all his beer from the mortgagee even after redemption, the covenant was void: *Noakes & Co. Ltd.* v. *Rice* (1902).

(c) *Collateral advantages* given to the mortgagee in the mortgage are enforceable, but *must cease upon redemption*. Thus if the mortgagor of an inn in addition to promising to repay the loan, also promises to buy all his beer from the mortgagee until redemption, such a provision is valid: ✱ *Biggs* v. *Hoddinott* (1898). But the covenant must cease to be binding as soon as the loan is repaid: *Noakes* v. *Rice*.

SECTION 72. PLEDGES AND MORTGAGES OF PERSONALTY

1. Mortgages of personalty. The method of mortgaging personalty is to transfer legal ownership to the mortgagee, subject to a condition for re-transfer on repayment of the loan. The method of mortgaging therefore depends on the method of transfer of legal title appropriate to the particular form of personalty.

(a) *Chattels are transferable by delivery without the need for any accompanying document,* but in order to provide the mortgagee with documentary evidence (while leaving possession in the hands of the mortgagor) a *conditional bill of sale* is normally used: *see* 3 *below.*

(b) *Choses in action are transferable by assignment,* either legal (under *L.P.A.*, *s.* 136) or equitable: *see s.* **28.**

In some cases *particular statutes* lay down special requirements for the assignment of particular choses in action, *e.g.* insurance policies, copyrights, etc., and these requirements would have to be observed in a mortgage of such a chose.

2. Pledge or mortgage. Where chattels are to be mortgaged, a conditional bill of sale must be used. But this procedure is not popular: *see* 3 *below.*

An easier method of using small chattels as security, is to *pledge* them, *i.e.* to deliver possession to the lender subject to a condition that he shall return the chattels on repayment of the loan. But pledging is only appropriate in connection with smaller chattels, which can be easily moved or stored. Larger chattels, such as pianos, motor cars, collections of furniture or paintings, etc., must normally be mortgaged by bill of sale.

3. Conditional bills of sale. An *absolute bill of sale* is a documentary assignment of chattels, giving title with or without delivery of the chattels comprised. Since chattels can pass by delivery, without documentation, and since most sales take effect in actual or constructive delivery, absolute bills of sale are rarely used. Their only use today is where the purchaser requires for some reason documentary evidence of his purchase, *e.g.* where he is buying goods for export and may have to prove to the customs authorities that he is the owner of the goods.

A *conditional bill of sale* is one used as documentary evidence of a *mortgage of chattels*, *i.e.* it transfers ownership to the mortgagee (while leaving the mortgagor in possession as bailee for the lender), subject to a condition that the chattels shall be re-assigned to the borrower on repayment of the loan.

4. Form of conditional bills of sale. These must comply with the requirements of the *Bills of Sale Acts*, 1878 *and* 1882, as follows:

(a) The bill must be by *deed*, attested by at least one witness; otherwise it is void.

(b) The bill must be *registered* at the Central Office of the Supreme Court within 7 days of creation; otherwise it is void.

(c) *Consideration* for the bill must be truly stated therein.

(d) *Interest payable* and date for repayment must be stated in the bill, together with any other conditions.

(e) The chattels comprised in the bill must be *inventoried*, and the inventory must be attached to the bill on registration.

(f) *The lender's remedy* under a conditional bill of sale which has been properly registered and drawn is seizure of the chattels. The *right to seizure* arises (i) on failure to repay the loan as agreed, (ii) on bankruptcy of the borrower, or (iii) on any fraudulent dealing by the debtor with the chattels with the intention of removing them from the lender's power, *e.g.* an attempted sale to another person.

NOTE: A conditional bill of sale takes its *priority* from the date of registration. Therefore a bill created earlier than a rival may rank after the rival if registered later.

Because of the technicalities and publicity involved, bills of sale are not popular forms of security. They are sometimes taken by professional moneylenders, but very rarely by non-professional moneylenders such as bankers.

From the borrower's point of view a pledge offers an easier way of raising money on security of chattels; the difficulty here is that a pawnbroker will not usually take a pledge of large and cumbersome chattels, which may then only be useful as security if someone can be found who is willing to take a conditional bill of sale, *e.g.* pianos, cars, collections of paintings, etc.

5. Pledges. A pledge of chattels involves *actual or constructive delivery* of chattels to the lender. Constructive delivery might be by giving the pledgee the key to a warehouse in which the goods are stored.

The pledgor remains the legal owner of the goods, and the pledgee becomes a bailee who must return the goods on repayment as agreed. The pledgor is entitled to demand a receipt for deposit of the goods.

The pledgee owes a *duty of care* for the goods while in his possession, and if they are lost or damaged through his negligence he must make good the loss. (But if the goods were taken from him by robbery with violence, he is generally excused from liability.) The pledgee generally has no right to use the goods deposited unless otherwise agreed.

The pledgee has a *possessory lien* over the goods entitling him to retain them until repayment, even if there is no written agreement stating the purpose of deposit.

6. Pawnbrokers. These are professional pledgees, who are required to be licensed under the *Pawnbrokers' Acts*, 1872 and 1960, to carry on business by lending money on security of goods pawned to them.

The *Pawnbrokers' Acts* (applying to loans of £50 or less) lay down the following rules:

(a) *A pawn-ticket* must be given for the pledge.
(b) Pawns are to be redeemable any time within *six months*, plus seven days of grace.
(c) *Pawns not redeemed* within this period: (i) if for less than 40s., belong absolutely to the pawnbroker, and (ii) if for more than 40s., must be sold by public auction. (Surplus moneys after the pawnbroker has deducted the amount of his loan, belong to the pledgor.)
(d) *If the loan exceeds* £5 the pawnbroker may make a special contract varying the provisions of the Act, providing such contract (usually in the form of a pawn-ticket) is signed by both parties.
(e) The pawnbroker must *deliver up* the goods on presentation of the pawn-ticket, and repayment of the loan. (He is entitled to presume that the person presenting the ticket is lawfully justified in claiming the goods.)
(f) If the goods are *destroyed by fire*, the pawnbroker is responsible for making good the pawner's loss. (Valuation is measured as the amount of the loan, plus interest, plus 25% of the loan.) He is not liable for war damage.

SECTION 73. LIENS

1. Definition. A lien is a right over the property of another arising *by operation of law* (independently of any agreement), and gives the lienor a right (a) to retain the property until the owner has settled some debt owed to the lienor (*a Common Law or possessory lien*), or (*b*) to sell the property in satisfaction of the debt (*an equitable lien*).

A lien must be distinguished from a deposit of chattels by way of pledge. A pledge is security derived from express agreement; a lien generally arises independently of agreement.

2. Common Law or possessory liens.
These arise where the creditor has *actual possession* of some of the debtor's property, and obtains a right to retain such property until an outstanding debt is paid.

NOTE:

(*a*) A Common Law lien *cannot arise independently of possession*, *i.e.* the creditor is not entitled to obtain possession solely for the purpose of claiming such a lien. (Cf. Equitable liens: *see 4 below.*)

(*b*) A Common Law lien is *exercisable only by detaining the goods* until the debt is paid, *i.e.* there is no right of sale, save in some exceptional cases where a right of sale is given by statute.

A statutory right of sale is given to innkeepers (*Innkeepers' Liability Act*, 1878), unpaid sellers of goods (*Sale of Goods Act*, 1893), and repairers (*Disposal of Uncollected Goods Act*, 1952).

(*c*) A Common Law lien is *extinguished* by (i) agreement, express or implied, (ii) payment of the debt, (iii) loss of possession, or (iv) taking security for the debt.

(*d*) A Common Law lien may be *general or particular*, *i.e.* may be available against any goods of the debtor coming into possession of the creditor, or only against the particular goods in connection with which the debt was incurred.

Thus a carrier has a particular lien for his freight charges, while stockbrokers and factors have general liens. A banker's lien is also a general lien: *see 5 below.*

3. Maritime liens.
A maritime lien is one attaching to a ship, in favour of the shipmaster (for disbursements and wages), seamen (for their wages), salvors (for charges in connection with salvage), etc.

The lien is exercised *against the ship* itself, not against the owners, and it arises independently of possession. A notice of lien is affixed to the ship, and proceedings may be taken in the Admiralty court to arrest the ship. If the lien is not discharged, the ship will not be allowed to leave harbour, and a court order for sale may be given to the lienor.

If the owner of a ship subject to a lien sells the ship, the purchaser takes it subject to the lien, *i.e.* becomes responsible for discharging the lien.

4. Equitable liens. Unlike Common Law liens these are *not founded on possession,* and can be exercised by a court order for *sale* of the property subject to the lien. But like all equitable rights they can be extinguished by the owner selling the property to a bona fide purchaser for value without notice of the lien.

They arise mainly in connection with the sale of land, *e.g.* a vendor of land who has given possession to the purchaser has a lien over the land for unpaid purchase money, and a purchaser who hands over a deposit before obtaining possession has a lien for his deposit.

5. Banker's lien. This is a *general possessory lien* arising at Common Law, but unlike other Common Law liens it gives the banker a *right of sale* of securities subject to the lien.

NOTE:

(a) *The lien arises out of a general course of dealing,* and covers "All securities deposited with them as bankers, by a customer, unless there be an express contract, or circumstances that show an implied contract, inconsistent with lien": *Brandao* v. *Barnett* (1846). (The lien therefore usually arises by implication from the relationship, but it appears that it may also be granted expressly unlike other liens.)

(b) Property subject to the lien includes *all securities coming into* the banker's possession in the ordinary course of dealing, *e.g.* promissory notes, bills of exchange, foreign bonds, etc. It does not cover securities deposited merely for safe custody, unless at some time the customer agrees to allow the banker to hold these as security for an advance (in which case they are subject to an equitable mortgage, rather than a lien).

(c) The banker's lien has been called an *"implied pledge"* (*Brandao* v. *Barnett*) which appears to confer a power of sale, at least in so far as it affects negotiable securities.

The Bills of Exchange Act, s. 27, provides that any person having a possessory lien over a bill is deemed to be a holder for value to the extent of his lien, and can therefore sell and transfer the bill.

GUARANTEES AND INDEMNITIES

SECTION 74. NATURE OF GUARANTEE

1. Definition of guarantee. A guarantee, or surety contract, is an undertaking "to be answerable for the debt, default, or miscarriage of another," ✳ *Statute of Frauds*, 1677, *s.* **4**.

Guarantees may be either *specific* or *continuing*.

(a) *A specific guarantee* relates to one isolated debt only. (Where a bank accepts a specific guarantee of a single loan, a separate account should be opened for that loan, otherwise the guarantee may be cancelled out by operation of the *Rule in Clayton's Case, see s.* **22**.)

(b) *A continuing guarantee* is one covering a series of transactions, *e.g.* a guarantee of an overdraft on a current account at a bank. (A bank, in order to enforce such a guarantee of an overdraft, should stipulate expressly in the guarantee form that the guarantee shall cover the *final balance*. Otherwise it will be interpreted as covering only the overdraft as it existed at the date of the agreement, and payments in after that date would thus reduce the guarantor's liability.)

2. Characteristics of guarantees.

(a) *Three parties:* principal creditor, principal debtor and guarantor (or surety).

(b) *Primary liability to pay* must attach to the principal debtor. The surety only becomes liable to pay if the debtor defaults.

(c) *The guarantor has no interest in the contract* between the principal debtor and the principal creditor, except in so far as he agrees to accept liability if the debtor fails to pay.

3. Form of guarantees. *The Statute of Frauds, s.* **4**, requires any contract of guarantee to be evidenced in writing, by some sufficient note or memorandum; *see s.* **11**. (This requirement does *not* apply where the guarantee is part of some larger transaction, *e.g.* a contract of agency.)

Guarantees require to be supported by consideration, but the consideration does not need to be *stated* in the written memorandum: *Mercantile Law Amendment Act,* 1856. (Thus the consideration may be proved by independent oral evidence if necessary.) Guarantee bonds do not require consideration.

NOTE:

   (a) *Representations made in order to assist someone to obtain credit* must be *in writing, personally signed* by the party making the representation. Otherwise the representation is not actionable: *Statute of Frauds Amendment Act,* 1828.

   (b) Guarantees must normally be *stamped* (6*d.*) within 14 days of being signed. Guarantee bonds (guarantees under seal) must be stamped 10*s.* within 30 days of execution.

4. Guarantees not uberrimae fidei. Neither the principal creditor nor the principal debtor are under any legal duty to disclose to the guarantor facts which might influence him against entering into the contract. Thus if A offers to guarantee B's bank account, the bank is under no obligation to reveal matters which show that B is a bad risk: *Wythes* v. *Labouchere* (1859).

BUT NOTE:

   (a) *Active misrepresentation by the creditor* (or by the debtor with the creditor's knowledge) will be grounds for rescission.

   (b) *Active concealment* of material facts may amount to misrepresentation, *e.g.* keeping silent about some facts so as to put facts disclosed into a deceptive light.

   (c) *Once the contract of guarantee* is made, the creditor owes a duty of the utmost good faith to the guarantor, who is entitled to be discharged if this duty is not observed.

     Thus the creditor must disclose material *facts* coming to his knowledge and affecting the guarantor's risk, but need not disclose *mere suspicions, e.g.* A guaranteed B's bank account, and B overdrew on the guaranteed account to pay off debts to another creditor. The bank suspected that A was being defrauded, but did not disclose this. HELD: They were under no duty to do so: *National Provincial Bank* v. *Glanusk* (1913).

   (d) *Guarantees in the nature of insurance* are *uberrimae fidei, e.g.* "fidelity guarantees" (of the character and good faith of some third person). Thus A gave a fidelity guarantee in respect of L to L's employer, B. B omitted to disclose that L had misappropriated some of B's money and was only being retained in employment in reliance on A's guarantee bond. HELD: L's former dishonesty should have been disclosed, and A was not liable on his guarantee: *London General Omnibus Co.* v. *Holloway* (1912).

5. Indemnity contracts.

An indemnity contract is one in which the indemnifier promises to preserve the other party from loss. *Unlike a guarantee* (a) it is a contract of primary liability, and (b) it does not require written evidence, and (c) there are only two parties, *i.e.* the indemnifier and the person he promises to indemnify.

In * *Birkmyr* v. *Darnell* (1704) guarantees and indemnities were distinguished thus:

A and B enter a shop and B asks X for goods on credit. Then (i) if A says to X, "Give B the goods, and if he does not pay for them I will," this is a contract of guarantee (since A will only become liable if B defaults, *i.e.* A's liability is secondary to B's); (ii) if A says to X, "Give B the goods and I will see that you get paid," this is an indemnity since A accepts the principal or primary liability for the debt.

6. Capacity to contract.

Capacity to guarantee is generally co-extensive with normal contractual capacity, but note:

(a) *A partner* as guarantor has no power to bind his firm unless (i) so authorised by his co-partners, or (ii) giving guarantees is part of the firm's normal business. Even where he has authority, he cannot bind the firm in a *guarantee under seal* unless (i) he is so authorised by deed (power of attorney), or (ii) all the partners sign the guarantee deed.

(b) *Guarantees by married women* are enforceable only against their separate estates. (Thus a bank considering a guarantee from a married woman cannot take her husband's status into account in assessing the value of her guarantee.)

(c) *Trading companies* have implied power to borrow money, but there is probably no implied power to give guarantees. (Thus a bank before accepting a guarantee from a company must examine the Memorandum and Articles of the company to make sure there is power to give guarantees.)

7. Position of creditor.

His rights against the guarantor are dependant on the terms of the contract. But a *continuing guarantee* by or to a *partnership* is revoked as to future transactions by any change in the constitution of the firm: *Partnership Act*, 1890, *s.* 18.

8. Joint and several guarantees. Sometimes several persons join in giving a guarantee, and the liability of such co-guarantors may then (depending on the agreement) be joint, or several, or joint and several.

    (a) *Joint guarantors:* Each guarantor is personally liable for the full amount, but the creditor has *only one cause of action* against them and should therefore sue all in one action. If he elects to sue just one of the guarantors, he cannot later sue the others since he has exhausted his one cause of action, and is taken as having waived his claims against the others: The rule in ✳ *Kendall* v. *Hamilton* (1879).

       Also on the *death* or *bankruptcy* of a joint guarantor, his estate is discharged from all liability. (As between themselves joint guarantors have a right of contribution for any sums paid beyond their fair share of liability.)

    (b) *Several guarantors.* Each is fully liable for the whole debt, and can be sued separately and successively, *i.e.* the creditor has *several* rights of action and the rule in *Kendall* v. *Hamilton* does not apply. Further, the death or bankruptcy of a several guarantor does not release his estate from liability for claims arising before the death or bankruptcy.

    (c) *Joint and several guarantors.* Here the creditor can either sue them jointly or separately and successively, and death or bankruptcy has the same effect as in (b) above. (From the creditor's point of view therefore a several, or joint and several guarantee is preferable, *e.g.* bank guarantees are nearly always drafted on the basis of joint and several liability.)

SECTION 75. POSITION OF THE GUARANTOR

1. Liability of the guarantor. *Arises* only when the principal debtor has defaulted, and not until then.

The surety's liability *depends* partly on the terms of the contract and partly on the following rules of law:

    (a) If the transaction between the creditor and the principal debtor is *void*, the surety is not bound by his guarantee, *e.g.* guarantees of loans to infants, which are themselves void under *Infants' Relief Act*, 1874, *s.* 1: ✳ *Coutts & Co.* v. *Browne-Lecky* (1947).

    (b) The creditor may be entitled to treat the guarantor as a *principal debtor*, unless he makes it clear that he is a surety only and only secondarily liable.

(c) The creditor is under *a legal duty not to prejudice the guarantor* in any way, *e.g.* by increasing his liability by allowing release of any co-guarantor. (In such a case the guarantor can demand release also: *see s.* **76** *below.*)

(d) *If the surety goes bankrupt,* the creditor can prove in the bankruptcy for the amount guaranteed. (Bank guarantees usually provide expressly for this contingency, and for the bankruptcy of the debtor.)

(e) When he has accepted liability to the creditor, the guarantor immediately acquires a *right of action against the debtor* for the value of the guarantee. But this right does not arise until he has *accepted liability* himself (even though he has not yet actually paid the creditor); *Ascherson* v. *Tredegar Dry Dock Co.* (1909). (Under the *Bankruptcy Act, 1914, s.* 24, discharge in bankruptcy does not release the debtor from liability to his guarantors: for discharge in bankruptcy *see s.* **78**.)

2. Rights of the guarantor.

(a) *Indemnification by debtor.* The surety can sue the debtor for all sums properly paid under the guarantee (with 4% interest), plus damages for any additional loss. But he cannot recover the whole value of the guarantee if he was only made to pay a smaller sum. (This right to compensation arises as soon as he actually accepts liability to the creditor; but he cannot sue the debtor until he has actually paid the creditor himself.)

(b) *Set-offs and counter-claims.* If sued by the creditor, the surety can avail himself of any set-offs or counter-claims which the debtor has against the creditor, *e.g.* where he is sued on a £1000 guarantee and finds that the creditor owes the debtor £200 for goods or services he is entitled to set-off the £200 against the guarantee and so reduce his own liability to £800.

(c) *Delivery of securities held by the creditor.* On paying his guarantee to the creditor, the surety is entitled to possession of any securities the debtor may have earlier deposited with the creditor in respect of the same debt, even if the surety did not know of them when he made his guarantee.

(d) *Hotchpot.* A co-guarantor who has received securities from the principal debtor (or creditor) must share the benefit of them with other co-guarantors, even though they may have been unaware of their existence when they became guarantors.

(e) *Contribution from co-guarantors.* If one surety pays the whole debt, he is entitled to compensation from co-sureties (in a joint, or joint and several guarantee), even if (i) their guarantees are contained in different instruments, or (ii) he did not know of the existence of the co-sureties when he signed his own guarantee.

This right is implied by equity, and is independent of contract. (It may however be modified by contract.)

SECTION 76. DISCHARGE OF GUARANTOR

Unless otherwise agreed, a guarantee is *automatically discharged* in the following circumstances.

1. Unauthorised variation of terms. The guarantor is automatically released if the debtor and creditor vary the contract between them, without the guarantor's knowledge and approval (even though the variation is not prejudicial to the guarantor).

EXAMPLE: A guaranteed D's overdraft. Without A's knowledge the bank allowed D to open a second account into which he paid substantial sums, while leaving his existing overdraft undiminished. HELD: This amounted to an unauthorised variation of the guarantee and A was discharged: *Nat. Bank of Nigeria Ltd*. v. *Awolesi* (1964).

2. Creditor relinquishes securities. If the creditor relinquishes securities of the debtor held by him in respect of the debt guaranteed, this automatically releases the guarantor (unless otherwise agreed).

3. Creditor omitting to do something to protect the surety. If the creditor omits to do something he reasonably should do for the protection of the guarantor, this operates as automatic release, *e.g.* where he fails to register an equitable mortgage granted to him by the debtor, since such a mortgage may be void if not registered (and the surety would be entitled to a transfer of such mortgage on payment of the guarantee).

4. Unauthorised extension of time to the debtor. If the creditor makes a binding agreement to grant the debtor an extension of time for payment of the debt, this automatically releases the surety.

EXCEPTIONS:

(a) Where the extension was *expressly or impliedly sanctioned* by the original guarantee agreement (as in Bank guarantees in some cases).

(b) *Where judgment has already been obtained* against the surety, and the principal debtor together.

(c) Where there are *several distinct debts*, extensions of time in respect of one debt will only discharge the surety in respect of that debt alone.

5. Release of co-surety, *i.e.* where the creditor discharges any co-surety, thus depriving the remainder of their rights of contribution against the surety discharged: *Smith* v. *Wood* (1929).

6. Revocation. This is only possible where the consideration for the guarantee is divisible, *i.e.* in continuing guarantees, which can always be revoked as to future liabilities (unless otherwise agreed).

Specific guarantees cannot generally be revoked, and revocation of a continuing guarantee does not affect liability for debts already incurred.

Also if the consideration for any guarantee is a *forbearance to* sue (*i.e.* a promise by the creditor not to sue the debtor for the debt, in reliance on the guarantee), it appears that the guarantee is irrevocable.

7. Release of debtor. Release of the debtor automatically releases the surety, unless the creditor expressly or impliedly reserves his rights against the surety in the original contract (as is usually done in Bank guarantees).

NOTE that if the debtor goes bankrupt and later obtains his discharge in bankruptcy this operates to release him from liability to the creditor in most cases, but it does not affect the liability of the guarantor.

8. Payment of debt by the debtor.

9. Death of guarantor. It depends on the terms of the contract whether his death will discharge his estate from liability under his guarantee. Thus bank guarantee forms usually stipulate that the guarantee shall remain operative until the bank receives *notice* of the guarantor's death.

Death of a joint guarantor discharges his estate from liability, but surviving joint guarantors remain liable.

10. Bankruptcy of guarantor. The creditor can prove for the debt in the guarantor's bankruptcy, even if the debtor has not yet defaulted in payment himself, and even if he has received (but not yet realised) securities from the debtor: *Bankruptcy Act*, 1914, *s*. 30 (3).

If the surety obtains his discharge in bankruptcy, this operates to release him from his guarantee in most cases: *B.A.*, 1914, *s*. 28 (2).

The bankruptcy of a joint guarantor does not relieve his co-sureties from liability.

11. Change in constitution of firm. A continuing guarantee given to a firm, or to a third party regarding transactions by a firm, is automatically revoked as to future liabilities by any change in the constitution of the firm, *e.g.* on the death or retirement of any partner: *Partnership Act*, 1890, *s*. 18.

12. Limitation Act, 1939, s. 2. The creditor's rights against the guarantor are statute-barred after 6 years (12 years if the guarantee was under seal), but time begins to run only when the debt becomes due from the principal debtor.

Thus bank guarantee forms usually stipulate that the guarantor shall not become liable until the bank formally notifies him that it proposes to call in his guarantee. Time then begins to run only after the banks makes this formal demand, even though the debtor may have become liable considerably earlier: *Bradford Old Bank* v. *Sutcliffe* (1918).

The Act also bars the guarantor's claim for indemnification against the debtor, and for contribution from co-sureties, after the limitation period has elapsed.

SECURITIES

1. What is a security, and what forms may it take? (69. 1, 2.)

2. Distinguish between legal and equitable interests in property, and explain how ownership of the various forms of property can be transferred at law. (69. 3; 70. 3.)

3. Distinguish between estates and interests in land. Has the mortgagee of land an estate or an interest, or may he have either? (70. 4, 5; 71. 2.)

4. "In some parts of Britain the entire title to land is registrable, and throughout the country charges on land can be registered." Explain this statement, and outline the registers referred to and the matters which can be registered therein. (70. 7, 8.)

5. How may (a) legal and (b) equitable mortgages of land be created today? (71. 2, 3.)

6. Explain briefly the remedies of a legal mortgagee. How do these differ from the remedies available to an equitable mortgage of land? (71. 5, 8.)

7. When does a mortgagee's power of sale (a) arise and (b) become exercisable. (71. 6.)

8. Write explanatory notes on: (a) Consolidation, (b) Tacking, (c) Attornment clause, (d) Sub-mortgage. (71. 9, 10, 12.)

9. Explain briefly the rules governing the priority of mortgages. (71. 11.)

10. What is the Equity of Redemption, and what is meant by a "clog on the equity"? (71. 14, 15.)

11. How can personalty be (a) mortgaged, and (b) pledged? What sort of chattels are suitable for pledging? (72. 1–5.)

12. Explain briefly the main provisions of (a) The *Bills of Sale Acts*, and (b) *The Pawnbrokers' Acts*. (72. 4, 5.)

13. What is a lien? Distinguish between Possessory, equitable and maritime liens. **(73. 1–4.)**

14. When if ever, does a lien confer a power of sale? **(73. 1–5.)**

15. Define a guarantee. How does it differ from an indemnity contract, and what form must it take? **(74. 1, 3, 5.)**

16. Guarantees are not *uberrimae fidei* contracts, but once formed a guarantee imposes similar duties upon the creditor. Explain. **(74. 4.)**

17. Distinguish between joint, and joint and several guarantees. **(74. 8.)**

18. What are the rights and liabilities of a guarantor under a contract of guarantee? **(75.)**

19. In what circumstances is a guarantor discharged from liability? **(76.)**

SPECIMEN QUESTIONS

1. In relation to unregistered land there are five registers kept in the Land Charges Department of the Land Registry. What are those five registers? In your answer explain briefly the nature of the principal charges entered upon each of the five registers. *Inst. of Bankers, Diploma Part II*, 1963. **(70. 8.)**

2. Explain the statement that the guarantor in respect of the debt, default, or miscarriage of another is entitled to insist upon a rigid adherence to the terms of his obligation.
In what circumstances is the guarantor discharged from his obligation under the guarantee? *C.I.S., Final, June* 1961. **(75. 1; 76.)**

3. In a guarantee is consideration necessary and, if so, when? How can the agreement be made and what rights has the surety after payment thereunder? *A.C.C.A., Intermediate, June* 1961. **(74. 3; 75. 2.)**

4. Mention the essential features of a continuing guarantee, and state the steps which must be taken to make such guarantee enforceable by action.
What are the rights of the guarantor, and in what circumstances are they exercisable? *C.I.S., Final, June* 1962. **(74. 1; 75. 2.)**

5. State the circumstances which will render a conditional bill of sale void. *A.C.C.A., Intermediate, June* 1964. (**72. 3.**)

6. State the essentials of a contract of guarantee.

A and Co. were stockbrokers who agreed with B that he should have half the commission earned as a result of his introductions and that he should pay half of any losses which might be sustained from them. Explain whether or not this is a contract of guarantee. *A.C.C.A., Intermediate, Dec.* 1963. (**74. 1–3; 39. 2.**)

7. (*a*) An executor finds that the deceased had, during his lifetime, given a continuing guarantee.

  (i) In what circumstances would the guarantee be revoked by death?
  (ii) If it is revoked, what action should the executor take?

(*b*) Jones gives Brown a continuing guarantee for the due fulfillment by a partnership firm, Robinson & Co., of its business transactions with Brown. A partner in the firm retires and another partner is taken in. What effect, if any, has the change in the partnership on Jones' guarantee? *C.A., Final, May* 1964. (**74. 1; 76. 9, 11.**)

8. When one of two sureties has paid the debt to the creditor what remedies are available to such surety against:

  (*a*) the debtor,
  (*b*) the creditor, and
  (*c*) the co-surety? *C.A., Final, May* 1962. (**75. 1, 2.**)

9. Explain the ways in which a mortgage may be made of:

  (*a*) chattels personal;
  (*b*) debts;
  (*c*) shares in a limited company.

State the rules for determining priority of successive mortgages in cases where the same property has been mortgaged to several lenders. *C.I.S., Intermediate, June* 1961. (**71. 11; 72. 1, 3, 28, 3, 4.**)

10. G signed a guarantee in respect of the banking account of C. The latter is unable to repay his overdraft, and the bank has demanded payment from G under his guarantee. G wishes to deny liability on the ground that the bank failed to disclose to him: (i) that C's wife had served a prison sentence and (ii) that C's wife had authority to draw on C's account. Advise G whether or not he is liable to the bank. *Inst. of Bankers, Diploma Part II, April* 1962. (**74. 4.**)

11. A customer has applied to his bank for an overdraft of £1000, and he has offered as security a life policy on his own life for £5000 with profits, the surrender value being £900.

Explain what is meant by "surrender value," and describe the steps which should be followed to enable the bank to obtain a legal mortgage of this policy. *Inst. of Bankers, Diploma Part II, April* 1964. (**55.** 2–4; **72.** 1.)

12. (*a*) Define a guarantee and explain how it differs from an indemnity contract.

(*b*) P orally hired A as his agent for the sale of some valuable paintings, and as part of the contract A guaranteed P against failure of any of A's clients to pay for the paintings they bought. State with reasons whether the guarantee is enforceable. *A.C.C.A. June* 1967. (**74.** 3 and 5; **29.** 2.)

PART SIX

BANKRUPTCY

BANKRUPTCY

SECTION 77. COMMENCEMENT OF PROCEEDINGS

1. Objects of bankruptcy. When a person is *insolvent* (*i.e.* unable to pay his debts as and when they fall due) either he or his creditors may *petition* for the court to take over the administration of his estate and its distribution among creditors. This procedure is called bankruptcy and is governed by the *Bankruptcy Act,* 1914, as amended.

The objects of bankruptcy are:

- (a) *To secure fair and equal distribution* of available property among the creditors.
- (b) *To free the debtor from his debts,* so that he can make a fresh start as soon as he is discharged by the court.
- (c) *To enquire into the reasons for his insolvency,* and so to deter people from rashly incurring debts they cannot pay.

2. Procedure in bankruptcies. For a debtor to be declared bankrupt he must first have committed one of the recognised *acts of bankruptcy*: *see 5 below.* The commission of such an act raises a presumption of insolvency and justifies presentation of a *petition* for the debtor's bankruptcy.

Procedure is then as follows:

- (a) *Presentation of petition* by a creditor, or by the debtor himself. To present a petition a creditor must be owed £50 or more; *see below.* The petition should be presented (i) *to the local county court* in whose jurisdiction the debtor has carried on business for the greater part of the previous six months, or (ii) *to the Chancery Division of the High Court,* if the debtor does not reside in England, or his whereabouts are unknown.
- (b) *A receiving order* is made out by the court if satisfied that the debtor appears to be insolvent. The receiving order

makes the Official Receiver (an officer of the Board of Trade) receiver of the debtor's property. The official receiver then (i) obtains a *statement of affairs* from the debtor, and (ii) conducts a *public examination* of the debtor as to the reason for his failure.

(c) *Creditors' first meeting.* The official receiver then summons the creditors to a meeting with the debtor to decide whether to accept any *composition or scheme of arrangement* he may wish to put forward, to save himself from bankruptcy. If he makes no offer, or the creditors reject what he does offer, the bankruptcy proceeds to the next stage. If they do accept, the bankruptcy normally ends there.

(d) *Adjudication order.* If no composition or scheme is accepted, the Court *adjudicates the debtor bankrupt.* His property then passes to his *trustee in bankruptcy* or, if none has been appointed, remains vested in the official receiver.

(e) *Discharge.* When all debts have been paid, or as much as can be, the debtor can apply for his discharge. He must first undergo a *public examination* to ensure that he has done all he can towards paying his debts, and if the court is satisfied it will order his discharge. This has the effect of freeing him from further liability on most of the debts still outstanding at his discharge.

3. Who may be bankrupted.

Any debtor can be bankrupted (subject to the special rules in 4 below).

A debtor is any person, whether a British subject or not, who at the time he committed an act of bankruptcy was (*a*) personally present in England, (*b*) ordinarily resident, or possessing a residence, in England, (*c*) personally, or through an agent, carrying on business in England, or (*d*) was a member of a firm which was carrying on business in England: *B.A.*, 1914, *s.* 1 (2).

A non-resident can only be bankrupted in England if he was (*a*) domiciled in England, (*b*) resident in England within one year before presentation of the petition, or (*c*) trading in England either personally, or through an agent, or as a member of a firm: *s.* 4. (A debtor is still "trading in England" as long as any of his trade debts are outstanding: *re Bird, ex parte the Debtor,* v. *I.R.C.* (1962).)

4. Special classes of debtors.

(a) *Infants* can be bankrupted for *debts enforceable* against them, *e.g.* for necessaries, and for taxes. Voidable contracts ratified after maturity are not sufficient to ground a petition. If an infant is a member of a *firm*, proceedings should be taken only against the adult members. (But all the firm's assets are available for the creditors, including the infant's share.)

(b) *Married women* are now fully bankruptable: *L.R. (Married Women & Tortfeasors) Act*, 1935, *s.* 1. But a husband cannot prove in his wife's bankruptcy for debts owed to him until all the other creditors have been paid, *i.e.* he is a deferred creditor.

(c) *Persons of unsound mind* can only be bankrupted with the consent of the court (or, if the act of bankruptcy was committed before he was certified, without consent of court).

(d) *Companies and partnerships.* Companies are wound up, not bankrupted. Partnerships can be bankrupted and the separate estate of each partner may be brought into the firm's bankruptcy: *see s.* **37** and *s.* **81.** 8.

(e) *Deceased persons* cannot be bankrupted. But if the deceased's estate is unable to meet his debts it may be *administered in bankruptcy*, *i.e.* the administrators can be compelled to follow approximately the same procedure as in bankruptcy.

(f) *Aliens: see* 3 *above.*

5. Acts of bankruptcy: B.A., s. 1. Before bankruptcy proceedings can be commenced against him, the debtor must have committed one of the following acts of bankruptcy:

(a) *Assignment or conveyance of his property to a trustee for the benefit of his creditors generally.*

NOTE:

(i) It must be a *conveyance or assignment*, *i.e.* an actual transfer. A mere contract to transfer is not enough.

(ii) It must affect *substantially all* the debtor's property.

(iii) It makes no difference whether assignment is honest or fraudulent.

(iv) *A creditor who has assented to it* cannot rely on such assignment as an act of bankruptcy.

(b) *Fraudulent conveyance, gift, or other transfer of any of his property.*

NOTE:

(i) Under this head *any kind of transfer* is sufficient; it need not be in favour of all the creditors, nor of all the debtor's property. But it *must be fraudulent.*

(ii) *"Fraudulent" means* seeking to prevent distribution in accordance with the bankruptcy laws. (This is a much narrower meaning than normally given to the word, which is usually intended to connote some intention to deceive.)

(iii) *Such conveyance etc. is void*, and the transferee must restore the property to the trustee in bankruptcy: *s*. 42.

(iv) *By s*. 172, *Law of Property Act*, 1925, a conveyance is also void if it is *intended to defraud* the transferor's creditors.

(c) *Fraudulent preference, i.e.* a transfer of any of the debtor's property with the intention of paying the recipient creditor in full in preference to other creditors. Such transfer is void: *s*. 44.

(d) *Departing or remaining out of England with intent to defeat or delay his creditors* (or leaving his residence, or otherwise hiding from his creditors, even though he remains in England).

"Intent to defeat," etc., must be proved by the creditors, but can be presumed from the circumstances, if they warrant it.

(e) *Seizure of goods by a sheriff*, under process of execution under a court order.

The goods must either (i) have been *sold*, or (ii) have been *held by the sheriff for at least 21 days* and the petition must be presented within 3 months thereafter.

(f) *Declaration by the debtor of his inability to pay his debts*.

The debtor may (i) file such declaration with the court, or (ii) present his own petition in bankruptcy, and either will constitute an act of bankruptcy.

(g) *Failure to comply with a bankruptcy notice*.

A bankruptcy notice is one served by a creditor who has obtained judgment for his debt, and demands payment and warns the debtor that a petition will be presented for his bankruptcy unless he pays within 7 days. But the debtor may resist the notice by (i) raising any *set-off or counter-claim* which was not available to him in the action in which the creditor obtained judgment, or (ii) *paying* the debt, or (iii) *giving adequate security*.

(h) *Notice by a debtor of suspension of payment of debts.*

The debtor may give the notice orally or in writing, and it will be grounds for a petition even if suspension is only temporary, or the notice is issued "without prejudice." The notice may not state expressly that suspension of payment is intended; it is sufficient if it gives a creditor reasonable grounds for believing that this is the intention: ✷ *Crook* v. *Morley* (1891).

6. The petition. A petition can be presented by the *debtor* himself (because of inability to pay debts), or by a *creditor*.

A creditor's petition (verified by affidavit) can be presented if (*s*. 4):

(a) *His debt is £50 or more.* Several creditors can present a joint petition if their debts together aggregate £50.

(b) *The debt is a liquidated sum* (*i.e.* an ascertained amount, not for instance a claim for unliquidated damages for breach of contract), payable immediately or in the future.

(c) *The act of bankruptcy relied on occurred within 3 months* before presentation of the petition.

(d) *The debtor is liable to English bankruptcy law: see 3 above.*

(e) *The act of bankruptcy is not one to which the creditor was privy, e.g.* not a deed of arrangement to which the creditor was a party: *see s.* **82**.

NOTE:

(i) *A secured creditor* can only petition if he relinquishes his security for the benefit of all the creditors, or if the security does not cover his debt fully.

(ii) *Several petitions presented simultaneously* can be consolidated and dealt with at one hearing: *B.A.*, *s*. 110.

(iii) *A petition can be dismissed if* (*a*) the petitioner's motive is improper, *e.g.* malicious: *re Shaw* (1901), or (*b*) the debtor's sole property is a life interest terminable on his bankruptcy: *re Otway* (1895), or (*c*) there are no assets and no reasonable likelihood of there being any: *re Betts* (1897).

(iv) A petition once presented can only be *withdrawn* with consent of the court: *B.A.*, *s*. 5 (7).

(v) Before hearing the petition (usually 8 days after presentation) the court may *stay all actions* or executions against the debtor's estate, and protect the available assets by making the Official Receiver their custodian: *B.A.*, *ss*. 8, 9.

7. The receiving order.

(a) *When made.* (i) The order can be issued immediately after presentation of a petition by the debtor himself, but (ii) if the petition is presented by a creditor, a formal court hearing is a necessary prerequisite.

(b) *Advertisement of receiving order.* The making of the receiving order must be advertised in the *London Gazette* and a local newspaper: *B.A., s.* 11. (Also, if the debtor owns any land, the receiving order should be registered as a land charge to prevent dealings with the land: *Land Charges Act,* 1925, *s.* 6.)

(c) *Effect of receiving order.* (i) The official receiver (an official of the Board of Trade attached to the court for bankruptcy purposes) becomes receiver of all the debtor's property, and may appoint a special manager of his business, if any. (ii) No actions can be commenced or continued against the debtor without leave of the court: *B.A., s.* 7.

NOTE: The receiving order does not make the debtor bankrupt. He only becomes bankrupt when the adjudication order is made: *see s.* **78,** 4.

(d) *Rescission of the receiving order* is allowed in the following circumstances:

  (i) Where the court sanctions a *composition or scheme* of arrangement: *B.A., s.* 16.

  (ii) Where it appears that the property should be distributed according to the *laws of Scotland or Ireland,* *e.g.* where a majority of the creditors in number and value, or the bulk of the debtor's property, is in Scotland or Ireland: *s.* 12.

  (iii) Where the court exercises its wide *discretion* to rescind under *B.A., s.* 108, *e.g.* where the debts are paid in full, or the court is satisfied that the receiving order should never have been made. (The fact that the creditors may ask for rescision is not binding on the court.)

8. Arrest of debtor: s. 23. The court may order the arrest of the debtor and the seizure of books, papers, goods, etc., if the debtor:

  (a) seems likely to *abscond,*

(*b*) seems likely to *remove or conceal goods*, or

(*c*) *fails to attend* any examination ordered by the court.

SECTION 78. PROCEEDINGS AFTER RECEIVING ORDER

1. Proceedings after receiving order.

(*a*) The debtor must submit a *statement of affairs* to the official receiver and this must be verified by affidavit.

(*b*) After submitting the statement of affairs, the debtor must attend the *first meeting of creditors*, at which he may offer any composition or scheme of arrangement he has in mind.

(*c*) After a private examination by the official receiver, the debtor must attend a *public examination*. This may continue, by successive adjournments, until his bankruptcy ends.

(*d*) If the creditors refuse to accept any composition or scheme offered by the debtor, the court will issue the *adjudication order* (which makes the debtor bankrupt, though commencement of the bankruptcy is back-dated to the date of the first available act of bankruptcy, *i.e.* up to as early as 3 months before the presentation of the petition).

2. Debtor's statement of affairs: s. 14. This (supported by an affidavit as to its truth and accuracy) must *set out* the debtor's debts and liabilities and the names of his creditors together with a list of his assets and such other matters as the official receiver may require.

The debtor has 7 *days* to prepare his statement (or 3 where the petition was presented by himself).

The statement may be inspected by any person claiming in writing to be a creditor entitled to payment in the bankruptcy (if any person falsely so states he is guilty of contempt of court).

If for some reason the debtor himself *cannot* prepare the statement, the official receiver may do so at the expense of the estate: *B.A.*, *s.* 74. If the debtor *refuses* to prepare a statement of affairs he can immediately be adjudicated bankrupt.

3. First meeting of creditors: compositions.

(a) *When summoned.* Within 14 days after the making of the receiving order the official receiver will summon and chair a meeting of the creditors, who will then decide whether or not they wish to have the debtor adjudicated bankrupt. The meeting is summoned by *written notice* to the creditors named in the statement of affairs, and by giving 6 days' notice, in the *London Gazette* and a local newspaper. The debtor must attend this meeting and answer any relevant questions as to his affairs.

(b) *Debtor's proposals.* At the meeting the debtor may put forward proposals, if any, for the payment of his debts, *i.e.* a composition or a scheme of arrangement. Such proposals must be submitted to the official receiver within 4 days after submission of the statement of affairs: *s.* 16.

If accepted by a *majority in number, and three-quarters in value,* of the creditors the proposals must then be submitted to the court for its approval.

(c) *Approval by court.* The court can approve or reject the proposals, but cannot vary them.

It must reject if of the opinion (i) that the proposals are unreasonable, (ii) that they will not benefit the general body of creditors, or (iii) that they do not obey the order of payments laid down by the Bankruptcy Act. The court also has a discretion to reject in other cases, if it appears just and equitable to do so.

(d) *Creditors bound.* Once approved by the court, a scheme or composition is binding on all the creditors. Its effect (so long as it is carried out) is to free the debtor from all debts provable in bankruptcy, and to release him from jurisdiction in bankruptcy.

(e) *Approval annulled.* An approved scheme or composition may be annulled by the court because of (i) default in payment, (ii) injustice or impracticality, (iii) fraud of the debtor.

4. Adjudication order.

If the receiving order is not rescinded and no scheme or composition is approved by the court, the court will issue the adjudication order declaring the debtor legally bankrupt.

(a) *When made.* The order must be issued if (i) *the creditors so resolved* at the first meeting, or (ii) at that meeting the creditors reached *no decision,* or (iii) there was *no meeting* for some reason, or (iv) *no scheme has been approved* within 14 days after conclusion of the public examination, or (v) the debtor fails to give a reasonable account of his affairs: *B.A., s.* 14.

(b) *Effect.* The debtor becomes bankrupt and all his property vests in his trustee in bankruptcy, and becomes divisible among his creditors.

(c) *Annulment.* The order may be annulled if (i) a scheme or composition is accepted after adjudication (*s.* 21), (ii) the adjudication for some reason should not have been made (*s.* 29) (iii) the debts of the bankrupt have been paid in full (*s.* 29). On annulment the property of the bankrupt revests in him. (Notice of annulment must be published in the *London Gazette* and a local newspaper.)

5. Meetings of creditors.

(a) *First meeting: (see* 3 *above*). If the creditors reject any scheme or composition put forward, they will usually at this meeting appoint the *trustee in bankruptcy* (upon whom falls the duty of paying the debts and managing the bankruptcy generally).

(b) *Voting at meetings.* No creditor can vote until he has proved his debt. A creditor entitled to vote can give a proxy (authority for someone else to attend on his behalf), which may be either (i) *a general proxy* to any adult employee to vote at any meeting (but not in order to secure any exceptional advantage for the appointor), or (ii) *a special proxy* to any adult to vote on the acceptance of any composition or scheme, the appointment of a trustee or committee of inspection, or any other specified matter. A proxy may not be used at any meeting unless deposited with the official receiver or the trustee before the meeting.

(c) *Resolutions.* (i) An *ordinary resolution* means a majority in value of creditors voting personally or by proxy at any meeting. (ii) *A special resolution* is a majority of three-quarters in value and more than half in number of creditors present personally or by proxy.

(d) *Chairman* is the official receiver at the first meeting, and the trustee thereafter. The chairman decides whether to admit proofs of any debt for the purpose of allowing a creditor to vote, etc.

6. Committee of inspection: s. 20. The creditors usually (but not invariably) appoint a committee consisting of not more than five and not less than three of their number, to supervise the trustee in his management of the bankruptcy. No member

K

may act on the committee until he has proved his debt and had proof admitted: see s. **81. 1.**

The committee must *meet at least once a month*, and the trustee or any member may call a meeting at any time. It may *act by majority* of members present at any meeting, and a majority of the members forms a quorum, *i.e.* the quorum will usually be three.

Appointment of members is terminated by (*a*) resignation, in writing, (*b*) bankruptcy, (*c*) absence from five consecutive meetings, (*d*) removal by ordinary resolution of a general meeting of creditors (of which 7 days' advance notice has been given).

If no committee is appointed, acts of the trustee usually requiring the consent of such committee require the consent of the Board of Trade.

The committee supervises the trustee in the execution of his duties, and he must submit his accounts to the committee for examination, *i.e.* (i) trading accounts (if any) every month, (ii) cash book every 3 months, or more often. (The committee must sign the books if satisfied with them.)

7. Discharge of bankrupt: s. 26. The bankrupt may apply in open court for his discharge at any time after adjudication. The creditors must be given 14 days' notice of the application, and they, the trustee or the official receiver can oppose it.

   (a) *Court's discretion.* The court has a wide discretion to decide how far, if at all, discharge shall be granted. *The court cannot grant an unconditional discharge where the bankrupt:*

       (i) Has been *convicted* of any offence in connection with the bankruptcy.

      (ii) Has assets amounting to *less than* 10*s*. in the pound on his unsecured liabilities (unless this is due to circumstances beyond his control).

     (iii) Has failed to keep proper *books and accounts* in business within three years immediately preceding the bankruptcy.

     (iv) *Has continued to trade* knowing himself to be insolvent.

     (v) Has contracted provable debts *without reasonable expectation* of being able to pay them.

     (vi) *Has failed adequately to account* for any loss or deficiency of assets.

    (vii) *Has contributed* to his own bankruptcy by gambling, extravagance or culpable neglect of his business.

(viii) Has brought a *frivolous action* which has resulted in judgment being given against him, or has put up a frivolous defence to an action against him by a creditor.

(ix) *Gave undue preference* to any creditor within 3 months before the receiving order.

(x) Has been adjudicated bankrupt, or has made any composition with creditors *on any previous occasion.*

(xi) Has been guilty of *fraud* or fraudulent breach of trust.

(b) *Kinds of discharge.* The discharge may be (i) *unconditional,* freeing the bankrupt from all further liability on his provable debts, (ii) *conditional,* having the same effect as (i) but subject to a condition that subsequently acquired property shall be disposed of in a certain way, (iii) *suspensive, i.e.* not becoming unconditional until after a certain period of time, or until the payment of certain debts, or (iv) *conditional and suspensive.*

8. Effect of discharge order: s. 28. The order discharges liability on all debts *except* (*a*) Crown debts (unless the Treasury consents in writing), (*b*) liabilities incurred by fraud, and (*c*) liabilities under a judgment for seduction, affiliation, or being co-respondent in divorce proceedings.

Non-provable debts are not affected by discharge and can be sued upon in the normal way, unless statute-barred or waived.

An order of discharge does not necessarily relieve from liability any co-debtor, or any surety for the bankrupt.

The order may be revoked by the court at any time on cause shown, provided that such revocation does not affect the rights of third parties acquired since the discharge, unless they were fraudulent. Thus if after discharge the debtor sold certain property to X, and the discharge was revoked some days later, the property could not be recovered from X unless it could be shown that he was a party to some fraudulent scheme with the debtor.

SECTION 79. THE TRUSTEE IN BANKRUPTCY

1. How appointed: B.A., s. 19:

(a) *By ordinary resolution of the creditors* (usually at their first meeting).

(b) *By the committee of inspection*, if the power has been delegated to the committee.

(c) *By the Board of Trade*, if 4 weeks after adjudication no appointment has been made by (a) or (b).

NOTE: *The official receiver* cannot be appointed as trustee in bankruptcy except (i) where the value of the estate is not likely to exceed £300, or (ii) to fill a temporary vacancy in the office of trustee, or (iii) where the estate is that of a deceased debtor, or (iv) where directed by the Board of Trade in exceptional circumstances.

(The appointment of a trustee must be *approved by the Board of Trade*, which may refuse to approve because of (i) some irregularity in the appointment, or (ii) because the person appointed is not suitable, *e.g.* has been convicted of dishonesty, or is too closely and intimately connected with the debtor or any creditor to be truly impartial.)

2. Duties of trustee.

(a) *To get possession* of all the debtor's property, and to make the most of the available assets.

(b) *To obey* the instructions of the creditors in general meeting, and those of the committee of inspection.

(c) To exhibit the *utmost good faith*.

(d) *To summon meetings* of creditors when required by one-sixth in value of them, or as directed by the creditors generally.

(e) *To convert* the bankrupt's assets into money as soon as possible.

(f) *To keep proper accounts* which can be inspected by any creditor (but not by the debtor). Such accounts must be submitted every 3 months to the committee of inspection (if any), and to the Board of Trade every 6 months. In addition a full statement of his dealings must be submitted to the Board of Trade every 12 months, or more frequently if directed.

    The accounts kept must include (i) *a record book* (minutes and proceedings of creditors' meetings, etc.), (ii) *a cash book* (receipts and payments from day to day, etc.), (iii) *trading accounts*, if he carries on the bankrupt's business: *s.* 85.

3. Powers of the trustee: ss. 55–58.

(a) *On his own authority* he may:

    (i) *Sell* all or any part of the bankrupt's property.

    (i) *Give receipts* for money.

(iii) *In any other bankruptcy,* draw and prove for a dividend owing to his bankrupt.

(iv) *Exercise any powers necessarily incidental* to his duties and execute any necessary instrument.

(v) *Bar any entailed interest* to which the bankrupt is beneficially entitled (so bringing it into the bankruptcy for the benefit of the creditors).

(b) *With permission* of the creditors, the committee of inspection or the Board of Trade, he may:

    (i) *Carry on the bankrupt's business* (but only so far as is necessary for beneficially winding it up, *e.g.* so as to sell it as a going concern).

    (ii) *Bring or defend* any action affecting the bankrupt's property.

    (iii) *Employ a solicitor* or other agent where necessary.

    (iv) *Mortgage* or pledge any of the bankrupt's property.

    (v) *Accept money* payable at a *future date* on sale of any of the bankrupt's property.

    (vi) *Agree a compromise* of any claim by or against the bankrupt.

    (vii) Refer disputes to *arbitration.*

    (viii) *Appoint the bankrupt to manage* his own property.

    (ix) *Make an allowance* to the bankrupt for the support of himself and his family, or any payment to him in consideration of his services in the winding up of his estate (subject to the court's power to reduce such payments).

4. Remuneration and expenses.

(a) *Remuneration.* The trustee is not automatically entitled to any remuneration, though payment is usually made. Remuneration is fixed by the *creditors* (or the committee of inspection, if so agreed) as a percentage of the amount raised for distribution: *s.* 82.

Remuneration may however be fixed by the *Board of Trade* if one-quarter in number or value of the creditors so request, or at the bankrupt's request (if the amount fixed by the creditors is too large).

(b) *Expenses.* A trustee is automatically entitled to his expenses. But if he litigates unsuccessfully he is generally personally liable for the costs of the action, unless the creditors have agreed to reimburse him.

5. Vacation of office.

(a) *Release by the Board of Trade* discharges the trustee from all liability: *B.A.*, *s.* 93. A trustee may apply to the Board at any time for his release and if it is refused he may then apply to the court.

(b) *Removal: s.* 95. A trustee appointed by the creditors may be removed by an ordinary resolution of a general meeting called for the purpose.

A trustee may also be *removed by the Board of Trade* for various reasons, *e.g.* misconduct, incapacity, lunacy, undue delay, etc. If the creditors disapprove of such removal they may apply to the court to set it aside.

(c) *Bankruptcy: s.* 94. If the trustee himself becomes bankrupt he is automatically removed from office.

(d) *Resignation* must be notified to a general meeting of creditors, who may accept or reject it.

SECTION 80. DISTRIBUTION OF PROPERTY

1. Property available: s. 30. The trustee is entitled to all the debtor's property except as stated in 2 below.

The title of the trustee to the property available extends back to the date of commencement of the bankruptcy.

Under the *Doctrine of Relation Back*, commencement of the bankruptcy is *the date on which the first available act of bankruptcy was committed*, within 3 months before the presentation of the petition: *s.* 37.

(a) *Property belonging to the debtor at commencement of bankruptcy.*

This includes (i) payments made to any creditor since commencement of bankruptcy, *i.e.* after the first available act of bankruptcy (under the doctrine of relation back), (ii) benefits of the bankrupt's existing contracts, except where these depends on the personal skill of the bankrupt.

(NOTE: *Relation back does not occur* regarding (i) money obtained by a creditor by sale of the bankrupt's property under a *writ of execution* either before the receiving order or before he has notice of the petition: *s.* 40. (ii) *protected transactions, i.e.* payments *by* the bankrupt to creditors in return for valuable consideration (provided these were made before the receiving order and without notice of an available act of bankruptcy), and bona fide payments *to* the bankrupt before the date of the receiving order and without notice of presentation of a petition: *ss*. 45, 46, (iii) sales of land to a bona fide purchaser for value without notice, who bought before the date of the receiving order and before registration of the petition in the Land Charges Registry: *Land Charges Act*, 1925, *s*. 3.)

(b) *Property acquired by or devolving on the bankrupt before his discharge and after the commencement of bankruptcy.*

Property coming to the bankrupt (i) after commencement of bankruptcy end before adjudication, vests in the trustee automatically, (ii) after adjudication, must be expressly claimed by the trustee.

(c) *Capacity to exercise all powers over property* which the bankrupt might have exercised for his own benefit.

(d) *Goods in the bankrupt's reputed ownership: s.* 38. This means: goods which at the commencement of the bankruptcy are (i) in his possession order or disposition, (ii) in his trade or business, (iii) by consent of the owner, (iv) under such circumstances that he is the reputed owner thereof.

NOTE:

   (i) *Goods* includes all chattels personal, but not choses in action (except debts due or growing due to the bankrupt in his business).
  (ii) Reputed ownership may be *excluded by trade custom, e.g.* hotel furniture is customarily hired and this custom could defeat the reputation of ownership: *re Parker* (1885).
 (iii) If the owner of hired goods *does not know* they are used in the bankrupt's business, the reputed ownership provisions do not apply.
  (iv) Possession by the *bankrupt's agent* suffices for reputed ownership.
   (v) If goods are taken by the trustee under *s*. 38 the owner can prove in the bankruptcy as a creditor for their value: *re Britton* (1907).

(e) *Property transferred gratuitously by the bankrupt to another person: s*. 42, *i.e.* "voluntary settlements" made:

   (i) within 2 years before commencement of bankruptcy, or

(ii) within 10 years (unless the bankrupt could pay all his debts in full at the time of transfer, without recourse to the property in question).

The following settlements are not voluntary, and are therefore not affected by bankruptcy:

(i) Settlements before and in consideration of marriage.
(ii) Settlements in favour of a purchaser for value.
(iii) Settlements for the wife or children of the bankrupt of property coming to him after marriage and by right of his wife.

   (*A settlement means* any gift or transfer of property made with the intention that it shall be retained by the grantee.)

(f) *Property used by the bankrupt to give fraudulent preference to any creditor over other creditors, within* 6 *months before becoming bankrupt.*

NOTE:

(i) There must be actual intention to prefer one creditor over another. (The burden of proving this lies on the trustee in bankruptcy, and he cannot claim back the property unless he can prove it.)
(ii) The transfer must be voluntary, *i.e.* not under pressure by the creditor, for instance under threat of legal proceedings.
(iii) A payment is not fraudulent if made (*a*) to revive a statute-barred debt or (*b*) by a trader in order to keep his business going, even though he knows he is insolvent at the time: *re Clay & Sons* (1895).
(iv) The burden of proving intention to prefer a creditor lies on the trustee in bankruptcy.
(v) If the fraudulently preferred creditor sells the property given him to an innocent third party, the purchaser gets a good title, though the creditor may be compelled to reimburse the estate.

2. Property not available. The following classes of property do not vest in the trustee for distribution among the creditors:

(*a*) Property held by the bankrupt as *trustee* for any *other* person.
(*b*) *Tools of the bankrupt's trade*, necessary apparel and bedding (for the bankrupt and his family) to the value of £20: *B.A., s.* 38.
(*c*) *Personal earnings*, provided they are not more than are necessary to maintain the bankrupt and his family.

(d) *Rights of action* to sue for damages for bo'dily harm, or for injury to credit or reputation. (Rights of action for injuries to property do vest in the trustee.)

(e) *Interests in property which are determinable on bankruptcy.*

(f) The benefit of *contracts requiring personal skill.*

(g) *Old age pensions,* and benefits under the National Insurance Acts.

NOTE: *Copyrights of authors* assigned to the bankrupt in return for royalty payments *do vest* in the trustee, but he must not dispose of them in such a way as to deprive the author of his royalties.

3. Discovery of bankrupt's property. The court can order the bankrupt, his wife, or any other person suspected of possessing information about, or possessing any of the bankrupt's property, to appear and be examined on oath and to produce any relevant documents, and may order delivery up of such property: *B.A., s.* 25.

4. Disclaimer of onerous property: s. 54.

(a) *Onerous property.* The trustee can rid himself of property which would be more trouble than it is worth, *e.g.* land subjected to burdensome covenants, stocks and shares in companies which may make calls upon them, unprofitable contracts, etc.

He cannot however disclaim the obligations and retain the rights in any property.

(b) *Form of disclaimer.* It must be in writing, signed by the trustee, and must be made (i) *within* 12 *months* after his appointment, or (ii) within 12 months after he becomes aware of the property (providing he did not become aware of it within one month of his appointment), or (iii) within such extended time as the court may allow.

(c) *Notice of disclaimer.* Any person interested in property which is likely to be disclaimed can compel the trustee to decide whether to disclaim or not, by serving notice on him requiring him to disclaim within 28 days or not at all.

(d) *Leases,* may not as a rule be disclaimed without leave of the court, *except* (i) where the bankrupt has not sub-let or mortgaged the premises, and the value is less than £20 per year and the trustee has served notice on the lessor giving him 7 days to appeal to the court against the disclaimer, or (ii) where the bankrupt has sub-let or mortgaged the property, but the trustee has served 14 days' notice on such sub-tenants or mortgagees giving them 14 days in which to appeal to the court against disclaimer.

(Failure to disclaim a lease which could properly have been disclaimed renders the trustee personally liable thereon.)

(e) *Effect of disclaimer* is to relieve the bankrupt's estate from all liabilities in connection with the property thenceforward. (It does not affect the rights and liabilities of other persons except insofar as is necessary to protect the bankrupt's estate, and the trustee. Disclaimer merely divests the trustee of the property, it does not vest in any other person, and any person interested in the disclaimed property can apply to the court for an order vesting the property in him.)

Any person harmed by disclaimer can prove in the bankruptcy for the amount of his loss.

SECTION 81. PAYMENT OF DEBTS

1. Proof of debts. Before he can be paid a creditor must prove his debt, as quickly as possible after the receiving order.

Proof is by a *statement of the debt* + *affidavit* asserting the creditor's claim and stating any surrounding circumstances. When proof is submitted, the *trustee must within* 28 *days* (*a*) admit liability, (*b*) reject it, or (*c*) require further evidence. (The creditor can appeal to the court against rejection.)

A secured creditor (such as a mortgagee) must disclose his security in his proof (if any) or he must surrender it for the benefit of the creditors generally. There is no need however why he should prove for his debt at all. He has in fact four choices: (i) to rely on his security and not prove, (ii) to realise his security and prove for the deficiency (if any), (iii) to surrender his security and prove for the whole debt, or (iv) to value his security and prove for any deficiency.

2. Provable debts. These are all debts and liabilities, present or future, certain or contingent, to which the debtor is subject at the date of the receiving order, or to which he may become subject before his discharge by reason of any obligation incurred before the date of the receiving order: *s*. 30 (3).

(The obligation to pay must have arisen before the receiving order even though the debt may not be payable till after that date.)

If the debt is contingent (*i.e.* dependant on the happening of some future event), the trustee must assess its value and make allowance for it. If the creditor disagrees with the assessment he can appeal to the court.

Ordinary debts rank *pari passu* among themselves and are paid rateably, *i.e.* as fully as possible from the funds available.

3. Debts not provable.

(a) *Unliquidated damages,* not arising out of breach of contract or breach of trust: *L.R. (Miscellaneous Provisions) Act,* 1934.

(b) *Debts due to any person who knew of an available act of bankruptcy* committed by the debtor, at the time the debt was incurred.

(c) Debts which *in the opinion of the court* are incapable of being fairly assessed.

(d) Debts contracted *after the date* of the Receiving Order.

4. Mutual dealings. Where in the course of dealings between the bankrupt and a creditor each has incurred liabilities to the other, the *trustee must strike a balance* and (*a*) if the balance shows a deficiency owing to the creditor, the debt must be paid, and (*b*) if the balance shows a credit in favour of the bankrupt, the creditor must pay this sum to the trustee: *B.A., s.* 31.

A creditor cannot claim any set-off against the bankrupt if, at the time of giving credit to the bankrupt, he had notice of an available act of bankruptcy.

The debts must be due between the same parties in the same right; thus a debt owed jointly by a partnership cannot be set off against a separate debt owed to one of the parties on his own: *re Pennington & Owen* (1925).

5. Priority of debts: s. 33. Debts must be paid by the trustee in the following order:

(a) *Official receiver's expenses,* and other costs occurring before the bankruptcy proceedings.

(b) *Trustee's expenses.*

(c) *Allowances to the bankrupt* by the trustee.

(d) *Trustee's remuneration* (if any).

(e) *Preferred debts:*

　　(i) *Rates* falling due within 12 months before the receiving order, and *taxes* assessed up to April 5th preceding the receiving order but not exceeding the amount due for one year.

   (ii) *Wages* of workmen and clerks, etc., for services rendered during the four months preceding the receiving order (not amounting to more than £200).

   (iii) *Accrued holiday remuneration* for employees on the termination of their employment before the receiving order.

   (iv) *National Insurance contributions* payable by the bankrupt employer as during the 12 months prior to the receiving order.

   (v) *P.A.Y.E. deductions* due from the bankrupt employer to the Crown.

(f) *Ordinary debts, pari passu.*

(g) *Deferred debts: see below.*

6. Deferred debts. The following debts are not payable until all the preferred and ordinary debts have been paid in full:

(a) Loans to a business at a rate of interest varying with profits: *Partnership Act*, 1890, *s.* 3.

(b) Amounts due to the seller of the goodwill of a business as a portion of profits (by way of annuity or otherwise).

(c) Loans by a husband to his wife (or vice versa) for trade purposes.

(d) Interest exceeding 5% p.a. under a moneylending contract: *Moneylenders Act*, 1927, *s.* 9.

(e) Claims by the trustees of any settlement avoided in the bankruptcy: *B.A.*, *s.* 42.

7. Distraint by landlord. A landlord has no priority for his rent unless he has distrained for it (*i.e.* seized the bankrupt tenant's goods and chattels found on the premises).

But if he has distrained the position is as follows:

(a) If he distrained before commencement of the bankruptcy, he can keep whatever he has obtained.

(b) If he distrained within 3 months before the receiving order, he can be made to pay the preferential creditors out of the proceeds of distraint. (He then steps into their shoes and acquires their priority.)

(c) If he distrains after commencement of the bankruptcy, he can distrain only for 6 months' rent accruing before the adjudication order. (For any balance owing, he must prove as an ordinary creditor.)

8. Bankruptcy of partnerships. A receiving order may be made against a firm, and it then operates as a receiving order against each individual partner also: *B.A.*, *s.* 119.

Procedure is as follows:

(a) *The partners submit* (i) Statement of Affairs for the firm, and (ii) each partner submits a Statement of Affairs for himself.

(b) *The first meeting of creditors* will be attended by the firm's creditors, and by the creditors of the separate partners.

(c) *Any composition offered* may be accepted by the joint creditors and rejected by the separate creditors, and vice versa.

(d) *One trustee is appointed* to manage the firm's bankruptcy and those of the partners. (But the joint creditors, and each group of separate creditors may appoint their own Committees of Inspection.)

(e) *The joint estate is applied* first in payment of the firm's debts; and the separate estates are applied first in payment of the separate debts.

(f) *The firm's creditors* are entitled to prove in the separate bankruptcies of the partners and receive dividends, but only after the separate creditors have been paid in full.

(g) *The separate creditors* are entitled to prove and draw in the firm's bankruptcy, but only after the firm's creditors have been paid in full.

(h) *If there is no joint estate* and no solvent partner, the firm's creditors can prove against the separate estates and rank equally with the separate creditors.

(i) *If the bankruptcy was started by a firm's creditor* petitioning against one of the partners separately (as he may do), he is entitled to rank in that partner's bankruptcy with the separate creditors.

(j) *Where one partner is carrying on a separate business*, and there are debts outstanding between his business and the firm, his estate can prove against the firm and the firm can prove against him (providing the debts were incurred bona fide in the ordinary course of trading).

SECTION 82. DEEDS OF ARRANGEMENT

1. Arrangements outside bankruptcy. Where a debtor is insolvent and wishes to avoid bankruptcy, he and his creditors may reach an agreement for the arrangement of his affairs for the benefit of the creditors (without pushing the debtor into bankruptcy).

The Deeds of Arrangement Act, 1914, applies to such agreements (whether under seal or not) made (*a*) for the benefit of creditors generally, or (*b*) by an insolvent trader for the benefit of 3 or more creditors. (The administration of the arrangement is entrusted to a trustee.)

Alternatively such agreement may take the form of a *composition with creditors,* *i.e.* a contract by which the creditors agree to accept (in complete discharge of their debts) a proportion of their claims, *e.g.* 15*s.* in each pound owed. (This composition, despite the rule in *Foakes* v. *Beer* (*see s.* 12) is binding on all creditors who assent to it; the consideration for it lies in the mutual interchange of promises by the creditors not to sue for the whole debt, *i.e.* mutual forbearances.)

2. The Deeds of Arrangement Act, 1914.

If an arrangement or composition is embodied in a document (whether under seal or not), it is *void* unless:

(*a*) It is registered at the Board of Trade within 7 days of execution, and is properly stamped: *Deeds Of Arrangement Act,* 1914, *s.* 2.

(*b*) It is assented to by a majority in number and value of the creditors (if made for the benefit of creditors generally) within 21 days of registration.

If the deed affects land it must also be registered at the Land Charges Registry, otherwise it will be void against a purchaser for value of the land: *L.C.A.,* 1925, *s.* 13.

(The time limits for registration may be extended by the court.)

3. The trustee under a deed.

He must within 28 days of registration file a statutory declaration that the necessary majority of creditors have assented to the arrangement: *D.A.A.,* 1914, *ss.* 2 and 3. (Once registered the deed can be examined by any person on payment of a fee.)

Unless all the creditors have assented to it, the trustee must not act under the deed for 3 months after its execution. The reason for this is that if the debtor subsequently becomes bankrupt (and the trustee in bankruptcy's title relates back to a date 3 months before the presentation of the petition), the trustee under the deed may be personally liable in the bankruptcy for any property he has disposed of under the deed of arrangement. (Though usually the trustee in bankruptcy, if satisfied as to the good faith of the trustee under the deed of arrangement, will remunerate the latter for his services and treat his actions as those of his own agent.)

NOTE:

   (i) If the deed of arrangement is void merely because it failed to receive the assent of the majority of creditors required, and if the trustee was unaware of this, he is entitled to be exonerated from liability in any subsequent bankruptcy.
  (ii) If the trustee acts when he knows the deed is void, he is liable to penalties at the rate of £5 per day.

4. Duties and accounts of trustee.

  (a) *Duties.* He must carry out the trusts stated in the deed, *e.g.* as to the distribution of the property assigned to him. He must pay creditors equally, except (i) those who can distrain for their claims, *i.e.* landlords, and (ii) preferential creditors.
        (The bankruptcy rules which go to swell the assets (*e.g.* the reputed ownership rule, the avoidance of voluntary settlements, the rules as to fraudulent preferences) do not apply in favour of the trustee under a deed, and his authority extends only to the actual property assigned to him.)
  (b) *Accounts.* He must account annually to the Board of Trade, and every 6 months to the assenting creditors. If a business is being carried on, a separate trading account must be rendered. His accounts are open to inspection by any interested person.
        An audit may be ordered at any time on application of a majority in number and value of the assenting creditors, up to 12 months after the rendering of the final accounts to the Board of Trade.

5. Deed of arrangement as act of bankruptcy. A creditor who has not assented to a deed or composition is not bound by it, and can sometimes use it as grounds for filing a petition in bankruptcy against the debtor: *see acts of bankruptcy, s. 71. 5.*

In order to be cited as an act of bankruptcy, the deed must be for the benefit of creditors generally. Any creditor not assenting to the deed may ground a petition upon it any time within 3 months of its execution. (The trustee can reduce this time to one month by serving notice of the deed on non-assenting creditors.)

BANKRUPTCY

1. What are the objects of bankruptcy, and who may be made bankrupt?

Explain briefly the course of proceedings in bankruptcy. (**77. 1–4.**)

2. Explain briefly the recognised acts of bankruptcy. What is their importance? (**77. 5.**)

3. When and by whom may a petition in bankruptcy be lodged? (**77. 6.**)

4. What is a Receiving Order? When is it made and what is its effect? (**77. 7.**)

5. What are the duties of the Official Receiver after a Receiving Order has been made? (**78. 1–3.**)

6. What meetings of creditors are held during a bankruptcy? (**78. 3, 5.**) How do creditors vote at such meetings, personally or by proxy? (**78. 5.**)

7. Explain the significance of (a) Adjudication Order, and (b) Committee of Inspection. (**78. 4, 6.**)

8. When may a bankrupt apply for his discharge, and what power has the court on hearing the application? Explain also the effect of discharge. (**78. 7, 8.**)

9. How is a trustee in bankruptcy (a) appointed, (b) removed, and (c) remunerated? (**79. 1, 4, 5.**)

10. What are the duties and powers of a trustee in bankruptcy? When can he act on his own discretion, and when does he need the sanction of the court or of the creditors? (**79. 2, 3.**)

11. What property of a debtor is available for distribution among his creditors in bankruptcy? (**80. 1.**) Explain in particular what is meant by "reputed ownership." What property is not available in bankruptcy? (**80. 2.**)

12. When does bankruptcy commence? Explain what is meant by the Doctrine of Relation Back. (**80. 1.**)

13. In what circumstances can a trustee divest himself of onerous property in a bankruptcy? (**80. 4.**)

14. What debts are provable in bankruptcy, and how is proof effected? (**81. 1, 2.**) Explain also what debts are non-provable. (**81. 3.**)

15. Explain what is meant by (a) mutual dealings, (b) preferred debts, (c) secured creditors. (**81. 1, 4, 5.**)

16. What debts are not payable until all preferred and ordinary debts have been paid in full? (**81. 6.**) Explain the position of a landlord who has distrained for rent owed by a bankrupt tenant. (**81. 7.**)

17. Where a member of a firm becomes bankrupt, how may this affect the other members of the partnership? Explain what happens when a partnership becomes bankrupt. (**81. 8; 77. 4.**)

18. X is insolvent but wishes to avoid bankruptcy. Advise him how he may reach an agreement with his creditors. If any creditor is dissatisfied with an agreement so made, what can he do? (**82. 1, 2, 4; 77. 5, 6.**)

19. Explain the position of a trustee under a deed of arrangement, noting particularly his duty as to the rendering of accounts. (**82. 2, 3.**)

SPECIMEN QUESTIONS

1. Explain the position of a trustee in bankruptcy in connection with the following matters:

(*a*) a lease held by the bankrupt;

(*b*) a claim by a bankrupt for damages arising out of a collision between a Post Office van and the bankrupt's motor car driven by the bankrupt;

(*c*) securities held by the bankrupt as trustee under a settlement created by his uncle;

(*d*) goods in the reputed ownership of the bankrupt. *C.I.S., Final, June* 1962. (**80. 1, 2, 4.**)

2. (*a*) Explain the protected transactions which are governed by sections 45 and 46 of the Bankruptcy Act, 1914.

(*b*) Is the following transaction protected, namely: the payment by a bank of a cheque drawn by a customer in favour of a third party if the payment takes place after the bank receives notice that the customer has committed an act of bankruptcy? *Inst. of Bankers*, 1964. (**80. 1.**)

3. When a receiving order has been made against a debtor, it is necessary to call a first meeting of his creditors.

(a) By whom and in what way is such a meeting summoned?

(b) What are the purposes for which the meeting is held?

(c) What information are the creditors entitled to receive in advance of the meeting? *C.A., May* 1966. (**78. 1–5.**)

EXAMINATION TECHNIQUE

QUESTIONS in Mercantile Law are of two types: (a) *text-book questions*—asking the student to expound or discuss a topic, *e.g.* "What is specific performance and in what conditions will it not be granted?" (b) *problems*—in which the facts of a case are given and the student is asked to apply the various appropriate rules of law and discuss the situation (or advise one of the parties), *e.g.* "P's agent, A, exceeds his authority in contracting with C, and does not tell C that he is acting merely as an agent. Discuss." (Or "Advise C.")

These two types of question require *slightly different approaches*, but the following general points should always be borne in mind:

(i) *First read the question carefully*, to make sure you understand precisely what is involved. (If in doubt, underline *key-words*, or note the points you think are involved on a separate piece of paper).

(ii) *Read the question a second time*, noting down any points which may be involved but are not actually mentioned in the question. For instance in the problem on agency stated above: "breach of warranty," "ratification," "agency by estoppel," etc.

(iii) *Shuffle the points you have noted into a logical sequence.* Thus in the agency problem above: (1) Agency, (2) Exceeding authority, (3) Breach of warranty of authority—damages; (4) Estoppel and Ostensible authority; (5) Undisclosed principal.

(Time spent on these preliminary stages is not wasted. It helps you to put your answer into logical order, saves you time in writing, and—most important—shows the examiner that you have taken the trouble to plan your answer instead of leaping into the question without preparation. It will also make your answer easier to mark, and go some way toward endearing you to the examiner.)

NOTE: *Citation of cases, etc.* In studying law you should *first* learn the facts and names of starred cases; *secondly*, the facts of other cases; *thirdly*, the names of all. If in an examination you cannot remember the name of a case but can remember the facts, cite the facts on their own. If you cannot remember either name or facts it is permissible to invent facts of your own to illustrate an argument, providing you make it clear that they are your own invention (and do not pretend they come from some fictitious

279

case). As to the method of incorporating cases in an answer, note the method used in the model answers below. (Remember always to *underline case-names* and references to statutes; this is a legal tradition, and it also helps attract the examiner's attention.)

Text-book questions. These test: (*a*) your memory of your text-book and notes; (*b*) your ability to organise your information. Therefore before answering you should assemble your information carefully, and then write it down in a logical sequence. Use short sentences; long sentences tend to confuse you if you are in a hurry (and are also harder for an examiner to read).

In Mercantile Law, text-book questions do not usually require a very detailed knowledge, but they do require that the information sought should be known *precisely*.

Example: "Summarise (or "state briefly" or "state" or "describe," etc.) the conditions and warranties implied in contracts for the sale of goods, and explain how these terms may be excluded."

Model answer: Under the *Sale of Goods Act*, 1893, the following conditions and warranties are implied in every contract covered by the Act (unless excluded by express agreement):

1. A condition that the seller has or will have the legal right to sell the goods at the time the property is to pass: *s.* 12 (1).

2. A condition, in sales by sample, that bulk shall correspond with sample and that the buyer shall have reasonable opportunity to examine and compare, and that the goods shall be free of any defect not likely to be apparent on reasonable examination: *s.* 15 (2).

3. A condition in sales by description (where the buyer merely describes what he wants and leaves it to the seller to select the goods) that the goods shall correspond with the description: *s.* 13.

4. A condition or warranty as to quality or fitness is only implied in the following cases:

   (*a*) Where the seller is a dealer in the goods sold, and the purchaser makes clear that he relies on the seller's skill and judgment, a condition is implied that the goods shall be reasonably fit for the purpose intended: *s.* 14 (1).

   (*b*) Where the seller is a dealer in the goods sold, there is an implied condition that they shall be of merchantable quality, *i.e.* of a quality generally acceptable: *s.* 14 (2).

   (*c*) An implied warranty or condition may be incorporated by the customs of a particular trade: *s.* 14 (3).

5. A warranty that the buyer shall enjoy quiet possession: *s.* 12 (2).

6. A warranty that the goods shall be free of any undisclosed charge or incumbrance in favour of any third party: *s.* 12 (3).

Any condition (main term) or warranty (subordinate term) implied by the Act can be excluded by express agreement: *s.* 14 (4). But exclusionary clauses are construed strictly against the party inserting them. The seller cannot avail himself of an exclusionary clause if he broke the contract in some other way: *Karsales Ltd.* v. *Wallis* (1956). Thus where printed conditions of sale excluded liability for misdescriptions, it was held that the express and written exclusion was cancelled by an express oral representation: *Couchman* v. *Hill* (1947).

Problems: This type of question tests: (*a*) your understanding of the application of basic rules of law to unfamiliar situations; (*b*) your ability to present a rational argument.

Consequently you should (i) state the points of law involved in the problem, (ii) decide whether they are in fact applicable to the particular circumstances, and (iii) state your decision as to who is liable (if asked), etc. The most important parts of this answer are (i) and (ii). You can still get a good mark on a problem question, even if you fail to reach a decision on point (iii) or reach a wrong decision.

Example: "A is P's agent for the purchase of certain goods, and is authorised to pay up to £100. In fact he buys the goods from X at a price of £120. Can X enforce the contract against A and/or P? Would it make any difference to your answer if A had concealed the fact that he was merely acting as agent for P?"

Model Answer: This question appears to involve two main points, namely (i) excess of authority by an agent, and (ii) the doctrine of the undisclosed principal.

Where an agent exceeds his authority, his principal incurs no liability to the third party, but the agent is liable for damages for breach of his implied warranty of authority: *Collen* v. *Wright* (1914).

The principal may however incur liability where:

(i) *He ratifies* the agent's transaction, in which case the agent ceases to be liable. Ratification is only possible where:

   (*a*) the principal had capacity to make the particular contract at the time the agent contracted, and at the time of ratification;

   (*b*) the agent contracted expressly as agent for the principal, naming him;

   (*c*) the principal was in possession of all material information or agreed to dispense with it.

(ii) *He is estopped* from denying the agent's authority to make the contract in question, *e.g.*

(a) where the principal has *held out* the agent as having authority to make the contract in question (for instance where the agent has in the past made such contracts with the principal's concurrence), or

(b) where the agent's *ostensible authority* covers the transaction in question, even though he has exceeded his actual authority (for instance where the agent occupies a position which normally carries with it authority to make such contracts, and the principal has imposed restrictions on that authority which are *unknown to X*).

Thus a factor has implied authority to sell goods in his possession, and can give a good title to a purchaser even though he was instructed not to sell the particular goods: *Factors Act*, 1889, *s.* 2.

The doctrine of the undisclosed principal would be applicable to the problem stated if A had concealed the fact of his agency. The doctrine is that in such a case the third party (here X) can enforce the contract against the agent, and on discovering the identity and existence of the principal has an alternative right of action against the principal.

In the problem therefore it is submitted that:

(i) X has a right of action against A for breach of his warranty of authority, and is entitled to damages whether the breach was innocent or fraudulent;

(ii) X has no right of action against P, unless P ratifies the transaction or is estopped from denying A's authority.

INDEX